The Life and Raigne

of King Edward the Sixth

BY JOHN HAYWARD

Frontispiece depicting King Edward as it appeared
in John Hayward, *The Life and Raigne of King Edward the Sixth* (1630).
Courtesy of The Newberry Library

The
Life and Raigne
of
King Edward the
Sixth

BY JOHN HAYWARD

Edited by Barrett L. Beer
Foreword by Lacey Baldwin Smith

THE KENT STATE UNIVERSITY PRESS

Kent, Ohio, and London, England

© 1993 by The Kent State University Press
Kent, Ohio 44242
All rights reserved
Library of Congress Catalog Card Number 92-26984
ISBN 0-87338-475-X
Manufactured in the United States of America

Library of Congress Cataloging-in-Publication Data

Hayward, John, Sir, 1564?–1627.
The life and raigne of King Edward the Sixth / by John Hayward ;
edited by Barrett L. Beer ; foreword by Lacey Baldwin Smith.
p.   cm.
Includes bibliographical references and index.
ISBN 0-87338-475-X (alk. paper) ♾™
1. Edward VI, King of England, 1537–1553. 2. Great Britain—
History—Edward VI, 1547–1553. 3. Great Britain—Kings and rulers—
Biography. I. Beer, Barrett L. II. Title. III. Title: Life and
reign of King Edward the Sixth.
DA345.H38 1993
942.05′3′092—dc20
[B]   92-26984

British Library Cataloging-in-Publication data are available.

Contents

Foreword

*E*VER SINCE the art of biography was perfected, royalty has attracted biographers like so many bears to the honey pot. The attraction derives from a threefold assumption: that sovereigns really do possess and exercise power for good and evil; that their lives are somehow richer, more intense, and more susceptible to corruption than those of common folk; and that the "royal throne of kings" is always marketable. Seventeenth-century writers would have added a fourth and, for them, more important element: that history, especially the deeds and decisions of the rich and powerful, was driven by a providential imperative which linked the past to the present by ties of causation and analogy. History, therefore, contained a moral lesson for the benefit of the living and was a mirror in which it could both discern God's purpose and comment upon itself. This last assumption gave to seventeenth-century biography a polemical and contemporary flavor now lost to the twentieth century. John Hayward and his generation of historical biographers and dramatists were writing about figures and events that had contemporary impact. Their works could be—indeed often were—censored, and the suspected hidden meaning of their histories could land unwary authors in jail.

It is hard enough even in the twentieth century to write about the Tudor dynasty. I speak with considerable experience, having written biographies of three Tudor kings and queens, and I can appreciate firsthand the task that Hayward set for himself when he elected to write *The Life and Raigne of King Edward the Sixth*. Even with the documentation available to us, which was unknown to the seventeenth century, it is difficult to isolate decision making and responsibility, to disentangle monarchs from their councillors, or to penetrate the friendless fog of self-interest and personal animosity that enveloped the courts of sixteenth-century sovereigns. Behind "the sceptre and the ball," "the tide of pomp," and the "bed majestical" lay concealed what kind of slavery, fears, and burdens? Even for a prince as intimately described as Elizabeth I, it is almost impossible to see through the glittering cake of ceremony and pageantry to the biological reality of constipation, body odor, and menstruation. For us the myth of the Tudors is historical fiction; for John Hayward it was historical reality because, almost without exception, the documents which shaped the seventeenth century's image of the past recorded only the public, not the private, lives of sovereigns.

Like any biographer, John Hayward struggled with the dichotomy implicit in the title of his work, the tension between a Life and a Raigne. What was the proper balance between the two, and to what extent did one explain the other? In the case of Edward VI the equilibrium was hopelessly out of balance because the child king, who lived only sixteen years and reigned six years, five months and nine days, never had a chance to rule and thereby generate the documentary pieces that create the jigsaw puzzle of historical personality. For Hayward, Edward remained forever a two-dimensional stereotype of unrealized potentiality: "in disposition . . . mild, gracious and pleasant, of an heavenly wit; in body beautiful . . . a miracle of nature" (275) that never reached maturity.

Where the center is hollow, the perimeter must bear the lesson of history so important to the seventeenth century, and Hayward established what is still the standard approach to Edward's reign—a study of divine-right kingship in which the powers of monarchy resided not in the head but in weak and corruptible servants surrounding the crown. Here was the making of tragedy both political and personal, and Hayward presents the reign as a three-act tragedy about Sir Edward Seymour, who was Duke of Somerset, Lord Protector of the realm, and senior uncle of the king. Of the sixty-six printed pages assigned to the life and times of Edward, fifty-two tell the story of the duke's tragic death brought about by the fatal interaction between the unholy ambitions of John Dudley, Earl of Warwick, and Somerset's character flaws inflamed by the unbridled vanity of his own wife, Anne Stanhope.[1] Seymour appears as a weak but affable gentleman whose rise to prominence under Henry VIII was the product not of talent but of extraordinary luck and faithful service. The newly appointed Lord Protector was a "tractable and mild" (301) nobleman who made the mistake of "gaping after the fruitless breath of the multitude" and was "more desirous to please the most than the best" (289). He proved to be an easy morsel for the barracudas that circled about the child king, the most dangerous being Warwick, who was a master of dissimulation, always ready to instigate "any mischief" to attain his "ambitious ends" and never hesitating to use "empty promises and threats to draw others to his purpose" (280).

The lopsided clash between the "good duke" and the "wicked earl" is only part of the unfolding drama. Hayward presents a second villain, this time close to the foolish duke's bedchamber. Anne Stanhope is depicted as a Lady Macbeth of Iagoesque proportions, "a devilish woman" who deliberately baited her husband's paranoia and "rubbed into the duke's dull capacity" (301) the belief that his younger brother, Thomas, was conspiring to depose the Lord Protector and was willing to perpetrate fratricide to do so. Somerset, "embracing this woman's counsel," yielded "himself both to advise and devise for [the] destruction of his brother" (302), thereby setting the stage for his own tragic end. Hayward could not document Warwick's role in what began as a family quarrel masterfully fueled by the duchess, but he sensed that the earl "had his finger in the business . . . so as the duke might thereby incur infamy and hate" (302) and make it possible for the earl to plot his rival's execution. Hayward's interpretation of the reign is in style far closer to theater than to history. He savagely overdraws the virtues and vices of his protagonists, but no amount of modern revisionism has been able to entirely dispel the sense of tragedy and the clash of personalities that he injected into the drama—it makes far too good reading.

Authors who tell "sad stories of the death of kings" in an age which viewed history as a reflection of itself could get into serious trouble. Hayward discovered this when he was closely interrogated by Elizabeth's council for having dedicated his newly published *Henrie IIII* to the troublesome earl of Essex. Although Henry IV was the founder of the Lancastrian line and his father was the dynastic source from which the Tudors claimed their Plantaganet blood and right to the throne, no amount of special Lancastrian pleading could entirely conceal the smell of high treason and usurpation in the actions of Henry Bolingbroke. Rebellion, even 200 years old, on the part of an overmighty and ambitious magnate was still a dangerous subject in 1599. The timing and dedication of Hayward's biography was singularly inopportune, and during the years between 1599 and

1601 the council intensified its search for hidden meaning in Hayward's narrative and constantly asked its author why he had dedicated such a story of rebellion to an earl who was in the process of harboring seditious thoughts and committing treason. There is a story told by Francis Bacon, who liked to record his literary conceits, that he saved John Hayward more than once from an indignant and suspicious Elizabeth, who regarded the biography as "a seditious prelude to put into the people's head boldness and faction."[2] On one occasion she asked Bacon whether the work and its writer might be deemed treasonous. No, he answered, there was no treason, only egregious felony for having plagiarized so much of the contents from Tacitus. At another time, when Elizabeth wanted to rack Hayward to discover the truth whether he had in fact written the biography and, if so, whether Essex had put him up to it, Bacon quipped: "Nay, Madam, he is a doctor, never rack his person, but rack his style." Fortunately Hayward escaped with only a spell in the Tower of London by way of punishment for participating in the dangerous craft of history writing. He lived to complete his *Life and Raigne of Edward Sixth*, a piece of historical literature which, despite the advances of modern scholarship, still sets the flavor of a reign steeped in drama and personal tragedy.

Lacey Baldwin Smith
Peter B. Ritzma Professor in the Humanities
Northwestern University

NOTES

1. These statistics come from White Kennet's *A Complete History of England*, 3 vols. (London, 1706), in which Hayward's *Edward the Sixth* is printed (2:273–328), the last eleven pages being incorrectly paginated.

2. "The Apology of Sir Francis Bacon, in Certain Imputations Concerning the Late Earl of Essex," in *The Works of Francis Bacon*, 10 vols. (London, 1826) 3:218.

Preface

ALTHOUGH Sir John Hayward rated a substantial biography by
Sidney Lee in the *Dictionary of National Biography*, he has ex-
isted until recently largely in the margins of early modern English
history. Now the important work of S. L. Goldberg, published in the
1950's, has been supplemented by D. L. Woolf's study of early
seventeenth-century historiography and a critical edition of both
parts of *Henrie IIII* by John J. Manning. Work remains to be done on
Hayward's political and religious writings, and his overall contribution to the intellectual life of the period needs to be viewed from a
broader perspective than that of a court historian.

Hayward's *King Edward* first came to my attention a number of
years ago when Lacey Baldwin Smith encouraged me to study the
life and political career of John Dudley, Duke of Northumberland.
Although I was not prepared to accept Hayward's assessment of
Northumberland at face value, it never occurred to me that anything
could be learned from examining manuscripts of an early seventeenth-century biography. Later, after discovering that the chronicles
of John Stow do not give a single, uniform interpretation of the Tudor
period and that the various editions offer important insights into the
author's historical thought, I returned to Hayward with an entirely
different outlook.

Unlike medievalists and literary scholars, early modern English
historians have been reluctant to probe much beyond the most
readily available text of contemporary chronicles and historical writings and have preferred to devote their time to the study of manuscripts. Although Victorian scholars thought otherwise and left
behind a rich legacy of edited texts, the major Tudor chronicles and
many other important historical works including Hayward's *King
Edward* are available only in the original editions or in unedited
reprints of these editions. Editorial and textual scholarship continues
to appeal less to historians than to students of literature, but the

recent appearance of a new edition of *Henrie IIII* suggests that attitudes are beginning to change.

My research has been supported by the Newberry Library, which allowed me to use its rich collection and to organize materials collected over several summers in England, and by the Institute for Bibliography and Editing at Kent State University. Librarians at the Newberry, British Library, University College London, and Kent State University were extremely helpful. Enquiries were answered by librarians at Trinity College, Cambridge, the Folger Library, and the Huntington Library and by several other scholars, including Professor Conrad Russell and Dr. Diana Greenway. I would also like to thank Professors Roger Manning, S. R. Reid, A. J. Slavin, and Mr. A. C. L. Hall for their assistance. As in the past, Lacey Smith has been generous with sound advice and helpful criticism.

Barrett L. Beer

Introduction

SIR JOHN HAYWARD'S LIFE AND WORK

Education and Legal Career

JOHN HAYWARD, best known as a historian, but also an important lawyer, political theorist, and religious writer, was born in Suffolk, probably in 1564. Little is known of his parents, but as the family had no recognized coat of arms, it may be assumed his father was not numbered among the leading gentry of the county.[1] Hayward's social origins are perhaps reflected in historical writings that reveal contempt for the common people, because a man of his family background could advance educationally and professionally only through ability and hard work and by dissociating himself from the culture and environment into which he was born. Hayward's will suggests that he was educated in the parish of Felixstowe, since he left money for the poor of that parish where, he said, "I received the means of my education."[2] From rural Suffolk he went on to Pembroke Hall, Cambridge, and graduated with a B.A. in 1581 and M.A. in 1584. He received an LL.D in 1591, which qualified him for a career in the ecclesiastical and admiralty courts.[3]

Sometime after completing his studies at Cambridge, Hayward married Jane Pascall of Springfield, Essex, daughter of Andrew Pascall, Esquire. A university education with prospects of success in the practice of civil law undoubtedly made this marriage possible, but the bride brought only a small marriage portion, probably because Hayward himself married with little family money behind him. Hayward and his wife lived for many years in the parish of Great St. Bartholomew, near Smithfield, and had only one daughter of whom there is any trace. When he prepared his will a year before his death in 1627, the daughter was dead, and he pronounced the marriage a resounding failure. He justified the modest legacy left to his wife on account of her "unquiet life" and "small respect towards me." One is tempted to interpret these accusations as veiled charges of adultery, but without any testimony from Lady Hayward or corroborating witnesses such speculation would be best avoided. Considering the tormented soul that Hayward publicized in his religious writings and the antipathy to women found in *The Life and Raigne of King Edward the Sixth,* Hayward may have been a less-than-perfect marriage partner. Hayward's personal life may have been unhappy, but he died possessed of substantial wealth accumulated undoubtedly by prudent living and a successful legal career.

Hayward's professional life began with the development of a large practice in the Court of Arches, where he was admitted as an advocate in 1595. His dedication of a devotional work to George Abbot, Archbishop of Canterbury, may have been Hayward's way of thanking Abbot for channeling legal work to him. He also practiced before the High Court of Admiralty but achieved greatest prominence as a civil lawyer in Chancery. A manuscript from 1604 referring to Hayward's participation in a debate on the precedence of "doctors and masters of the chancery before serjeants at lawe" identifies him as a Master in Chancery, thirteen years before the date given by Brian Levack.[4] As one of twelve Masters, Hayward was recognized as "a senior legal officer" of the Crown. He was knighted by James I in 1619 and subsequently served on the High Commission for the Province of Canterbury. Hayward was called before the House of Commons in 1626 to testify about his role in the trial of Sir Robert Howard, MP. The latter had been excommunicated for adultery with the daughter of Sir Edward Coke but allowed to take his seat in Parliament without receiving Holy Communion. With wealth from a successful legal career, Hayward invested in London property and the Bermuda and Virginia companies.[5]

Political Thought

Hayward's political thought has been studied primarily in the context of absolutism and divine-right monarchy, but the whole corpus of his writings has never been analyzed systematically. Since the pioneering work of J. W. Allen, first published in 1928, scholars have concentrated on a single work, *An Answer to the First Part of a Certain Conference Concerning Succession* (1603), in which Hayward defended James I's right of succession against the Jesuit, Robert Parsons, who wrote under the pseudonym R. Doleman.[6] In defending the Stuart claim against Roman Catholics, Hayward also reaffirmed arguments dating back to the reign of Henry VIII that supported the royal supremacy in ecclesiastical affairs. The only study that carries the inquiry beyond Allen is Levack's *The Civil Lawyers in England: 1603–1641*, where Hayward's advocacy of absolutism is seen as atypical of his profession. Although Hayward drew upon the *Corpus Juris Civilis*, he "placed relatively slight emphasis on his analogy between Roman and English government."[7] Levack's examination of Hayward's first historical work, *Henrie IIII* (1599), revealed significantly different political principles. In place of forthright advocacy of monarchical authority, Hayward deceptively articulated conflicting political principles through speeches placed in the mouths of several persons, a technique that attempted to conceal the author's own views. Therefore, it is difficult to fault the conclusion that Hayward's absolutism resulted as much from his desire to gain favor from James I as from disinterested scholarly reflection on the foundations of royal authority.[8]

If Hayward's defense of absolutism was self-serving, *A Treatise of Union of the Two Realms of England and Scotland* (1604), which promoted the king's interest in Anglo-Scottish union, may be seen in a similar light. A pronounced fear of popular rebellion and social chaos that runs through Hayward's political and historical works, on the other hand, would seem to reveal Hayward's own inner anxiety rather than a desire to ingratiate himself with the king.[9] As early as 1606 Hayward wrote that the "multitude" was weak, fierce, and mutable with regard to religion and observed that the sixteenth-century Anabaptist, John of Leiden, "a tailor by trade, set all Germany in uproar and in arms."[10] The English rebels of 1549 were also "base and degenerate" although clerical leaders of the Western Rebellion possessed "some academical training." The rebels, according to Hayward, sought to transform the state, but "whether reformed or deformed they neither cared nor knew."[11] He concluded that seditious men were most dangerous when they have "broken awe" or have been tempted with well-intentioned promises of reform.[12] Hayward's remedy for the threat of social chaos required a strong monarchy, religious unity, and a responsible nobility committed to a regime of law and order.

Religious Thought

On the basis of published titles, editions, and issues, it is arguable that Hayward enjoyed his greatest success as a religious writer. Between 1601 and 1650, *Sanctuarie of a Troubled Soule, David's Teares,* and *Christ's Prayer upon the Crosse for His Enemies* appeared in no fewer than nineteen different versions. These three devotional books reflect little or nothing of Hayward's historical, legal, or political interests; thus they remind us that Hayward was an extraordinarily complex thinker, one who could function on several different levels without his diverse interests intersecting in any significant way. Hayward's approach to religion is biblical, not historical, and he shows no interest in the early development of the Catholic church, the Reformation, or the Church of England. His devotional works studiously avoid doctrinal controversy as well as criticism of individual persons. The strongest echo of Hayward's historical writings is found in the generous citation of classical writers whose arguments are never supported by references to prominent theologians. He offers an interesting example of an educated layman whose religion grew out of biblical Christianity and a Protestant writer who appears to have been indifferent to Luther and Calvin as well as leading Anglican apologists.[13]

Considering that *Sanctuarie of a Troubled Soule* first appeared at the time of Hayward's imprisonment for offending Queen Elizabeth with *Henrie IIII*, it is likely that his loss of liberty kindled a spiritual rebirth.[14] In *Sanctuarie* and the other books, man faces God as a solitary individual without the support of church or clergy. Like Luther, Hayward suffered a profound awareness of his sins and turned to the *Bible*, but he never spells out the exact nature of his transgressions. His devotional writings, therefore, offer little insight into his personal life or his career as a lawyer and historian.

Sanctuarie of a Troubled Soule, Hayward's first and most frequently reprinted devotional work, is also the longest. Although the 1604 and 1607 editions have no dedication, later editions (1616, 1636, 1650) were dedicated to George Abbot, who served as Archbishop of Canterbury from 1611 to 1633, because of "some dependency, both of myself and my profession upon your grace."[15] Hayward explained that his book was the result of prayer and meditation on the sabbath.

The two-part work, which in its enlarged versions runs to 800 pages, reveals the depth of Hayward's despair. "O, bottomless sea of misery and sorrow wherein I have plunged myself," he wrote, "I acknowledge indeed that among all, and above all sinners, I am wretched. I acknowledge that I am unable to satisfy for my sins."[16] As a "weak and wretched worm," Hayward approached God, hoping that He would receive "my sacrifice of prayer and praise [and] inflame it with the comfortable heat of thy love."[17]

In the introduction to *David's Teares*, Hayward explained that after completing *Sanctuarie* and "finding it to have taken root and life for some continuance, I could not conceive any better employment of those hours which I have resolved to sequester for exercises in this kind, than in making my conceptions legible upon those Psalms of David which lively [*sic*] describe both the form and force of true repentence."[18] Through devotional study he sought a quiet contented life free from anguish and ambition.[19] Looking back over his life from the vantage point of 1622, Hayward lamented that none of his own "productions" fully satisfied him and added that the approval of others was no warrant to "my own judgment, tender and severe in what I do."[20] He proceeded to offer an extended commentary on two penitential Psalms, 6 and 32. Using language of the new scientific age, Hayward observed that the knowledge of God is "the foundation of our spiritual building, the first wheel of the clock; the first moveable sphere, which causes the motion of all the rest."[21] Consistent with his newly acquired peace of mind, Hayward wrote, "All the sins of the world are more easily consumed by the mercy of God than is a drop of water in a hot fiery furnace."[22] The posthumously published edition of 1636 was expanded to include Psalm 130 where Hayward refers to life in prison, a reflection that probably recalls his punishment after the ill-fated publication of *Henrie IIII* in 1599. He speaks of prison as the place where "all the filth of a city doth draine" and likens his own life to a prison from which he seeks deliverance.[23]

Christ's Prayer upon the Crosse for His Enemies, first published in 1623 and dedicated to Lady Anne Caesar, is the shortest of Hayward's devotional writings. The book contains his "sabbath exercises" for the year and was intended to supplement *David's Teares*, which he hoped to expand. The text "Father forgive them for they know not what they do" is the subject of extended commentary. At the end Hayward returns to his own distress, begging God to hide him from the world and "take me into the secret retreats of thy bosom to dwell."[24]

Hayward's devotional writings are part of a large body of religious work that, "far from being a special interest on the periphery of literature, was at the very center."[25] Hayward's contemporary, Francis Bacon, praised English achievements in the field of biblical commentary and interpretation, especially the "rich and precious works of positive divinity that were collected upon particular texts of scriptures in brief observations."[26] In her study of this literature, Helen C. White calculated that a little more than half of the 130 books entered in 1630 at Stationers' Hall, London, were religious in nature and that at least a dozen were "in purpose and scope clearly devotional."[27] More recently, Patrick Collinson identified private devotion as a prominent aspect of the "voluntary religion" that characterized the Jacobean church.[28] In another context Hayward's university education and devotional writing reveal an identification with Christian humanism, while his retreat from the active life into spirituality and contemplation reflects the conservative religious impulse of the early seventeenth century described by Margo Todd.[29]

Historical Writings

A major historian of the early seventeenth century, John Hayward wrote four historical works, each of which is biographical. Only two of these books were published during the author's lifetime, *The First Part of the Life and Raigne of King Henrie the IIII* (1599) and *The Lives of the III Normans, Kings of England* (1613). *The Life and Raigne of King Edward the Sixth* was first published in 1630, three years after Hayward's death, while *Annals of the First Four Years of the Reign of Queen Elizabeth* was not published in its entirety until 1840.[30] As recently as 1991 John J. Manning edited the unpublished Folger Shakespeare Library manuscript of *The Second Part* of the life of Henry IV and combined it with a scholarly edition of part one. Unlike contemporary chroniclers such as John Stow, who produced large works surveying centuries of English history, Hayward wrote short books that combined narrative with analysis and interpretation. The 1630 edition of *King Edward* is only 180 pages in length, while *The Lives of the III Normans* runs to 314 pages. Hayward also edited and wrote an introduction to Sir Roger Williams, *The Actions of the Lowe Countries* (1618). He complained that the manuscript, owned by Sir Peter Manwood, had come to him "in a ragged hand, much maimed both in sense and in phrase," but added that his editorial work had restored the text to the "style and meaning" of the author.[31]

Modern historiographers recognize Hayward as the first English scholar to write "politic history," an approach introduced earlier in Renaissance Italy by Machiavelli and Guicciardini. The politic historian wrote in a succinct, epigrammatic style and emphasized ways that the past might be used to achieve political objectives.[32] As Levack has shown, Hayward combined politic history with his knowledge of the civil law to make a significant contribution to legal history. He denied that the common law was immemorial and showed how William I had changed English law and introduced new legal language.[33] Yet his identification with the new history did not preclude a major role for Providence in human affairs. Providentialism, although rooted in medieval traditions, survived not only in Hayward but in the historical works of the Earl of Clarendon.[34]

The utilitarian aspect of politic history is evident in the staffing of Chelsea College, which was founded by James I as a "spiritual garrison" to defend the Church of England and the Protestant religion against the threat of Rome.[35] Although Chelsea College failed to achieve its objectives as a result of opposition from the two universities, the appointment of Hayward and William Camden as historiographers shows that the king expected historians to rise above disinterested scholarship, antiquarianism, or merely chronicling the past. Hayward's annals of the early years of Elizabeth was the only one of his historical works that actually supported the established church, and he certainly achieved more wealth and fame during his lifetime as a master in the Court of Chancery than as a practitioner of politic history. Yet politic history, with its emphasis on the role of great men, brought Hayward distinction as an early contributor to the development of English biography. His books on Henry IV and Edward VI fall short of what literary critics call "pure biography," but Hayward successfully demonstrated that it was possible to examine important political issues and reach a large reading public through biographical writing.[36]

Although his first published book, *Henrie IIII*, focused on the court politics of the later Middle Ages, it created such controversy that the author was imprisoned by order of Queen Elizabeth. Dedicated to the Earl of Essex, Hayward's *Henrie IIII* severely criticized Richard II, who was deposed in 1399. After recording the king's death, Hayward observed, "And thus do these and the like accidents daily happen to such princes as will be absolute in power, resolute in will, and dissolute in life."37 On the other hand, Hayward has the dying king prophesy doom for Henry IV and the usurping Lancastrian dynasty.38 Henry IV is the principal subject of the book, but he falls well short of heroic stature. While Hayward recognizes that Henry was unjustly deprived of his inheritance, he questions his right to seize the throne. Hayward offers a carefully balanced assessment of Henry's role in the death of Richard, yet his references to the Irish, Scots, and the common people of England are consistently contemptuous. The commons, according to Hayward, were "void of cares, not searching into sequels, follow the mighty, [and] flatter the prince."39

The queen's government took little interest in Hayward's deft handling of the major characters or in the social context in which he placed the narrative. Neither were contemporaries aware that Hayward's *Henrie IIII* introduced the new politic history to the English reading public. The book nevertheless created a sensation, selling 500 or 600 copies within three weeks. The queen's government demanded that the dedication to Essex be removed when the book was reprinted and subsequently seized and burned 1,500 copies of another reprint. The declining fortunes of Essex explain the queen's dislike of this book. Hayward was interrogated about the purpose of his writings and imprisoned at the Tower of London in 1600. He may not have regained his freedom until the accession of James I. Although the recently published second part of the life of Henry IV was never examined by Elizabethan authorities, John J. Manning has argued that it shows that the original portion "was intended as part of something more than a 'seditious prelude.'"40

The Lives of the III Normans, Kings of England appeared ten years later when Hayward, having successfully gained the favor of the king, looked ahead to even better fortune through the patronage of Henry, Prince of Wales. Prince Henry sent for Hayward and encouraged him to write about the royal family's Norman ancestors. The prince's complaint about the lack of historical books on English subjects offered great hope to Hayward, who had already written "of certain of our English kings." But Henry's death on November 6, 1612, came as a devastating blow.[41] The completed version of *The Normans* was dedicated to Prince Charles, but Hayward never advanced into the inner circle of the future king's favorites and never published another biographical work.

In *The Normans*, Hayward wrote that "ambition, a reasonless and restless humour" made Harold a difficult and obstinate man.[42] After a lengthy examination of Duke William's right to the throne of England, Hayward concluded that "his propinquity in blood to King Edward" was decisive.[43] While the laws of the new king were exceedingly harsh for the defeated Anglo-Saxons, Hayward noted that Norman writers praised the Conqueror's clemency and mercy.[44] The influence of Hayward's scholarship survives in a modern biography of William the Conqueror by David C. Douglas, which concludes with an extended quotation from *The Normans*:

> Verely, he was a very great Prince: full of hope to undertake great enterprises, full of courage to atchieue them: in most of his actions commendable, and excusable in all. And this was not the least piece of his Honour, that the kings of England which succeeded, did accompt their order onely from him: not in regard of his victorie in England, but generally in respect of his vertue and valour.[45]

In contrast with his works on Henry IV and the Norman kings, Hayward's *Annals of the First Four Years of the Reign of Queen Elizabeth* is incomplete, covering only the years 1558 to 1562. It resembles earlier chronicles in that it is organized around four regnal years but focuses on topics within each year and is not strictly chronological. Beginning with Queen Mary languishing on her death bed, Hayward describes the accession of Elizabeth and the subsequent religious settlement. His account of the second year concentrates on Scottish affairs, while the third year is more of a potpourri that includes relations with Mary Queen of Scots, an anecdote relating the punishment of a self-proclaimed messiah active in London, and a detailed description of the fiery destruction of the steeple of St. Paul's after it was struck by lightning. The fourth and final year focuses primarily on Anglo-French relations but concludes with trivia such as the birth of a pig having "hands and fingers like a man child."[46]

Throughout *Annals*, Hayward writes as a devoted and enthusiastic admirer of the queen, not as a man who unjustly suffered imprisonment at her hands. His lengthy treatment of the reestablishment of the Church of England is similarly approving and uncritical and significantly anticipates modern revisionist scholarship by arguing that Protestantism enjoyed extensive public and political support from the beginning of the new reign.[47]

The earliest reference to the *Annals* dates from 1612 when Hayward presented a manuscript entitled "Certain Years of Queen Elizabeth's Reign" to Henry, Prince of Wales, together with a manuscript of the Norman kings. Prince Henry found the latter to be a "perfect work" and ordered its publication, but he left no recorded judgment on the first manuscript. "Not long after he died," wrote Hayward, "and with him died both my endeavors and my hopes."[48] The manuscript of "Certain Years" must have been similar or identical to the *Annals*, which is John Bruce's transcription of British Library, Harleian MS 6021. At the time of presentation to Prince Henry, Hayward said that the work was finished but did not explain why he limited the study to the early years of the reign. If the work was truly completed, it is easy enough to understand why it was unsuitable for publication. If Hayward meant that only the initial part of a larger work was finished and ready for the prince's examination, he may have decided to abandon the project after his patron died. S. L. Goldberg noted that the *Annals* was the closest Hayward ever got to writing contemporary history and found the work "freer in arrangement and more classically formed than Camden's."[49] A less sympathetic assessment by F. J. Levy concluded that the *Annals* was a failure because the author had been unable "to nerve himself sufficiently to give up the annalistic structure altogether."[50]

SIR JOHN HAYWARD AND KING EDWARD VI

The Life and Raigne of King Edward the Sixth, the earliest biography of the king, first appeared in 1630, three years after the death of the author. It was printed for John Partridge, a prominent London bookseller who traded in astrological books on the eve of the Civil War. There are no known connections between Hayward and Partridge, and the book contains no dedication, because "This [book] comes out into the world after the death of the father; a posthumous, and is not like to find any patron, but the love and affection of thee (favorable reader)."[51] It is not easy to explain why a biography of Edward VI should have been published in 1630. Obviously no competing books had to be taken into account, but it is difficult to see how the events of Edward's reign were of particular relevance to readers of that year.[52] Whatever the reason for the first edition, sales must have been good enough to justify a second edition six years later. The entirely new edition of 1636 was printed by Robert Young for Partridge and included a portion of Hayward's previously unpublished *Annals.* The third and last printed edition of *King Edward* was included in White Kennet's *A Complete History of England with the Lives of All the Kings.*[53]

It is likely that copies of *King Edward* circulated fairly extensively before 1630 because at least five manuscript copies have survived. Since none of the manuscripts is written in the hand of Hayward, there is no reason to believe that he ever saw them. Differences in spelling as well as more substantial variations in content, organization, and arrangement indicate that none of the surviving manuscripts was used as printer's copy for the printed editions.

Harleian MS 6021 at the British Library contains a complete text of *King Edward* and consists of eighty-six closely written pages. This manuscript is included in a volume of historical tracts dating from the reign of Edward VI to James I. *King Edward* is followed in the bound volume by texts of Leicester's *Commonwealth,* written in a different hand, and *Annals.* A second complete manuscript is found in folios 14–123 of Trinity MS 0.4.2 at Trinity College, Cambridge. The article on Hayward in the *Dictionary of National Biography* refers to this manuscript as part of Gale's manuscripts in the same location. The volume containing *King Edward* once belonged to Sir Kenelm Digby (1603–1665), who has no known associations with Hayward. Digby's library was in France at the time of his death and was later purchased by the Earl of Bristol.[54] A third copy, consisting of eighty-four folios, is contained in MS XXXII at Dulwich College in London.[55]

Odgen MS 34 at the Science Library of University College London contains an incomplete manuscript of *King Edward.* The volume includes the bookplate of Ernest E. Baker, who presumably owned it before it was acquired by C. K. Ogden (1889–1957).[56] Pasted inside the cover is what appears to be a cutting from a nineteenth-century sale catalogue stating that this is "the original autograph manuscript, neatly written on both sides of 50 folio sheets, with numerous marginal notes of reference by the author, circa 1615, in the same volume." Written in pencil above the words "original autograph manuscript" is "contemporary," and the date "1615" has been crossed out and replaced with "1620." The Ogden manuscript contains pages 1–101 of the 1630 edition and ends abruptly in the middle of a sentence.

Another incomplete manuscript is found in MS V.b. 164 at the Folger Shakespeare Library in Washington, D.C. Longer than the Ogden manuscript, the Folger, consisting of eighty-five folios, includes pages 1–164 plus additional material from the 1630 edition. The Folger manuscript is the most problematical of the manuscripts because it differs significantly from the other versions. It omits significant sections of the 1630 edition but includes material not found elsewhere. For example, the Folger manuscript offers more information on the invasion of Scotland, contains quotations from Polybius and Tacitus, adds a paragraph on enclosures, and gives different and slightly more favorable assessments of Thomas, Lord Seymour and the Duke of Northumberland. Internal evidence leaves no doubt that it is a copy of another text; this text may have contained the additional materials, or the copyist had access to other sources which he included without giving a reference to them. The unique characteristics of the Folger manuscript suggest the possibility that Hayward himself prepared more than one version of *King Edward* before his death.

The Harleian manuscript is the most valuable for supplementing and correcting the printed text, while the incomplete Ogden manuscript deviates the least from the edition of 1630. The manuscripts supply missing and incorrect words that improve the readability of the book. The Harleian manuscript, for example, gives a complete list of the peerages granted at the beginning of the reign (5), and it corrects the error that Lady Jane and Lady Katherine were both the eldest daughters of the Duke of Suffolk (172). Numerous numerical differences may be found concerning the number of troops and ships deployed and differences in amounts of money. The Harleian manuscript relates that the English navy burned several towns on the north side of the Firth of Forth in 1548, while the 1630 edition omits this wanton devastation in Scotland (39). The most important textual

differences, however, concern the character and reputation of political leaders. Only the Folger and Harleian manuscripts mention that
the jurors trying Sir Thomas Arundell received no meat or drink
while confined to a house (143) and remind the reader that the Garter
taken from Lord Paget and given to the Earl of Warwick, eldest son
of Northumberland, was later restored to him (143). Severe criticism
of Sir William Cecil included in the Folger, Harleian, and Trinity
manuscripts has been deleted from the 1630 edition. At one point
Hayward wrote that Cecil's fortunes wanted nothing but moderation
to use them (128) and at another that many of his actions at the time
of the king's death "affected little matter of praise" (173). Although
Hayward could scarcely have been more hostile to Northumberland,
the Harleian and Trinity manuscripts contain a passage that says the
duke was "a cunning dissembler for a time but a sure paymaster in
the end," which remained unprinted (176).

An examination of the printed editions and manuscripts of *King
Edward* leaves major questions unanswered. First of all is the question of dating. When did Hayward complete his work and when
were the manuscripts written? Paleographical evidence is not very
helpful, since few paleographers are prepared to commit themselves
to dates within thirty years. On the basis of handwriting alone, the
Trinity manuscript might be dated as early as the late sixteenth
century, but the likelihood is that the manuscripts belong to the
years 1600 to 1630.[57] Since Hayward died in 1627, that is obviously
the last year in which he could have completed his work. Internal
evidence offers more clues than the handwriting. References to
James I and the need for improved relations with Scotland make it
unlikely that the surviving manuscripts were written before 1603.
The reference to Robert Cotton as "knight baronet" (3) indicates
that the surviving manuscripts and the printer's copy were written
after 1611, the year from which Cotton's title dates. Hayward's
reference to *The Lives of the III Normans, Kings of England*, published
in 1613 (177), also suggests that *King Edward* was written after 1611,
although it is not known when *The Normans* was actually written.
The death of Prince Henry in 1612 ended Hayward's hopes for
advancement at court and possibly encouraged him to devote himself more fully to the practice of law and to the writing of religious
books. These indicators therefore suggest that *King Edward* was
written after 1611 and before 1620.[58]

The above conjectures, based on paleographical analysis and internal evidence, assume that Hayward wrote the book about the same time as the manuscript copies were made. Since no autograph manuscript survives, it is possible that Hayward began work much earlier, revised and added to early drafts, and produced a final version upon which the 1630 edition is based. A reference to Cuthbert Tunstall, Bishop of Durham (d. 1559), in the Harleian manuscript as a man who was still famous for his learning, a remark that was modified in the edition of 1630 (46, 137), would support the possibility that Hayward began *King Edward* before the death of Elizabeth, perhaps as early as the 1580s when he was a student at Cambridge. A marked shift of emphasis after the execution of the Duke of Somerset in January 1552 indicates that Hayward composed *King Edward* in two stages:

> After these times few matters of high nature or observable note happened in England during King Edward's life. Of these I will select such as I esteeme most fit for history, both being publique and as contained matter of some regard, not always observing the just order of time, but sometime coherence or propinquity of matter. (143)

These comments also suggest that Hayward may have changed his approach after he returned to an incomplete manuscript that had been begun earlier. Although his principal source, the king's journal, does not end until November 1552, Hayward may have lost interest in his subject and simply brought it to a quick conclusion.

Our inability to determine exactly when Hayward wrote *King Edward* obviously creates severe difficulties in explaining why he chose to write about the last Tudor king. Since the author does not give his reasons, the only alternative is to consider the character of the book in the context of the period when it was most likely written. It is quite easy to reject any notion that Hayward wrote *King Edward* for religious reasons. Hayward's work, unlike other characterizations of Edward VI, does not portray him as the young Josiah or the champion of English Protestantism. Indeed it is difficult to find any connection at all between the views expressed in Hayward's *Annals* and devotional writings and his treatment of the Reformation in *King Edward*. The work has a distinct didactic and moralizing tone which suggests that it was intended to be an instructional manual for states-men and rulers.[59] Commenting on an engagement during the invasion of Scotland, Hayward said, "Certainly a commander should not carelessly cast himself into danger, but when either upon necessity or misadventure he falls into it, it much enhances both his reputation and enterprise if he behaves himself" (21). At another point Hayward warns that a noble should not abandon his "public charge" to engage in personal combat (26). The frequent use of moralistic maxims is further evidence of the work's didactic character.

If the book were written as an instructional manual, for whom was it intended? One important clue is found as Hayward recounts the failure of Protector Somerset to unify the crowns of England and Scotland through military conquest of the northern kingdom. Union with Scotland, according to Hayward, was "reserved unto a more peaceable and friendly time, so for a person in whose progeny it hath taken deep and durable root" (28). The reference to James I and his children is unmistakable. Because of Hayward's association with Prince Henry, he is the most likely choice. On the other hand, it is far from clear what Prince Henry was to learn from Edward VI and the mid-Tudor era. Since Hayward did not emphasize the king's role in the Reformation, he was hardly a triumphant monarch that Hayward would want Prince Henry to emulate. The Edwardian conquest of Scotland was a failure, and the king never defeated either France or Spain.

Hayward, however, may have been more interested in his own times than the Tudor era. In a conversation with Prince Henry, he said that when writing history, "I did personally bend and bind myself to the times wherein I should live."[60] If Hayward was actually offering cryptic comments on early Stuart politics, a wide range of imaginative interpretations presents itself. Perhaps Hayward used Northumberland to warn against the danger of court favorites such as Robert Carr, Earl of Somerset, or George Villiers, the future Duke of Buckingham. Hayward's association with Thomas Howard, Earl of Arundel, may have encouraged him to recommend the older nobility, especially the Howards in preference to the likes of the sixteenth-century Dukes of Somerset and Northumberland.[61]

Sir Roy Strong suggested that Prince Henry cultivated Hayward as a rival to William Camden and asked, "Was Hayward being cast by Henry as his historian viewing history through the eyes of the

Elizabethan war-party?"[62] If Strong is correct, more emphasis might be given to Hayward's efforts to demonstrate Edward VI's potential military prowess. Since there is no evidence that Hayward's manuscript was actually presented to the prince, it is likely that Hayward did not complete his work before Henry died suddenly in 1612. Another possibility is that Hayward himself recognized that Edward VI was an ill-chosen model for Prince Henry and abandoned the work in favor of more promising projects. This would help explain the abrupt ending of the book and why it remained unpublished. Hayward had high hopes of winning favor from Prince Henry and may have decided that this book was doomed to failure after his death. While *King Edward* could have been written or revised for the benefit of a number of other persons, including Prince Charles, the fact remains that it is impossible to say with certainty for whom it was intended or learn what hidden messages it contains.[63]

At the beginning of the book, Hayward states unequivocally that the manuscript journal of Edward VI was his principal source. "These memorials written with King Edward's hand (which now shall be the ground of this history) were imparted unto me by the great treasurer of English antiquities, Sir Robert Cotton" (3).[64] Careful examination reveals that Hayward made extensive but selective use of the journal. For example, he rejected completely the king's assessment of the Dukes of Somerset and Northumberland. Hayward used the king's account of the trial of Somerset but offered his own legal interpretation. For topics such as Lord Grey's campaign against rebels in Oxfordshire, the sweating sickness of 1551, and diplomatic negotiations with the Dukes of Saxony and Mecklenburg and the Marquis of Brandenburg, Hayward followed the king very closely. He was the first historian to consult the journal, and therefore his work superceded all previous accounts of the reign of Edward VI.[65]

Hayward's acquaintanceship with Sir Robert Cotton also gave him access to other manuscript sources, including the king's articles for the reform of the council (146–48),[66] a collection of arguments for and against "erecting a mart in England" that would compete against Antwerp (148–53),[67] letters relating to diplomatic negotiations with the French in 1550,[68] and possibly an account of the trial of Somerset in 1551.[69] In addition to the manuscripts provided by Cotton, Hayward acknowledged that he had consulted other authorities including the Bible, Caesar, Cicero, Eusebius, Livy, Pliny the Younger, Tacitus, and sixteenth-century political theorist Francois Hotman. "Writers of either nation" are mentioned as sources of the carefully balanced account of the English invasion of Scotland in 1547. One of these writers was William Patten, whose *Expedition into Scotland* (1548) was also used by John Stow and Holinshed;[70] Hayward's authority on Scotland was most likely George Buchanan.

John Strype, Hayward's seventeenth-century critic, analyzed *King Edward* and determined that the author drew upon three printed sources—Holinshed, Patten, and Nicholas Sanders—in addition to the king's journal. As Sanders was a widely denounced Roman Catholic polemicist, his *De Origine ac Progressu Schismatis Anglicani Liber* (1585) was an unlikely source for Hayward. Strype believed that the Caesarean birth of the king was a "popish invention" first circulated by Sanders, who in turn served as Hayward's authority.[71] Several modern historians, citing sources that predate Sanders, now accept the Caesarean birth as factual.[72] Strype found further evidence of Sanders in Hayward's criticism of Hugh Latimer for preaching against Thomas, Lord Seymour, the brother of Protector Somerset.[73] While it cannot be shown that Hayward never read Sanders, the criticism of Edwardian clergy so troubling to Strype—who was himself a cleric—did not stem from pro-Catholic sympathies on Hayward's part. In view of his career as a civil lawyer and his association with two Jacobean bishops, George Abbot and Tobie Matthew, it is also difficult to present a convincing argument that Hayward was anticlerical. Sanders, unlike Hayward, charged that the guardians of the king had introduced the "Zwinglian heresy" into the realm, argued that God had frustrated the heretical policies pursued by Protector Somerset and the Duke of Northumberland, and concluded that the reign of Edward VI was "calamitous."[74] While the political and religious views of Hayward and Sanders were strikingly different, their accounts of the fall of Thomas Seymour and their praise for the Henrician catholic bishops, Stephen Gardiner and Cuthbert Tunstall, were quite similar.[75]

Fewer questions arise in demonstrating Hayward's use of the second edition of Holinshed. This chronicle, revised and enlarged after the author's death, includes materials added by its compilers, especially John Stow and John Hooker. In drawing information from Holinshed, Hayward had access to the work of those who contributed to it, and he was probably familiar with Stow's *Annals of England* (1605) and the writings of Richard Grafton and John Speed.[76] Hayward, however, used these accounts as historical sources and did not follow the organization or chronology of any single work. Hayward's independence may be seen in his treatment of Anglo-Scottish relations and the Edwardian Reformation and in his hostility toward the Dukes of Somerset and Northumberland. Nevertheless, the influence of Holinshed is extensive. Hayward based his narrative of the Western Rebellion of 1549 on John Hooker's account in Holinshed. Details from Holinshed about the Norfolk Rebellion, led by Robert Kett, were also used extensively by Hayward. Holinshed and other Tudor chroniclers emphasized narrative details, but Hayward developed an original, provocative interpretation of the reign of Edward VI that set his history apart from the earlier works.

Hayward makes two contradictory statements that summarize his assessment of Edward VI, conclusions that confound any historian attempting to study the last Tudor king. At the beginning of the book, Hayward says that Edward is "rather to be admired than commended" (3), but ends with the words "this history I have built for the monument of his unperishable fame" (180). If the virtues and achievements presented by Hayward are examined carefully, the first conclusion seems more accurate than the second. The qualities ascribed to Edward are consistently conventional and might be praised in many previous monarchs: Edward was loving and loved, he possessed great knowledge of affairs, and he practiced clemency and Christian charity. Because the king kept a personal journal, Hayward boldly compared him with Julius Caesar. Hayward was unable to identify many positive achievements for a monarch who ruled for over six years. The king failed to unify England and Scotland; his role in restoring order after the most extensive rebellions of the century was minimal, and he was ineffectual in controlling both Somerset and Northumberland.

Hayward does, however, support the argument of W. K. Jordan that Edward became more active in governmental affairs during the last years of his reign.[77] Hayward also anticipates the revisionist argument of Jordan that the king strongly favored the "devise" that disinherited his half sisters and willed the crown to Lady Jane Dudley. The decisive issues, according to Hayward, were the king's love of Jane and his commitment to the Protestant church that had been established with his vigorous support. As this final effort met with resounding failure, it is difficult to see what achievements contributed to Edward's "unperishable fame."

Upon close examination, Hayward's work is less a study of the life of Edward VI than a narrative of conflict among leading court nobility. The principal characters are the Dukes of Somerset and Northumberland, not the king. Hayward's conception of political history goes little beyond the interaction of great men, a drama that is greatly oversimplified by concentrating on only two major characters and relegating all others to the periphery of the historical stage (15, 141). In his view, conflict among the nobility weakened a country that required strong leadership to control a population that was savage and disorderly (148). While Hayward recognizes Edward Seymour's fitness for appointment as lord protector in 1547, the reader is also told from the very outset that the protector was "little esteemed either for wisdom or personage or courage of arms" (15). Somerset failed, according to Hayward, not only because of character defects, but because he courted the popularity of the vulgar masses and submitted himself to a wicked wife (45, 81, 137).

Somerset was married to Anne Stanhope, "a woman for many imperfections intolerable, but for pride monstrous, [and] she was exceeding both subtle and violent in accomplishing her ends" (82). Dominated by his jealous and overbearing wife, Somerset imprisoned and executed his brother, Thomas, Lord Seymour. Hayward's condemnation of women goes far beyond his profound dislike of the duchess. When Somerset acted upon her counsel, Hayward belittled her advice as "a woman's counsel indeed and nothing the better." His prejudice against women reached a climax when he wrote: "O Wives! The most sweet poison, the most desired evil in the world. Certainly as it is true as Syracides[78] saith, that there is no malice to the malice of a woman, so no mischief wanteth where a malitious woman beareth sway . . ." (84).

The nobility denounced Somerset as a "bloodsucker" and a "parricide" after the death of his brother, and gradually misfortune destroyed him as well. Hayward presents the decline and fall of Somerset in the form of a five-act tragedy (85ff). He charges the protector with a long list of misdeeds, including allegations that he wanted to be king, but curiously chooses Richard, Lord Rich, the lord chancellor, to deliver the most damaging blows in a speech to the mayor and aldermen of London (129, 86ff). As Hayward follows Somerset's career to its inevitable conclusion, he laments the passing of a faithful weakling who fell by the sinister machinations of a rival noble.

The evil genius who dominates *King Edward* is John Dudley, Earl of Warwick and Duke of Northumberland, a cunning monster who is the embodiment of Hayward's hatred of the court nobility. At the very beginning of the book, Hayward boldly assigns to Northumberland qualities which—like those of Somerset—determine the whole course of his subsequent career. Hayward's Northumberland was of "ancient nobility" (an inaccurate characterization), "comely in stature and countenance," and possessed of "great spirit," traits that masked "his ambitious ends" (16–17). In a few powerful sentences Hayward created the Northumberland who survived for centuries in a wide variety of historical works.[79] And once created, the wicked duke merely fulfilled his destiny. Northumberland's lust for absolute power accounts for the tragedy of Somerset, while Dudley was "sotishly mad with over great fortune" as he induced the king to disinherit his sisters (129, 34, 76, 173). An intriguing reference to Northumberland's son, Robert, Earl of Leicester, suggests that Hayward may have created the father in the image of the son. When Robert became one of six gentlemen of the privy chamber, Hayward denounced him as the heir of his father's hatred against persons of nobility and added that Robert subsequently became a cruel monster of the Elizabethan court. Hayward connects Robert's appointment to the privy chamber with the king's death, alleging that shortly after Robert appeared "the king enjoyed his health not long" (128–29).

Two major events of the reign, the Protestant Reformation and the rebellions that engulfed the country in 1549, are handled very differently. Although Hayward was a writer of devotional books and clearly understood the importance of religion in a well-governed commonwealth, his account of the Reformation under Edward VI is extremely brief. Citing classical authorities, Hayward argued that religious change should proceed slowly and carefully lest social upheaval result. He approved of the religious changes under Henry VIII because they came about "quietly," but held that greater caution should have been exercised by Edward as he and his father were "not equal either in spirit or power" (43–44).[80] Hayward criticized church leaders, including Thomas Cranmer and Hugh Latimer, and observed that "neither religious persons are fit men for arms, nor arms fit means either to establish or advance religion" (37), views that identify him with the more peaceful Jacobean era, not the Reformation of the sixteenth century. His treatment of the Reformation is significantly different from that found in *Annals of the First Four Years of Queen Elizabeth*, where he deals sympathetically and at great length with the Anglican religious settlement of 1559.

In contrast to his neglect of the Edwardian Reformation, Hayward saw popular rebellion as a major aspect of the reign. Like Stow and other Tudor chroniclers he attributed the revolts to rapid religious change and government policy restricting enclosures. Although Hayward feared and despised the common people, he surprisingly argued that the rebellions were caused "more by default of governors than the people's impatience to live in subjection" (53). He also recognized the strengths of the rebel tanner, Robert Kett, and condemned Sir Anthony Kingston's haughty contempt for the law and brutal reprisals during the pacification of the West of England (64). For an advocate of absolutism, Hayward unexpectedly considered at great length the government's conciliatory offer to negotiate with the Norfolk rebels. To appease them the king offered to summon a parliament in which four to six rebels would be permitted "to present bills of their desires" (68–70). Hayward's commitment to a regime of law and order, however, was unequivocal. He rejoiced at the defeat of the rebellions of 1549 and attributed the failure of subsequent disturbances to the commons' inertia and their memory of humiliating defeat (103).[81]

Although Hayward emphasized domestic political and social conflicts, *King Edward* plays an important role in the emergence of the concept of British history, as he shows that the English invasion of Scotland in 1547 was rooted in older rivalries and attitudes that were declining in the early seventeenth century (27). His narrative of Anglo-Scottish relations begins with an account of the birth of Mary Stuart in 1542 that is identical to that in his *Annals*. And as it is not known for certain which work was completed first, it is impossible to say where the narrative first appeared. Hayward is favorable toward Somerset's Scottish policy supporting the marriage of Edward to Mary and offering the Scots "equality both in liberty and privilege" (14). Later, when this policy led to war, Hayward strives for fairness in the hope that there would be no further conflict between the two nations. At the beginning of his long account of the Battle of Pinkie, he wrote, "I intend to describe this battle fully, not to derogate thereby anything from the one nation or to arrogate to the other" (22–23). The Scots suffered a crushing defeat at the hands of Somerset's army, but Hayward is at pains to demonstrate the heroism of the defeated army and praise the integrity of its commanders.[82]

The Life and Raigne of King Edward the Sixth is an excellent example of a historical work that despite severe criticism has retained its influence centuries after the death of the author. The earliest and most hostile critic was John Strype, who compiled an extensive list of factual errors, including an incorrect birth date for the king. Strype objected to Hayward's "framing" of speeches, a practice that allowed an author to invent or improvise elaborate orations for rhetorical effect. Hayward certainly improved on the speech of George Stadlow to the citizens of London in 1549, while, contrary to Strype's assertion, Lord Rich's bold denunciation of Protector Somerset was a highly imaginative reconstruction of a speech that was actually given.[83] Strype also favored a more sympathetic assessment of the Dudley and Seymour families and faulted Hayward's neglect of parliamentary legislation.

In reality Strype may have been less bothered by questions of detail or interpretation than by Hayward's hostility toward the Reformation and clerical leaders such as Hugh Latimer and Thomas Cranmer. Strype acknowledged that Hayward was "esteemed for his writings of English history" but found his temper was "not well qualified for an historian, being touchy and morose, censorious, conceited, and too much aspiring." However, after reading the devotional book *David's Teares*, Strype could not deny Hayward's personal humility.[84] Early twentieth-century historian A. F. Pollard, like Strype, questioned Hayward's historical authority but noted his use of original manuscripts.[85] More recently, F. J. Levy found *King Edward* disappointing while praising Hayward as the best example of a "politic" historian.[86]

Most of the criticism of *King Edward* has been the work of scholars whose own approach to history was confessional or who wished to emphasize the limitations of seventeenth-century historiography. Whatever its shortcomings, *King Edward* is significant as the earliest biography of the last Tudor king, a work that was not superceded until the twentieth century. Literary historian Donald A. Stauffer recognized the stature of Hayward as a biographer and political historian of the English Renaissance and ranked him together with Sir Thomas More, Lord Herbert of Cherbury, and Sir Francis Bacon.[87]

Bacon's greatness as a philosopher enhanced the reputation of his biography of Henry VII, but in *King Edward* Hayward was more skillful and enterprising in the use of original sources.[88] As a "politic" historian, Hayward towers above contemporaries who practiced antiquarianism or defended political and religious orthodoxies. For a short book, *King Edward* is amazingly diverse. Its subjects include personal tragedy, political intrigue, diplomacy and warfare, domestic violence, and problems of economic growth. Hayward's male chauvinism, bold character sketches, provocative interpretations, and pragmatic inconsistencies fascinate even those who utterly reject his arguments. For these reasons it is easy to agree with Norman Scarfe's conclusion that *King Edward* is "the most interesting of all Hayward's works."[89]

EDITORIAL PROCEDURE

In the preparation of the text, the edition of 1630 has been collated with four manuscripts:

> British Library, Harleian MS 6021
> Folger Shakespeare Library, MS V.b. 164
> Trinity College, Cambridge, MS 0.4.2
> University College London, Ogden MS 34

Letters, numbers, and words inserted from a source other than the 1630 edition have been placed in square brackets and identified in the notes. Spelling, capitalization, and punctuation have been preserved with the following exceptions: contractions and abbreviations (including the ampersand) have been extended, and the letter "j" has replaced "i" according to modern usage. Italics that appear erratically in the 1630 edition, but are entirely missing in the manuscripts, have been omitted. The modern pound sterling symbol has been introduced and used consistently, and monarchs' names are written using Roman numerals, such as "Henry VIII" and "Charles V." A few minor typographical errors have been silently emended. Page numbers refer to the 1630 edition.

The text has been edited as a historical document, and therefore the notes are intended primarily to assist in historical study. In addition to identifying differences between the 1630 edition and the manuscripts, reference is made to copies of the first edition at the Newberry Library, the British Library (shelf mark 1578/8702), the microfilm of the copy at the Yale University Library, and to the second edition of 1636. The notes do not identify numerous variations in spelling, capitalization, punctuation, paragraphing, and organization that occur in the manuscripts. Since the important persons, places, and events mentioned in the text are either identified internally or can be readily identified using the authorities listed in the Bibliography, lengthy descriptive notes have been avoided.

The editor has attempted to prepare a more complete text than has previously appeared in print. As no authorial text has survived and because the 1630 edition was published posthumously, it is not possible to say which version of the text is closest to Hayward's intentions.

NOTES

1. The best account of Hayward's career may be found in the introduction to John J. Manning, *The First and Second Parts of John Hayward's The Life and Raigne of King Henrie IIII* (London: Royal Historical Society, 1991). In addition to Sidney Lee's account in the *Dictionary of National Biography*, aspects of Hayward's life are discussed in John Bruce, ed., *Annals of the First Four Years of the Reign of Queen Elizabeth, by Sir John Hayward* (London, 1840); Margaret Dowling, "Sir John Hayward's Troubles over His *Life* of Henry IV" *The Library* 4th ser., 11 (1930–31): 212–24; and Norman Scarfe, "Sir John Hayward: An Elizabethan Historian, His Life and Disappointments," *Suffolk Institute of Archaeology* 25 (1952): 79–97. Diarmaid MacCulloch, *Suffolk and the Tudors: Politics and Religion in an English County, 1500–1600* (Oxford: Clarendon Press, 1986), indexes no Haywards among gentry of the county. The revised *Short Title Catalogue* contains an excellent bibliography of Hayward's published works.

2. Public Record Office, PROB11/152.

3. Brian P. Levack, *The Civil Lawyers in England; 1603–1641: A Political Study* (Oxford: Clarendon, 1973), 16–21, 237; John Venn, *Alumni Cantabrigienses*, 10 vols. (Cambridge: Cambridge Univ. Press, 1922–54), Pt. 1 of 2. See also A. L. Attwater, *Pembroke College, Cambridge: A Short History* (Cambridge: Cambridge Univ. Press, 1936), and H. C. Porter, *Reformation and Reaction in Tudor Cambridge* (Cambridge: Cambridge Univ. Press, 1958), for the religious background of Hayward's education.

4. Bruce, ed., *Annals*, xvii. British Library, Add. MS. 22,587, fos. 33–35, "Of the precedencye of Doctors and Masters of the Chancery before serieaunts at lawe. . . ."

June 22, 1604. Levack, *The Civil Lawyers in England*, 237. See also G. D. Squibb, *Doctors' Commons: A History of the College of Advocates and Doctors of Law* (Oxford: Oxford Univ. Press, 1977), 30n. 2, 170; and W. J. Jones, *The Elizabethan Court of Chancery* (Oxford: Oxford Univ. Press, 1967), 103–17. Manning, ed., in *King Henrie IIII*, suggests that the manuscript is retrospectively dated (13n. 45).

5. Levack, *The Civil Lawyers in England*, 175; R. G. Usher, *The Rise and Fall of the High Commission* (Oxford: Clarendon, 1913), 345; Conrad Russell, *Parliaments and English Politics, 1621–1629* (Oxford: Oxford Univ. Press, 1979), 277; Manning, ed., *King Henrie IIII*, 7–17.

6. See J. W. Allen, *A History of Political Thought in the Sixteenth Century* (London: Methuen, 1928), 256–62; J. P. Sommerville, *Politics and Ideology in England, 1603–1640* (London: Longman, 1986), 21–68; S. L. Collins, *From Divine Cosmos to Sovereign State* (Oxford: Oxford Univ. Press, 1989), 103–8; and Gordon Schochet, *The Authoritarian Family and Political Attitudes in 17th-Century England* (New Brunswick, N.J.: Rutgers Univ. Press, 1988).

7. Levack, *The Civil Lawyers in England*, 88–90.

8. Ibid., 114.

9. Collins, *From Divine Cosmos to Sovereign State*, 107.

10. *Report of a Discourse concerning Supreme Power in Affaires of Religion* (London, 1606), 12–14.

11. John Hayward, *King Edward* (London, 1630), 54–56.

12. Ibid., 59.

13. References to religious leaders in Hayward's historical works are discussed below.

14. See Manning, ed., *King Henrie IIII*, 8–9.

15. John Hayward, *The Sanctuarie of a Troubled Soule* (London, 1616).

16. Ibid. (1636), 11, 57.

17. Ibid. (1607), A3r, after number 17.

18. John Hayward, *David's Teares* (London, 1622), A2.

19. Ibid., A5v-6r.

20. Ibid., "to the reader."

21. Ibid., 105. Hayward anticipates the language of N. Grew, *The Anatomy of Plants* (1682) quoted in *New Cambridge Modern History*, 14 vols. (Cambridge: Cambridge Univ. Press, 1961) 5:57.

22. Hayward, *David's Teares*, 164.

23. Ibid. (1636), 547–48.

24. John Hayward, *Christ's Prayer* (1624), 159. See Thomas Cogswell, *The Blessed Revolution: English Politics and the Coming of War, 1621–1624* (Cambridge Univ. Press, 1989), where this work is related to James's foreign policy (42).

25. Helen C. White, *English Devotional Literature: Prose, 1600–1640* (Madison: Univ. of Wisconsin Press, 1931), 10.

26. W. A. Wright, ed., *The Advancement of Learning* (Oxford: Clarendon, 1926), 264.

27. White, *English Devotional Literature*, 11.

28. Patrick Collinson, *The Religion of Protestants: The Church in English Society 1559–1625* (Oxford: Clarendon, 1982), 247–52.

29. Margo Todd, *Christian Humanism and the Puritan Social Order* (Cambridge: Cambridge Univ. Press, 1987), 206–22.

30. A portion of this book was included with the 1636 edition of *King Edward* and was in the same year published separately as *The Beginning of the Reign of Queene Elizabeth*, British Library shelf mark, 1417 a. 21.

31. D. W. Davies, ed., *The Actions of the Low Countries by Sir Roger Williams* (Ithaca, N.Y.: Cornell Univ. Press, 1964), 8. The most recent edition is included in John X. Evans, ed., *The Works of Sir Roger Williams* (Oxford: Clarendon, 1972). Neither editor searched for the manuscript from which Hayward worked nor considered his editorial skills.

32. S. L. Goldberg, "Sir John Hayward, 'Politic Historian,'" *Review of English Studies* NS, 6 (1955): 235; F. J. Levy, *Tudor Historical Thought* (San Marino, Calif.: Huntington Library, 1967), 252; and D. R. Woolf, *The Idea of History in Early Stuart England* (Toronto: Univ. of Toronto Press, 1990), 106–15.

33. Levack, *The Civil Lawyers in England*, 148–50. See also J. G. A. Pocock, *The Ancient Constitution and the Feudal Law* (Cambridge: Cambridge Univ. Press, 1987), 258–85.

34. Michael G. Finlayson, "Clarendon, Providence, and the Historical Revolution," *Albion* 22, 4 (1990): 607–32.

35. Thomas Fuller, *The Church History of Britain*, 6 vols. (1845. Reprint. Westmead, Eng.: Gregg, 1970), 5, 387.

36. P. M. Kendall, *The Art of Biography* (New York: Norton, 1965), 93–94. John Garraty, *The Nature of Biography* (New York: Knopf, 1957), 69.

37. Hayward, *Henrie IIII*, 136.

38. Ibid., 133.

39. Ibid., 96.

40. Manning, *The Life and Raigne of King Henrie IIII*, 1–5; Scarfe, "Sir John Hayward," 82–86.

41. Hayward, *The Lives of the III Normans*, A2r.

42. Ibid., 32.

43. Ibid., 43.

44. Ibid., 103.

45. David C. Douglas, *William the Conqueror* (Berkeley: Univ. of California Press, 1967), 376.

46. Bruce, ed., *Annals*, 107.

47. Ibid., 14, 24.

48. Hayward, *The Lives of the III Normans*, A3r.

49. Goldberg, "Sir John Hayward," 240.

50. Levy, *Tudor Historical Thought*, 267.

51. The quotation is from "to the reader." For bibliographical details see *Revised Short Title Catalogue*, Henry R. Plomer, *A Dictionary of the Booksellers and Printers Who Were at Work in England, Scotland, and Ireland from 1641–1667* (London: Bibliographical Society, 1907), and "The Eliot's Court Printing House, 1584–1674," *The Library* 4th ser., 2 (1921): 175–84. Partridge was ordered not to sell copies of the first edition for more than 16d. or forfeit his rights.

52. The 1630 edition was published before the birth of Prince Charles on May 29.

53. White Kennet, *A Complete History of England with the Lives of All the Kings*, volume 2, London, 1706, 1719.

54. M. R. James, ed., *The Western Manuscripts in the Library of Trinity College, Cambridge*, 4 vols. (Cambridge: Cambridge Univ. Press, 1902) 3:249. For the career of Digby, see the *DNB* and *Private Memoirs of Sir Kenelm Digby* (London, 1827).

55. George F. Warner, ed., *Catalogue of the Manuscripts and Muniments of Alleyn's College of God's Gift at Dulwich* (London, 1881), 353. The manuscript is described as "a contemporary copy, written in two hands, neither of which is the author's autograph."

56. Ernest E. Baker, FSA, was the nephew and legatee of J. O. Halliwell-Phillipps (1820–1889), a prominent collector of books and manuscripts and a biographer of Shakespeare.

57. The possible early date of the Trinity manuscript was suggested by Mr. David McKitterick, Librarian of Trinity College. Dr. Diana Greenway and Professor Roger Manning were kind enough to offer their opinions on Harleian MS 6021.

58. According to Bruce, ed., *The Lives of the III Normans* dates from September 1612 (*Annals*, xxi). For connections between Hayward and Prince Henry, see Roy C. Strong, *Henry, Prince of Wales, and England's Lost Renaissance* (New York: Thames and Hudson, 1986); and Elkin C. Wilson, *Prince Henry and English Literature* (Ithaca, N.Y.: Cornell Univ. Press, 1946). Further insight into the date of composition is offered by the comment of James Mountague, Bishop of Winchester, who stated in his preface to the collected works of James I, published in 1616, that he saw the journal of Edward VI in the king's library. Hayward claimed to have obtained access to the journal through the good offices of Sir Robert Cotton. The unanswered question is whether Cotton obtained the journal from the king's library or whether the manuscript had passed into Cotton's own collection at the time it was studied by Hayward. See John Gough Nichols, ed., *Literary Remains of King Edward the Sixth*, 2 vols. (London, 1857), 1:i.

59. See Philip Styles in Levi Fox, ed., *English Historical Scholarship in the Sixteenth and Seventeenth Centuries* (Oxford: Dugdale Society, 1956), 50.

60. Hayward, *The Lives of the III Normans*, A3r.

61. See Kevin Sharpe, *Sir Robert Cotton: 1586–1631* (Oxford: Oxford Univ. Press, 1979), who notes that Arundel directed Cotton and Hayward to plan a history of his ancestors (139).

62. Strong, *Henry, Prince of Wales*, 148, 224; see also Wilson, *Prince Henry and English Literature*, 151.

63. See Annabel Patterson, *Censorship and Interpretaton: The Conditions of Writing and Reading in Early Modern England* (Madison: Univ. of Wisconsin Press, 1984), 44–48, 65.

64. Nichols, ed., *Literary Remains* 1:i-ii; Sharpe, *Sir Robert Cotton*, 139, 209.

65. John Speed, *Historie of Great Britain* (London, 1632), states that he knew of the existence of King Edward's journal but does not say that he actually saw it. Speed thought the journal continued to the death of the king (1105).

66. British Library, Cotton MS, Nero C.x, fos. 86–89. Printed in W. K. Jordan, ed., *The Chronicle and Political Papers of King Edward VI* (Ithaca, N.Y.: Cornell Univ. Press, 1966), 181–84.

67. Ibid., fos. 85ff. in Jordan, ed., *Chronicle and Political Papers*, 168–73.

68. Diplomatic negotiations with the French, January to February 1550. British Library, Cotton MS, Caligula E.iv., fos. 203ff. printed in Barrett L. Beer and Sybil M. Jack, eds., *The Letters of William Lord Paget of Beaudesert, 1547–63 Camden Miscellany XXV* (London: Royal Historical Society, 1974), 81–97.

69. Cotton may have given Hayward access to British Library, Harl. MS 2194, which contains an account of Somerset's trial.

70. Printed in A. F. Pollard, ed., *Tudor Tracts, 1532–1588* (New York: E. P. Dutton, n.d.), 53–157.

71. John Strype, "Animadversions upon Sir John Hayward...," in *Ecclesiastical Memorials* (Oxford, 1822) 2:ii, 181. Further criticism of Hayward may be found in Strype's notes in *A Complete History of England with the Lives of All the Kings and Queens...* (London, 1706), 2. Strype's critique was based exclusively on the printed editions.

72. J. J. Scarisbrick, *Henry VIII* (London: Eyre and Spottiswoode, 1968), 353, and John Guy, *Tudor England* (Oxford: Oxford Univ. Press, 1990), 142, support Hayward's position. Nichols, ed., *Literary Remains* 1:xxiv; J. A. Froude, *History of England* (London 1893) 3:77; A. F. Pollard, *Henry VIII* (London, 1925), 360; and W. K. Jordan, *Edward VI, The Young King* (London, 1968), 36 disagree. See also Audrey Eccles, *Obstetrics and Gynaecology in Tudor and Stuart England* (Kent, Ohio: Kent State Univ. Press, 1982), who states that no successful Caesarean section on a living woman was recorded in England until 1793 (113–15) and J. H. Young, *Caesarean Section: The History and Development of the Operation from Earliest Times* (London: H. K. Lewis and Co., 1944), 8–9.

73. Strype, "Animadversions upon Sir John Hayward." In *Ecclesiastical Memorials*, 190.

74. Nicholas Sanders, *The Rise and Progress of the English Reformation* (Dublin, 1827), 193, 231–32, 224.

75. Ibid., 233, 229, 247.

76. For a discussion of relationships between these chronicles, see Barrett L. Beer, "John Stow and the English Reformation, 1547–1559," *Sixteenth Century Journal* 16, 2 (Summer 1985): 257–71, and "John Stow and Tudor Rebellions, 1549–1569," *Journal of British Studies* 27 (Oct. 1988): 352–74.

77. Hayward, *King Edward*, 146, 160–64; W. K. Jordan, *Edward VI: The Threshold of Power* (London: George Allen and Unwin, 1970), 402–55.

78. Sirach, author of *Ecclesiasticus*.

79. See Barrett L. Beer, "Northumberland: The Myth of the Wicked Duke and the Historical John Dudley," *Albion* 11 (1979): 1–14; Beer, *Northumberland: The Political Career of John Dudley, Earl of Warwick and Duke of Northumberland* (Kent, Ohio: Kent State Univ. Press, 1973); and Dale E. Hoak, "Rehabilitating the Duke of Northumberland: Politics and Political Control, 1549–53," in *The Mid-Tudor Polity c. 1540–1560*, edited by Robert Tittler and Jennifer Loach (Totowa, N.J.: Rowman and Littlefield, 1980), 29–51.

80. Modern historians, especially G. R. Elton, do not accept Hayward's view that the Reformation under Henry VIII was achieved with little opposition. See Elton, *Policy and Police: The Enforcement of the Reformation in the Age of Thomas Cromwell* (Cambridge: Cambridge Univ. Press, 1972), 1–45.

81. For a study of these rebellions, see Barrett L. Beer, *Rebellion and Riot: Popular Disorder in England during the Reign of Edward VI* (Kent, Ohio: Kent State Univ. Press, 1982).

82. See J. G. A. Pocock, "The Limits and Divisions of British History," *American Historical Review* 87 (1982): 311–36; Bruce Galloway, *The Union of England and Scotland: 1603–1608* (Edinburgh: J. Galloway, 1986), 31, 40, 47; and Brian Levack, *The Formation of the British State* (Oxford: Clarendon, 1987), 43, 81, 88.

83. George Stadlow's speech is cited by several authorities including Foxe, Grafton, and Holinshed and here by William Maitland, *The History of London* (London, 1772), 1:240. John Stow, *Annals of England* (London, 1605), mentioned Rich's speech but gave no details (1010). For a discussion of invented speeches, see Barbara J. Shapiro, *Probability and Certainty in Seventeenth-Century England* (Princeton: Princeton Univ. Press, 1983), 146–47.

84. Strype, "Animadversions upon Sir John Hayward," 197–98. There is no evidence that Strype examined any of the manuscripts of *King Edward*.

85. A. F. Pollard, *England under Protector Somerset* (London, 1900), 301, 335.

86. Levy, *Tudor Historical Thought*, 258–66.

87. Donald A. Stauffer, *English Biography before 1700* (Cambridge: Harvard Univ. Press, 1930), 45–48, 279.

88. See Goldberg, "Sir John Hayward," 240–41; F. J. Levy, ed., *The History of the Reign of King Henry the Seventh [by] Francis Bacon* (Indianapolis: Bobbs-Merrill, 1972), 41, 51–52.

89. Scarfe, "Sir John Hayward," 96.

Sir John Hayward
in *The Life and Raigne of King Edward the Sixth* (1630)
Courtesy of the Newberry Library

The Life and Raigne
of King Edward the Sixth

*T*HIS NOBLE PRINCE, whose Storie is here deliuered, seems to
have had the same aduersitie of fortune in his life and death,
which he had at his birth. For as he was destituted of the helpes of
nature at his entrance, and was faine to haue his way made into the
world with a knife; so in his life was there continuall imployment of
either Sword or Axe; of that, either at home against his Rebells, or
against his enemies abroad; of this, vpon his Nobles, and particularly
vpon his owne vncles by the mothers side, of which the Duke of
Somerset's case is very remarkable. As his birth was violent, and his
reigne troublesome, so was his death praemature, and not without
suspicion of some practice; of which, (besides vulgar rumour,) Car-
dan[1] in calculating his scheme, seemes to haue some jealous conjecture. For whether he diuined it by his art in Astrology, or
apprehended it by the course and carriage of businesse, hee made a
dangerous praediction: when hee foresaw, that the King should
shortly dye a violent death, and (as he reporteth) fled out of the
kingdome for feare of further danger. Howsoeuer, he was as noble a
branch as euer sprung out of the Royall stocke, worthy (if so it had
seemed good to God) of a more fauourable birth, a quieter reigne,
and a longer life. But as the notable accidents in his tumultuous times
doe deserue to be recorded, so doth the King himselfe for his sweet
condition, for his minde as innocent as his years, for his rare endowments well deserue to be commended to euerlasting memory; that
he may bee permanent so much the longer in the life of an history,
by how much the threed of his naturall life was cut shorter by the
Fates. And indeed as he had the birth of Caesar, so had he beene
worthy to haue had the fortune and fame of Caesar; but a better

conclusion. This history is left vs from the pen of a worthy Author, of whom we haue another essay in Henry IV. This comes out into the world after the death of the father; a Posthumus, and is not like to finde any Patron, but the loue and affection of thee, (fauourable Reader) to which I commend it, and thee to God.

[Page 1] Edward King of England the sixth of that name of the Norman Race, was borne at Hampton Court the [6][2] of October 1537 being the only surviving sonne of King Henry VIII by Jane his third wife, daughter to Sir John Seymer Knight. And because King Henry did take her to wife, after the death of Katherine his first wife, from whom he had beene divorced, no question nor conceit was cast, but that this issue betweene them had right to succeede.

All reports do constantly runne, that he was not by naturall passage delivered into the world, but that his mothers body was opened for his birth, and that shee dyed of the incision on the fourth day following. After which sort men brought [Page 2] forth, were by the ancient Romanes esteemed fortunate; and commonly proved great enterprisers with happy successe. For so Plinie writeth: Auspicatius enecta matre nascuntur, sicut Scipio Africanus prior natus. These were called Caesones and afterwards Caesares as Plinie, Festus Pompeius, Solinus [Valerius][3] and Titius Probus affirme. Quia caeso matris vtero in lucem prodiissent.[4]

In this maner was Caeso Fabius borne, whom Livy reporteth to haue beene thrice Consull; first with Lucius Aemilius next with Sp. Furius, and thirdly with T. Virginius. Thus also was Scipio borne, who by reason of his braue atchieuements in Africke, was surnamed, Scipio Africanus prior. But in that Plinie affirmeth, that he was the first who was called Caesar, a caeso matris vtero, he seemeth to haue made a slippe. For before him and somewhat before the warres with the Samnites, one Claudius was surnamed Caesar, because he was in that fashion brought into the world.[5]

In ancient times these births were esteemed sacred to Apollo, as Servius noteth out of these words in Virgill.

> Inde Lycham ferit exectum cum [iam][6] matre perempta,
> Et tibi Phoebe sacrum.[7]

And therefore, Aesculapius because he was ripped from his mothers wombe, was feigned to be the sonne of Apollo; as Servius vpon another place of Virgill hath observed. For this cause also in the ancient state of Rome, things consecrated to[8] Apollo, were kept by the familie of the Caesars [because the first of that familie came by such passage into this light].[9] That Julius Caesar was so borne it is an vncontrouled Report. But that he was the first of the familie of Caesars, who was so either named or borne. It is a thicke mistie error supported chiefly by some men of excellent judgement in their owne professions, but childishly vnskilfull in anything besides. Plinie writeth[10] that his Father was surnamed Caesar; who having borne the office of Praetor, determined his life by suddaine death.

What would haue beene either the fortunes or endeavours of King Edward he never attained to yeares of proofe. Assuredly both for the time of his age and raigne, he is rather [Page 3] to bee admired then commended, whereby he raised an high expectation for times to ensue. In one point hee was like the like borne Julius Caesar. For as Caesar in the middest of his greatest actions, wrote an exact and curious Commentary of all his notable enterprises by Armes. So this Edward during all the time of his Raigne, but most especially towards the end, kept a most judicious Journall of all the most principall passages of the affaires of his [state].[11] These memorialls written with King Edwards hand (which now shall be the ground of this historie) were imparted vnto me by the great Treasurer of English antiquities, Sir Robert Cotton Knight Baronet, who as he hath beene a most industrious, both collector and conseruer of choice peeces in that kinde, so is he most ingenuously free, to communicate the vse of them to others.

This young Prince was brought vp among nurses, vntill he arriued to the age of sixe yeares, when he had passed this weake and sappie age, he was committed to Dr Coxe, who after was his Almoner, and Master John Cheeke men of meane birth, but so well esteemed for virtue and learning by reason of the place of their employment that they might well be said to be borne of themselues. These having equall authority for instruction of the young Prince and well agreeing bare equall stroake in divers faculties. Dr Coxe for knowledge of Divinity, Philosophy and gravitie of manners; Master Cheeke for eloquence in the Latine and Greeke tongues. But for other sufficiencies (so farre as it appeares by the bookes which hee wrote) pedantique enough. Others also were appointed to acquaint him with the vse of the most respected forraigne languages, all jointly

endevouring to infuse into him knowledge and vertue by some
mixture of honest delight.

Vnder these teachers the Prince thrived so well that in short time
he spoke the French tongue perfectly. In the Latine tongue he could
declaime vpon the suddaine no lesse both readily and purely then
many who were reputed [Page 4] amongst the most learned of these
times. He attained not only commendable knowledge but speech in
the Greeke, Spanish and Italian languages: having alwaies great
judgment in measuring his words by his matter: his speech being
alike both fluent and weightie, such as best beseemed a Prince, as
for naturall Philosophie, for Logicke, Musicke, Astronomie, and
other liberall sciences his perfections were such that the great Italian
philosopher Cardane, having tasted him by many conferences and
finding him most strongly to encounter his new devised paradoxes
in Philosophie, seemed to be astonished betweene admiration and
delight, and divulged his abilities to be miraculous. These his ac-
quirements by industrie were exceedingly both enriched and enlarged by many excellent endowments of nature. For in disposition
he was milde, gracious and pleasant, of an heavenly wit, in body
beautifull, but especially in his eies, which seemed to haue a starrie
liuelynes and lustre in them, generally hee seemed to be as Cardane
reported of him A MIRACLE OF NATURE. [In a word hee was
one that to prayse fully, were fully to sett downe, whatsoeuer perfection nature or art cann possibly bring forth].[12]

When he was few moneths aboue nine yeeres of his age, great
preparation was made either for creating or for declaring him to be
Prince of Wales, Duke of Cornewall, and Count Palatine of Chester.
In the middest whereof King Henry his Father ended his life of a
dropsie accompanyed with a spreading [sore][13] of his thigh. Herevpon Edward Earle of Hartford and Sir Anthony Browne knight of
the order and Master of the horse were forthwith dispatched by the
residue of the counsaile, to the young King then lying at Hartford.
These came vnto him and the next day brought him to Enfield,
neither with preparation nor traine any more then ordinarie. Here
they first declared vnto him and to the Lady Elizabeth his sister, the
death of King Henry their father. Vpon which tidings they both brake
forth into such vnforced and vnfained passions, as it plainely appeared that good nature did worke in them, beyond all other respects.
Never was sorrow more sweetly set forth, their face seeming [Page

5] rather to beautifie their sorrow, then their sorrow to clowde the beautie of their faces. Their young yeares their excellent beauties, their louely and liuely enterchange of complaints in such sort graced their griefe: as the most yron eies at that time present were drawne thereby into societie of their Teares [without any difference, whether the kinges death concerned them in particulare or not].[14]

The next day following being the last of Januarie the young king advanced towards London. The Earle of Hartford riding next before him and Sir Anthony Browne behinde. The same day he was proclaimed King and his lodging was prepared within the Tower. He there was received by the Constable and Lieuetenant on horse backe without the gates, and vpon the bridge next the Ward-gate by all the chiefe Lords of his counsaile. These attended him to his chamber of presence and there swore allegiance vnto him.

Here he remained about three weekes, and in the meane time the counsaile appointed vnto him by his Fathers will dayly sate for ordering the affaires of the Kingdome. Among these the Earle of Hartford was elected and forthwith proclaimed protector of the Realme, and governour of the kings person vntill he should accomplish the age of eighteene yeares. To this office he was deemed most fit, for that he was the kings vnckle by the Mothers side, very neere vnto him in bloud, but yet of no capacitie to succeede; by reason whereof his naturall affection and dutie was lesse easie to be over-carryed by Ambition. A few daies after the Lord Protector knighted the king within the Tower, and immediately the king stood vp vnder his cloath of estate, tooke the sword from the Lord Protector and dubbed the Lord Maior of London knight. Herehence ensued diverse other advancements in honour. For Sir Edward Seymer Lord Protector and Earle of Hartford, was created Duke of Somerset. The Lord William Parre Earle of Essex was proclaimed Marquis of Northampton. [Sir John Dudley Lord Lisle was created Earle of Warwick and made Lord Chamberlain of England, Sir Thomas Writhisley, Lord Chancellor was created Earle of Southampton.][15] Sir Thomas Seymer the kings vnckle was made Lord of Sudley and high Admirall of England. Sir Richard Rich was made Lord Rich Sir William [Page 6] Willoughby Lord Willoughby of Parreham, and Sir Edmund Sheffield, Lord Sheffield of Buterwike. And because high titles of honour were in that time of the Kings minority sparingly granted because dignity then waited vpon desert, which caused it againe to be waited on by respect, every of these testified for others, that it was the pleasure of the Kings Father before his death, that these titles should thus bee conferred.

During this time the body of King Henrie was with honorable solemnities conveyed from London to Sheene and thence to Windsore and there buryed within the Colledge. All his officers brake their staues and threw them into the graue, but at their returne to the tower, new staues were delivered vnto them, this solemnitie being finished the king vpon the nineteenth of February 1547 rode in great state from the Tower to the Palace of Westminster, and the day following was crowned by the Archbishop of Canterbury assisted with other Bishops and all the chiefe nobilitie of the Realme, about the twenty-ninth yeere of the Empire of Charles V and the 33 of the Raigne of Francis I of France and in the fifth yeere both of the raigne and age of Marie Queene of Scotland.

The same day a generall pardon was granted to all persons as it hath beene vsuall at coronations. But by some envious oppositions or for some other causes vnknowne six onlie were excepted. The Duke of Northfolke, Cardinall Poole, Edward Lord Courtney eldest sonne to the Marquesse of Exceter, Doctor Pates, Master Fortescue and Master Throgmorton. But they overlived that envie and had their pardons afterwards in the first yeere of the Raigne of Queene Marie. A few daies after the Earle of Southampton Lord Chancellor of England, for being opinatiue (as it was reported) and obstinately opposite to the rest of the Lords in matters of counsaile, was removed both from his office of being Chancellor, and from his place and authority in counsaile, and the great seale was delivered to Sir William Pawlet[16] Lord St John, who [Page 7] was Lord great Master of the Kings houshold. But this wound of disgrace never left bleeding, vntill it was stopped by the Protectors fall.

It is certaine that from the first entrance of this King, to his raigne never was King either more loving to others, or better beloved generally of all. The one whereof proceeded from the goodnes of his disposition, the other from many graces and vertues illustrious in him, for besides his excellent beauty and modestie beseeming a Prince, besides his sweet humanity the very life of mortall condition, besides a naturall disposition to all literature, whereto he seemed rather borne then instructed, many noble and high virtues sparckled in him, especially Clemencie, Courage, Care, and knowledge in affaires of state.

To Clemencie he was much enclined, especially in matters of blood, and most especially if it were for Religion, a vertue so much the more esteemed, by how much it had beene lesse vsed before, insomuch that albeit hee was most earnestly affected to that religion wherein hee had beene brought vp, yet none were executed in his time for other religion, but only two blasphemous Heretickes, Joane Butcher and George a Dutchman.[17]

And when Joane Butcher was to be burned, all the counsaile could not procure him to set his hand to the warrant. Wherefore they employed Thomas Cranmer Archbishop of Canterbury to deale privatly with him for his subscription. But the King remained firme both in reason and resolution, affirming that [religion cannot be supported with bloud and][18] that he would not driue her headlong to the Divell, but because Heretickes for the most part haue a straine of madnesse, he thought it best to apply her with some corporall chastisements which with respit of time might happely reduce her to good order. The Archbishop was violent[19] both by perswasions and entreaties, and when with meere importunity he [did prevaile].[20] The King in subscribing his name said, that he would lay all the charge thereof vpon the Archbishop before God. Not many yeares passed, but this [Page 8] Archbishop also felt the smart of the fire, and it may be that by his importunity for bloud, hee did offend, for a good thing is not good if it be immoderatelie desired or done.

His courage did appeare in the great delight he tooke in representations of Battailes, Skirmishes, Assaults, and of all kinde of military exercises, his judgment was great either for errors or fine contriuances in the field. And no actions of Armes were executed in his time, but he would perfectly vnderstand, by what aduantages on the one side or ouersights on the other euent succeeded. He tooke great pleasure in exercises of actiuity whereto he much trained his servants. And to that end he often appointed challenges among them for wrestling, leaping, running, riding, shooting at roues,[21] and at rounds and such like games, and at riding and shooting, would sometimes be of one of the sides. He had 100 archers of his ordinary guard, who once mustering before him shot two arrowes euery man together against an inch board of well seasoned timber. All stroke through the board, and their arrowes stucke in another board behinde, and divers pierced both the boards; generally none might be of his guard, but besides of tall and comely stature, such as were either good archers or wrastlers or casters of the barre or leapers or runners or of some other man-like qualitie. He was exceeding skilfull in fortifications, and bestowed great cost in strengthening Calleis, Berwicke, and other parts thereabout. He knew all the principall ports in England, Scotland, Ireland, France, and other countries not farre distant, how they lay, when the tyde served, what vessels of burthen they could receiue and what windes served for entrance.

Touching his care and knowledge in affaires of state, nothing was more conspicuous in him. He was much conversant amongst his counsaile, and would well vnderstand what matters passed their judgments, and vpon what grounds. In matters discoursed by them, he would often encounter [and ouerrule]²² their reasons, and adde most liuely reasons of his owne. In [Page 9] so much that at last they made an order that no matters of weight, should be debated vnlesse he were present. Admirable he was to collect the speeches and opinions of many, and to draw their differences to a true head, alwaies bending himselfe rather judiciously to resolue, then by doubts and distinctions to perplex a businesse, he had a chest whereof he alwaies carryed the key about him, for keeping record of such matters as were concluded by his counsaile. And embracing businesse for part of his solace, hee appointed set times with Doctor Coxe Master of his Requests for speeding poore mens causes without tedious attendance or delay. Of all the Magistrates Justices and Gentlemen of sort within his realme, he knew by their names, their housekeeping, their religion and manner of life. Hee was skilfull in the exchange beyond the seas, and in all the circumstances and practices thereof. And so was he both skilfull and provident in matters of the Mint at home. To Embassadors hee would giue answere vpon the suddaine and touch both orderly and fully vpon every part of their orations, to the delight and admiration of all the hearers. He much frequented sermons and penned notes with his owne hand, his notes hee cyphered with greeke characters to the end that they who waited on him should not read them. His disports were ingenuous and man-like whereby he alwaies learned somewhat. And yet as well from these as from his businesses of state, he dayly reserved some houres for his private studies and exercises with his Teachers. These endeavours fell vpon so excellent a capacitie that in every short distance of time, he made incredible increase both in learning and experience of affaires and consequentlie in loue of all men.

Presently after that he was setled in his governement, Dr Wotton the kings Embassador resident with the Queene Dowager of Hungarie, regent of the Low Countries vnder the Emperor was discharged of that attendance and addressed to the Emperors court, there to reside Embassador for the king insteed of Doctor Bonner Bishop of London, and of Sir [Page 10] Francis Bryan who were called home. He was furnished with instructions that being first informed from the former Embassadors as wel of the general state of the Emperors court as of such particuler intelligences as might serue to advance the kings intentions, he should deal with the Emperor to declare al Scots for his enimies, except such as should be friends to the King, which should appeare by his safe conduct. That because it had bin agreed betweene the Emperor and the late King of England, that the yeare next ensuing they should with [like joint][23] forces, inuade the Territories of the French King, he should moue the Emperor to aduise of some order and forme for those proceedings. That whereas the Duke of Lorraine had bin late before at the Emperors court, and made some ouerture for peace or truce, between the Emperor and the French King, he should be informed by Sir Francis Bryan of the whole estate of that businesse and awaite opportunity to put the Emperor in remembrance, that it had been couenanted betweene him and the King of England, that neither of them should treat of peace or truce with the French King, or any other common enimy without consent of the other, and that the King of England had well obserued that article in refusing to giue eare to the French embassador making overture for such a treatie. That whereas it had beene agreed betweene him and the King of England, that either of them should send certaine ships to sea well manned and apparelled for fight, which all that yeere had beene performed by the king, whereas the Emperor shifted the default vpon his officers, in case he should not cause the said Navy to be forthwith furnished, he should awaite occasion to sollicite the same. Lastly that he should carry a nimble eare as well touching any variation in all these matters, as for other occurrences in France, Spaine, Italie, Almaine and thereof advertise the king.

But notwithstanding all these cautions and preventions of peace, or truce betweene the Emperour and the French, the king of England finding the Emperor slow in his [Page 11] performances and much suspecting his secret ends entertained a treatie of peace with France, but secretly and a farre off, and to bee governed as occasions should vary, and in regard hereof agreement was made, that all ships and goods which had bin surprised at sea by the English vpon the French, or by the French vpon the English since the beginning of that treatie should be freely discharged. And albeit the English had great aduantage in value of reprisalls, as being alwaies both more strong and actiue at sea, yet the king by his proclamation commanded that forthwith restitution should be made.

Hostility being thus suspended with France, preparation was made for warres against Scotland, the occasion whereof did thus arise.

Mary Styward sole daughter and heire to James V King of Scots began her raigne ouer the Realme of Scotland vpon the 18 of December 1542, being then not aboue 7 daies olde, so as the Sunne no sooner almost saw her an infant then a Queen and no sooner was shee a Queene, but she was desired of Henry then King of England, to be assured in marriage to Prince Edward his only sonne, being then not much aboue 6 yeares of age. Vpon this ouerture the gouernor of Scotland assembled the nobility of the Realme at Edenburgh, where after much debatement of the comodities or discommodities like to ensue, they concluded in the end that in March then next ensuing a Parliament should be held to giue perfection and forme to that businesse.

In the meane time Sir Ralph Sadler knight was sent embassador from England to the Gouernor and other Lords of Scotland, who followed his charge with so good diligence and advice that in the same parliament, authority was giuen to William Earle of Glancorne, Sir George Douglasse, Sir William Hamilton, Sir James Leirmouth, knights, and to one of the secretaries of state, to conclude this marryage. These commissioners came into England with whom before the end of Julie, the same yeere all covenants were concluded, instruments of the contract of marriage interchangeably sealed and [Page 12] sworne, and a peace established for ten yeares, which time expyred both the Prince and the Queen should be of age to consent.

The French King all this time was so enteartined with warres against the Emperor that he had no sence of these proceedings, but when he vnderstood that these agreements were passed as well for marriage as for peace he bent his best endeuour to dissolue them both. First with intention to impeach both the greatnesse and strength of the English nation; after with desire to winne this marriage for Francis who afterwardes was King of France. To this purpose the French king sent for Mathew Earle of Levenoxe,[24] who then serued vnder his pay in Italie and furnished him with mony, forces, and friends, and aboue all with many encouragements to take vpon him brauely the honour of his house, and Ancestors, to remoue the Earle of Arraine from the Regency of Scotland, and to reverse such pactions as he had made. The Earle at his first arrivall in Scotland was joyfully received, as a man most[25] engaged in domesticall factions. He alwaies vsed curtesie and modestie disliked of none, sometimes sociablenes and fellowship well liked by many, generally he was honoured by his nation and well reputed by strangers, in favour of him the Pope sent the Patriarch of Apulia his Legat into Scotland, who in the Popes name did faithfully assure, that both forces and mony should be sent into Scotland to resist the English. Hee drew the greatest of the Cleargie on his side who were most powerfull to draw on others. On the other side the king was not negligent to support his party with supplies, whereby great troubles ensued in Scotland, which fell not within the times that I haue in hand.

In the end the Earle of Arraine abandoned the king of England, and applyed himselfe only to the French by reason whereof, the Regencie was confirmed to him which otherwise he had bin vpon adventure to loose. And as the Earle of Arraine did forsake the English and adjoine to the French, so the Earle of Levenoxe, being forsaken by the French, applyed [Page 13] his service wholy to the English, which did not only continue but much encrease the calamities of Scotland, during the time of King Henries raigne.

King Henrie at the time of his death gaue a speciall charge to the Lords of his counsaile, that they should omit no endevours whereby the said marriage might be procured to take effect. Herevpon they pursued this quarrell in the same state the king left it. But before they attempted any thing by Armes, the Lord Protector assailed the Scottish nobility with a friendly letter. Herein he remebred them of the promises, seales, and oathes, which by publike authority had passed for concluding this marriage, that these being religious bonds betwixt God and their soules, could not by any politike act of state be dissolved, vntill their Queene should attaine vnto yeares of dissent. Hee farther added that the providence of God did then manifestly declare it selfe, in that the male princes of Scotland failing the kingdome was left to a daughter, and in that King Henry [alsoe amonge his manie wiues][26] left only one sonne to succeed. That these two princes were agreeable both for yeares and princely qualities, to bee joyned in marriage, and thereby to knit both Realmes into one. That this vnion as it was like to bee both easily done and of firme continuance so would it be both profitable and honourable to both the Realmes. That both the easinesse and firmnes might be conjectured, for that both people are of the same language, of like habit and fashion, of like qualitie and condition of life, of one climate, not only annexed entirely together, but severed from all the world besides. For as these are sure arguments that both descended from one originall, and had bin vnder one governement, so (by reason that likenes is a great cause of liking and of loue) they would be most forceable meanes both to joine and to hold them in one body againe, that the profit would rise by extinguishing warres betweene the two nations, by reason whereof in former times victories abroad haue bin impeached invasions and seditions occasioned, the confines of both Realmes laid wast or else made a nurserie of rapines, robberies, and murthers, the [Page 14] inner parts often deepely pierced, and made a wretched spectacle to all eies of humanity and pittie. That the honour of both Realmes would encrease as well in regard of the countries sufficient to furnish not only the necessities but the moderate pleasures of this life: as also of the people great in multitude, in bodies able, assured in minde not only for the safetie, but the glory of their common state. That hereby would follow assurance of defence, strength to enterprize, ease in sustaining publike burthens and charge. That herein the English desired no preheminence, but offered equalitie both in liberty and priviledge, and in capacitie of offices and imployments, and to that end the name of Brittaines should be assumed indifferent to both nations. That this would be the accomplishment of their common felicitie, in case by their evill either destinie or advice they suffered not the occasion to be lost.

The authority and reasons of this letter weighed much with persons of most weighty judgements, but others more powerful in that state partly vpon vaine hope in regard of the young yeares of the

king, partly vpon feare of alteration in religion, and partly in favour
of their ancient amitie with the French, and doubting to be brought
vnder by the English, were altogether carryed another way, yet they
dispatched an Embassador into England, but neither was any thing
done, neither do I finde what was propounded to haue bin done.

Herevpon diverse hostilities began to be practised. And first a
small ship of the kings called the Pensie hovering at sea, was assailed
by the Lyon a principall shippe of Scotland. The fight began farre
off and slow, but when they approached, it grew very furious, wherein
the Pensie so applyed her shot, that therewith the Lyons ore loope
was broken, her sailes and tacklings torne: and lastly, shee was
boarded and taken. But as shee was brought for England, shee was
cast away by tempest and negligence neere Harewich haven, and
most of her men perished with her. I would not haue staide vpon
this small adventure, but that it seemed a presage to the succeeding
warre, wherein the English acquired a glorious victorie, but [Page
15] lost the fruit thereof, by reason of their stormie disorders at home.

Many such small actions were enterprised dayly, which were but
scattering drops in regard of the great tempest which did ensue. For
in the meane season an armie was prepared for invasion of Scotland,
vnder the fortune and commande of the Lord Protector. The
souldiers first assembled at Newcastle and were there mustred by
the Earle of Warwicke. [To this place the lord protector rode from
London in post, after whose arriuall they forthwith marched in file
to Barwick.][27] Heere they sojourned three[28] daies in which time the
kings fleete arrived, consisting of 65 Bottomes, whereof one galley
and 34 tall ships were well appointed for fight, the residue served
for carriage of munition and victuals. Of this fleete Edward Lord
Clinton was Admiral and Sir William Woodhouse his Viceadmirall,
in this time also a generall muster was taken and order appointed for
the March.

In the whole armie were betweene 12 and 1300 thousand foot,
1300 men at Armes, 2800 light horse, being such men for their goodly
personages, their ready horses their braue apparell, their armour and
weapons, as never before was an armie set forth into those parts in
all points better appointed. The Lord Protector being Generall,
represented the person and Majestie of the king. The Earle of
Warwicke was Lieutenant generall. The Lord Gray of Wilton was
Marshall of the field, and captaine generall of the horsemen.

[Sir Francis Bryan was lieftenant of the high horsemen.][29] Sir Ralph Vane Lieutenant of all the men at Armes and Dimilances, Sir Ralph Sadler was generall treasurer, other gentlemen had their particuler charges. But vpon the Generall and the Earle of Warwicke both the hopes and hazards of the maine adventure did wholy turne. And because much shalbe said of these two hereafter, because during the raigne of king Edward they were the principall actors in every sceane, I will briefly declare both what persons, and of what demerits at that time they were.

Edward Seymer Duke of Somerset, Lord Generall was a man little esteemed either for wisedome or personage, or courage in armes. But being in favour with king Henry and by [Page 16] him much imploied, was alwaies observed to be both faithfull and fortunate as well in giving advise, as in managing a charge. About fiue yeares before hee being Warden of the Marches against Scotland, the invasion of James V was by his direction encountred, and broken at Solome Mosse,[30] whereof diverse of the Scottish nobility were taken prisoners. The yeare next after, hee and the Earle of Warwicke with a handfull of men to speake of, fired Lieth and Edenburgh, and returned by a leasurely march 44 miles through the body of Scotland. The yeare next ensuing he invaded the Scottish borders, wasted Tiuedale and the marches and deformed the country with ruine and spoile. The yeare then next following, being appointed to view the fortifications vpon the marches of Caleis, he not only did that, but with the hardy approach of 7000 English men raised an armie of 21000 French, encamped over the River before Bulleine, wanne their ordinance, carriage, treasure and tents, with the losse only of one man, and returned from thence by land to Guisnes, wan in his way within shot and rescue of Arde the castle of Outing, commonly called the red pile. The yeare next ensuing this, he invaded and spoiled Picardy, began the forces[31] of Newhaven, Blacknesse and Bullingberge and so well applyed his endeavours, that in a few weekes and before his departure they were made tenible, vpon these and other like successes, his succeeding fortunes were esteemed alwaies rather new, then strange, and his onlie presence was reputed a sufficient surety for an army, and yet did he never rise hereby, either into haughtines in himselfe, or contempt of others, but remained courteous and affable, choosing a course least subject to envie betweene stiffe stubbornes and filthy flattery never aspiring higher then to be the second person in state.

John Dudley Earle of Warwicke was a man of ancient nobilitie, comely in stature and countenance,[32] but of little gravitie or abstinence in pleasures, ye sometimes almost dissolute, which was not much regarded, if in a time when vices began to grow into fashion, a great man was not over severe.[33] He was [Page 17] of a great spirit and highly aspiring, not forebearing to make any mischiefe the meanes for attaining his ambitious endes. Hereto his good wit and pleasant speeches were altogether serviceable, having the art also by emptie promises and threats to draw others to his purpose,[34] in matters of armes he was both skilful and industrious, and as well in fore-sight as resolution present and great. Being made Lord Lieutenant of Bulloine, when it was first taken by the English, the walls sore beaten and shaken, and in very truth scarce mainetaineable, he defended the place against the Dolphine whose armie was accounted to consists of 52,000 men. And when the Dolphine had entred the base towne, not without slaughter of divers of the English, by a braue sally he cast out the French againe with the losse of above 800 of their men esteemed the best souldiers in France. The yeare next ensuing when the French had a great fleete at sea for invasion of England, he was appointed Admirall and presented battaile to the French Navy, which they refused and returned home with all their threats and cost in vaine. Hereupon he landed 5000 men in France, fired Treport, and diverse villages there abouts and returned to his ships with the losse only of one man. To say truth for enterprises by armes, he was the Minion of that time, so as few things he attempted, but he atchieved with honour, which made him more proud and ambitious when he had done.[35] Generally he alwaies encreased both in estimation with the King, and authority among the Nobility, doubtful whether by fatall destinie to the state, or whether by his vertues, or at least by the appearances of vertues.

Now the Generall in this voyage was diligent and carefull and to perfect all practises which might serve to advance the adventure, as to give good contentment to all the Souldiers. These also were of good confidence and cheere, as well out of their owne courage, as for the skill, valour, and fortune of their commanders. And first every souldier was commanded to take with him provision for foure daies, and so were let out of Berwicke and encamped about two flight [Page 18] shootes[36] off the town upon the sea side towardes Scotland. The Lord Clynton also put to sea with his fleet, alwayes holding his course with the army to relieve them if neede should require. Here proclamation was made in three parts of the field, declaring the causes of this journey, and offering not only peace, but love and rewards to all such as would either advance or favour the marriage betweene the two princes. Hereof it was conceived that the Scots had good intelligence, having some factors doubtlesse at this mart, albeit (as wisdome was) they did not openly trade.

The next day they began to march, wherein the Lord Gray and Sir Francis Bryan led above 800 lighthorsemen as a scout a mile or two before the army, aswell to give advertisement of appearance or approach of enimies as to provide lodging both commodious and safe. Sir Francis Bryan was so regardfull of his charge as he never disposed any matter of weight but first he acquainted the Generall therewith, neither did he at any time forsake his saddle, untill the army were quartered, and seated in such order, as if any alarme should be given, the horsemen might issue forth without disturbance of the foote, and the Avauntguard without shufling with the battaile or Arriere, next to the light horsemen followed the Avantguard, in number between 3 and 4000 foote, 100 men at armes and 600 light horsemen led by the Earle of Warwicke. The Battaile followed consisting of about 6000 foote, 600 men at armes, and about 1000 light horsemen conducted, by the Lord Generall himselfe. Lastly followed the Arrier wherein were betweene 3 and 4000 foote, 100 men at armes and 600 light horse under the conduct of the Lord Dacres a lively aged gentleman no lesse setled in experience then in yeares. Upon one wing the Artillery was drawn being 16 peeces, every peece having his guard of pioners to plain the waies, the other wing was made by men at armes and demilances for the Avantguard and halfe the battaile riding [Page 19] about two flight shoote[37] from their side. The other halfe of the battaile and the whole flancke of the Arrier was cloased by the carriages being 900 cartes, besides wagons. The residue of the men at armes and Demilances marched behinde.

In this order both beautifull and firme they marched two daies using no hostility, least peace thereby might happely be hindred. The second day they arrived at a place called the Peathes, a valley stretching towards the sea 6 miles in length, about 20 score in breadth above, and 5 score in the bottome wherein runnes a little river. The bankes are so steepe on either side, that the passage is not direct, but by paths leading sloopewise, which being many the Place is thereupon called the Peathes. It was given forth in the army that here the Scots prepared to resist them, howbeit no forces appeared. Only the Pathes were cut in divers places with traverse trenches, which much encumbred the carriages untill the Pioners had leveld them againe. Assuredly a small power joyned to the advantage of the place might have troubled the English very much. For albeit no resistance was made yet the English had much to doe in surmounting the naturall difficulties of the place, the greatest part of one day.

Passage being made the generall summoned three castles that were neere. One desperate of succor and not desirous to dispute the defence presently yeelded, but two stood upon their adventure. So the Cannon was planted a breach made and the place entered, but, then the moderation of the Generall was both unusuall and unexpected, in sparing the Defendants lives, for it hath bin a long observed law of the field: That if a small company of better courage then judgement, will contrary to all mililtary discipline maintaine a feeble place against royall forces, if they will offer to impeach the purposes of an army, which they have no reason to thinke themselves able to resist, after battery presented they put themselves out of all ordinary expectation of mercy and so [Page 20] Caesar answered the Advaitici, Civitatem conservatarum, si privsquam aries murum attigisset sede dissent.[38] And so the Duke d'Alua much blamed Prosper Columnus for receiving a castle upon conditions after he had beaten it with the Cannon. And in this case I conceive the law of God to be understood; which spareth not those citties that will not yeeld untill they be beseiged, meaning doubtlesse when the defendants have little reason to thinke themselves able to make defence, I will not involve in silence with what a sodaine strategem of wit, the defendants of one of these peeces escaped extremities, when they understood both that they were not able to defend themselves, and that their obstinacy had excluded all hope of pardon. They made petition that they might not presently be slaine; but have some time to recommend their soules to God, and afterwards be hanged, this respite being first obtained their pardon did more easily ensue.

Upon the first newes of the approaches of the English and all truths enlarged by report. The Governor of Scotland was somewhat appalled, as neither furnished at that time with forraine aide, nor much trusting his forces at home yet resuming his accustomed courage well acquainted with both fortunes,[39] he sent his heralds through all parts of the realme, and commanded the firecrosse to be carried (an ancient custome in cases of importance) namely two firebrands set in fashion of a crosse and pitched upon the point of a speare, therewith proclamation to be made that all men above 16 yeares of age, and under 60 should resort forthwith to Muscleborough with convenient provision of victuals with them.

Hereupon they flocked to the place in so great multitudes that it was thought fit not only to stay further resort, but making choice of the most serviceable, to discharge divers of the rest.

Now as the English directed their way towards the place where they understood the Scots assembled, they came to [Page 21] a river called Lynne crossed with a bridge of stone. The horsemen and carriages passed through the water, the foote men ouer the bridg, which because it was narrow the army was long in setting over. The Avantguard marched forth and the battaile followed but as the Arriere was passing over, a very thicke mist did arise. The Earle of Warwick having before espyed certaine plumpes of Scottish horsemen ranging the field returned towards the Arriere to prevent such danger as the thicknesse of the mist, the neerenes of the enimy, and the disarray occasioned by the narrownes of the bridg might cast upon them. The Scots conjecturing (as it was) that some personage of honor staied to have a view of the Arriere, called to the English to know if any noble man were neere, for that one whom they named (well knowne to be of honourable condition) would present himselfe to the Generall in case he might safely be conducted. Certaine young souldiers not used to such traines made rash and suddaine answere that the Earle of Warwicke was neere, under whose protection he might be assured. Hereupon they passed the water placed 200 of their prickers behinde a hillocke, and with 40 more cast about to finde the Earle. Now the Earle espying 6 or 7 of them scattered neere the army and taking them to be of the English sent one to command them to their Arraie, and to that end himselfe rode an easy pace towards them followed only with 10 or 12 on horsebacke. He that had beene sent before was so heedlesse either to observe, or to advertise what they were that the Earle did disover them to be enimies untill he was in the middest among them.

Certainly a commander should not carelesly cast himselfe into danger, but when either upon necessity or misadventure he falleth into it, it much advanceth both his reputation and enterprise if bravely he behave himselfe. Now the Earle espying where he was gave so rude a charge upon a captaine of the Scots named Dandy Care, that he forced him to turne, and chased him above 12 score at the lances [Page 22] point. Herewith the residue retyred deceitfully towards the place of their Ambush, from whence issued about 60 more. Then the Earle gathered his small company about him, and with good countenance maintained the fight. But the enimy in the end whether preceiving some succors advancing from the army where the Alarme was then taken, or whether intending to draw the English further into their Ambush, turned away an easy pace. The Earle forbad his men from following, fearing a greater ambush behind the hill as in truth there was. At his returne he was received with great applause by the English souldiers, for that he did so well acquit himselfe in the danger, whereinto by error and not by rashnes he had bin carryed. One of his men was slaine, another hurt in the buttocke, a third named Vane so grievously hewne that many thousands have dyed of lesse then halfe his hurts, whereof notwithstanding, he was cured afterwards; of the Scots 3 were taken prisoners and presented to the generall by the Earle, of whom one had received many entertainments and curtesies in England.

I may happely be thought tedious in setting downe these occurrences which may seeme small. But besides that in actions of armes small matters are many times of very great moment, especially when they serve to raise an opinion of commanders, I intend to describe this battaile fully, not to derogate thereby anything from the one nation or to arrogate to the other. From what honor riseth upon event of a battaile, when oftentimes the smallest accident overthroweth a side? And when victory doth more often fall, by error of the vanquished then by valor of the victorious. But my purpose is to make it appear what myseries both nations have avoided, and what quietnesse and security they have attained by their peaceable union, when as either of them being able to bring such forces into the field for their mutuall ruine, they may now doe the like for their common either glory or necessity. Againe this battaile being partially [Page 23] described heretofore by the writers of either nation and not without uncivill termes, I will now set it forth so indifferently and fairely as I can. Lastly this battaile is not slightly to be slipped over, being the last (wherein I pray that I may prophesie truly) that was or ever shall be strooke betweene the two nations. But I returne to my purpose.

Now the Scottish horsemen began to hover much upon the English army, and to come pricking about them sometimes within the length of their staves, using some liberty of language to draw the English from their strength. But the Generall of the English knowing right well, that the Scots were expert in tumultuous fights, restrained his horse from falling forth, and maintained a close march untill they came to Salt Preston by the Frith. Here they encamped within view of the Scottish army, little more then two miles distant from them. About a mile from the English another way, the Scottish horsemen were very busy, upon a hill, and emboldened much partly upon their former approaches, and partly by the neerenesse of their army, but cheifly upon an opinion which they conceived, that the English horsemen were young and unskilfull, and easy to be dealt with, came upon the English with encreased troopes, to the number of 1200 besides 500 foote which lay in ambush behind the hill. The Lord Gray and Sir Francis Bryan impatient of braveries obtained leave of the Generall a little to assay them, and so as they came scattered upon the spurre within a stones cast of the English and were beginning to wheele about, the Lord Gray with some troopes of lighthorsemen charged them home. These were forthwith seconded by certaine numbers of dimilances and both backed with about 1000[40] men at armes. The Scots meant not to depart before they had done their errand wherefore turning their faces boldly maintained the fight, three houres and more. In the end overlaied with numbers they were put to flight and chased almost to the [Page 24] edge of their campe, in this fight the chiefest force of the Scottish horsemen was defeated, to their great disadvantage afterwards. The Lord Hume by a fall from his horse lost his life. His sonne and heire with two Preists and 6 gentlemen were taken prisoners, and about 1300 slaine. Of the English one Spanish hackbutter was hurt, and three captaines of the light horse, by unadvised pursuite were taken prisoners.

The day next following the Lord Generall and the Earle of Warwicke rode towards the place where the Scottish army lay to view the manner of their encamping, as they were return[ing][41] an herald and a trumpeter from the Scots overtooke them, and hauing obtained audience the Herald beganne, that he was sent from the Lord Governor of Scotland partly to enquire of prisoners, but cheifly to make offer, that because he was desirous to avoide not only profusion[42] but the least effusion of Christian blood, and for that the English had not done any vnmanlike outrage or spoile, he was content they might returne, and should haue his safe conduct for their peaceable passage.

Then the Trumpeter [said][43] that the Lord Huntly his master sent message by him, that aswell for breefe expedition, as to spare expence of christian blood, he would fight vpon the whole quarrell either with 20 against 20 or with 10 against 10 or more particularly by single combate betweene the Lord Generall and himselfe, which in regard the Scots had advantage both for number and freshnesse of men, in regard also that for supply, both for provision and succors they were at home, he esteemed an honourable and charitable offer.

To the Herald the Lord Generall answered that as his comming was not with purpose or desire to endammage their Realme, as he was there, he would neither intreat nor accept of him leaue to depart, but would measure his marches in advancing or retiring, as his owne judgment, guided by advice of his counsaile should deeme expedient.

[Page 25] To the Trumpeter he returned answere, that the Lord Huntley his master was a young gentleman full of free courage, but more desirous of glory then judicious, as it seemed, how to win it. That for number of Combatants it was not in his power to conclude a bargaine, but was to employ all the forces put under his charge to the best advantage that he could, that in case this were a particular quarrell betweene the Governour and him he would not refuse a particular combat, but being a difference betweene the 2 kingdomes, it was neither fit, nor in his power either to vndertake the [adventure][44] vpon his owne fortune, or bearing a publike charge to hazard himselfe against a man of private condition.

Then the Earle of Warwicke said, I marvaile Trumpeter that thy master would make his challenge so fond, as he might well knowe it could not be accepted. For tell mee Trumpeter, can he thinke it fit, that he, to whose charge is committed the command of all this Army abroad, and at home the Kings person and protection of all his Realmes, should vndertake a combate with a particular man. But he might haue found others his equals amongst vs, by whom he might haue beene assured that he should be answered? And (therewith

turning his speech to the Lord Generall) vnder your Graces favour,
I accept the challenge. And bring me word Trumpeter that thy master
will performe with mee as thou hast said, and thou shalt haue 100
crownes for thy travaile.

Nay, answered the Lord Generall, you haue a great charge in the
Army, which vpon a private mans challenge you must not abandon.
But Herault tell the Lord Governor, and the Lord Huntly, That we
haue entred your country with a sober company (for so the Scots
terme a thing that is meane) your army is both great and fresh, but
let them appeare vpon indifferent ground, and assuredly they shall
haue fighting enough. And bring me word Herault that they will so
doe, and I will reward thee with 1000 crownes.

This Earle of Huntley was a man young, bold, adventerous, of
very good resolution and skill in Armes. But this [Page 26] challenge
was so farre beyond the point both of direction and honor, that the
English that knew his noble spirit, did beleeue that his name was
therein abused, which hee manifested to be true by disavowing it
openly afterwards. For it is not fit that a man should abandon his
publike charge to vndertake both the office and danger of a private
Souldier. And therefore the like challenge of Tullus was refused by
the commander to the Albanes.[45] For that the contention was not
betweene their persons, but between the Citties of Alba and Rome.
So Sertorius was refused by Metellus, Antonius by Augustus, and
John Emperor of Constantinople by a king of Scythia. So Antonius
Caracalla by reason of his often challenges, was esteemed not to be
so valiant as vaine. And herevpon the histories of our times forbeare
not to blame Charles V, Emperour, Henry VIII, king of England, and
Francis I, king of France, for that they often adventured rather as
Souldiers then as Commanders.

But doubtless the Lord Governour made a most honourable offer,
and the rather for that it was conceiued by the English, that he held
himselfe no lesse assured of victory then he was of his owne resolution to fight, whereto it seemed that he wanted not good reason,
cheifly vpon confidence of his owne forces, and partly vpon expectation of 12 Gallies and 50 ships well appointed out of France to
assayle the English at their backs. All the chiefe Captaines yeelded
to the same advice of giving battaile, as out of their owne judgements,
because they saw it agreeable to that which the Lord Governor had
determined. To these the residue attributed so much, that albeit

diverse were of a different opinion, yet they chose rather to condemne their owne vnderstanding then to question theirs.

During this enterparlance the Scots discharged 4 great shots
against the English campe, without harme as it happened, but not
without breach of the Laws of the field, whereby not only publike
messengers are priviledged to passe without either danger or scorne,
but vntill they haue discharged their [Page 27] message all hostilty
should surcease. Howsoeuer this happened the Generall of the English army vnwilling to bee behind in any equall or honourable offer
sent letters to the Lord Governour of Scotland. Wherein he desired
him and the residue of the Scottish nobility to consider, That both
armies consisted of Christians, to whom nothing should be more
deere then peace, nothing more detestable then effusion of humane
blood. That the cause of this warre did not proceed from ambition,
avarice, or hate, but from desire of perpetuall peace betweene their
people and nations, which could no way so firmely be knit as by
knitting their Princes together in marriage. That many other respects, set aside their King for his birth, his yeares, his royall estate,
his princely personage, education, and qualities was such a marriage
for their Queene, that a more convenient could not be found, that
in case all the Nobility of Scotland were not of one minde. The
English would bee content that their Queene should bee brought
up amongst them, vntill she should be of age to make her owne
choice. Provided that in the meanetime she should not bee transported to any forraigne country, or any agreement made for any other
marriage. That vpon this condition there should be an abstinence of
hostility, for all that time, and they would in quiet manner withdraw
their army, and repaire all dammages which indifferent Commissioners should adjudge.

No answere was hereto returned, but rumors ran freshly among
the Scottish souldiers, that the intention of the English was to take
away their Queene by force, and vnder pretence of marriage to
reduce the kingdome vnder their dominion, and verily it may seeme
almost incredible that all these faire ouertures, made by men well
esteemed for honest dealing, could take no place, that nothing could
moue the Scots to forsake their distant and heavy helps, and to
embrace friends, both ready and at hand. But besides that, the long
continued warres betweene the English and the Scots, had then
raised invincible jealousies and hate, which long continued peace

hath since abolished, I doe herein [Page 28] admire the vnsearchable working and will of God, by whose inflexible decree the vnion betweene the two Realmes did not then take effect, when by the death of King Edward it should haue beene of short continuance, (as by the death of Francis II, the vnion betweene France and Scotland did suddenly dissolue) but was reserued vnto a more peaceable and friendly time, so for a person in whose progeny it hath taken deepe and durable root. And so for that time no conditions of peace being regarded, both sides addressed themselues to their adventure.

The places where the two Armies lay encamped, were divided by the river Eske, the banks whereof were almost so deepe as the bankes of the Peathes mentioned before. The Scots lay somewhat neere the one side and the English about two miles from the other. The English first raised their Campe, and began to march towards the river Eske, intending to possesse a hill called Vnder-Eske, which commanded the place where their enimies lay. The Scots conjecturing so much, cast their Tents flat vpon the ground, passed the River and mounted the Hill before the English could come neere. Hereupon the English turned aside to another hill called Pinkenclench, which afterwards fell much to their Advantage, aswell for that they were then in place to bee ayded by their ships which rode neere in Edenburgh Frith, as also for that they gained thereby the advantage both of winde and sunne, a great part of the strength of an Army and lastly for that their enimies were therby cast into a cruell errour.

For no sooner did they espy the English turning from them, but forthwith they were of opinion that they fled towards their shipping. This surmise was first occasioned for that the English ships remoued the day before from Lieth to Muscleborough Frith, which was conceiued to be for taking in their foote and carriages, that the horsemen might with lesse encumbrance and more hast returne backe vpon the spurre. Hereupon they had appointed the same [Page 29] night, (whose darknesse would haue encreased the feare) to haue giuen a camisado[46] vpon the English. But vnderstanding that they were well entrenched hauing good escout abroad and sure watch within, they brake that purpose, but vpon this declining of the English from them, the conceit did againe reuiue, not only as a thing desired, but because the English were inferior vnto them in number, and had trauailed farre, and were well knowne to grow short in their provisions. Yea when they were discerned to make stand vpon the first ascent of

Pinkenclench hill, the conjecture ran that their flight, was only deferred vntill they might couer their disorders by the dead darkness
of the night. Maruailous security and alwaies dangerous, when men
will not beleeue any bees to be in a hiue untill they haue a sharpe
sense of their stings.

And thus the Scots heaued vp into high hope of victory, tooke the
English fallen for foolish birds fallen into their nette, and seeming
to feare nothing more then that they should escape, forsooke their
hill and marched into the plaine directly towards the English. Here
the Lord Governor put them in remembrance, how they could neuer
yet be brought vnder by the English, but were alwaies able either
to beate them backe, or to weary them away. He bad them looke
vpon themselues and vpon their enimies, themselues dreadfull, their
enimies gorgeous and braue, on their side men, on the other spoil,
in case either through slownesse or cowardise they did nor permit
them to escape, who (lo now) already haue begun their fight.[47]

The whole army consisted of 35 or 36,000 men of whom they
made three battailons. In the Auantgard commanded by the Earle
of Angus about 15,000 were placed, about 10,000 in the battaile, over
whom was the Lord Governor and so many in the Arriere, led by the
valiant Gordone Earle of Huntley. Hackbutters they had none, no
men at armes but about 2000 horsemen, prickers as they are termed,
fitter to make excursions and to chase then to sustaine [Page 30] any
strong charge. The residue were on foote well furnished with Jacke
and skull, pike, dagger, bucklers made of boorde, and sliceing swords,
broad, thinne and of an excellent temper. Every man had a large
kercheife folded twice or thrice about the necke, and many of them
had chaines of latten drawne three or foure times along their hoses
and doublet sleeues, they had also to affright the enimies horses, big
rattles couered with parchment or paper, and small stones within,
put vpon staues about three els long. But doubtles the ratling of shot
might haue done better service.

The Earle of Angus led the Avantguard with a well measured
march, whereupon the Lord Governor commanded him by a messenger to double his pace, thereby to strike some terror vnto the
enimy. Himselfe followed with the battaile a good distance behinde,
and after came the Arrier well nigh euen with the battaile on the left
side, the avauntguard was flanked on the right side with 4 or 5 pieces
of Artellery drawne by men, and with 400 horsemen prickers on the

left. The battaile and Arriere were likewise guarded with Artillery in like sort drawne, and about 4000 Irish Archers brought by the Earle of Argile, serued as wing to them both, rightly so termed as being the first who began the flight.

The Generall of the English and the Earle of Warwicke were together when the Scots thus abandoned the hill, which they espying gaue thankes to God, holding themselues in good hope of the euent, forthwith they ordered the artillery, and taking a louing leaue departed to their seuerall charge, the Generall to the battaile, where the Kings standard was borne, the Earle to the Avantguard, both on foote, protesting that they would liue or dy with the souldiers, whom also with bold countenance and speech (which serue souldiers for the best eloquence) they put in minde of the honour, their ancestors had acquired, of their own extreme disgrace and danger if they fought not well, that the justice of their quarrell should not so much encourage as enrage them, [Page 31] being to revenge the dishonor done to their King, and to chastise the deceitfull dealings of their enimies, that the multitude of their enimies should nothing dismay them, because they Who come to maintaine their owne breach of faith, besides that the checke of their consciences much breaketh their spirit, haue the omnipotent arme of God most furious against them.

Herewith arose a buzzing noise among them as if it had bin the rustling sound of the sea a farre of, euery man addressing himselfe to his office, and encouraging those who were neerest vnto them. The Earle ranged his Avauntguard in Array vpon the side of the hill, expecting vntill the enemy should more neerely approach. The generall after he had ordered his Battaile, parte vpon the hill, and parte vpon the plaine, somewhat distant from the Avantguard on the right side, mounted the hill to the great artillerie, to take a view of both the Armies, and to giue directions as occasions should change. The arrier stood wide of the battaile vpon the same side, but altogether vpon the plaine. The Lord Gray Captaine of the men at Armes, was appointed to stand somewhat distant from the Avantguard on the left side in such sort as he might take the flanke of the enimie, but was forbidden to charge, vntill the foot of the Avantguard were buckled with them in front, and vntill the battaile should be neere enough for his reliefe.

Now after that the Scots were well advaunced in the field, marching more then an ordinary pace, the great shot from the English ships, and especially from the galley began furiously to scoure among them, whereby the Master of Grime and diuers others about were torne in peices; especially the wing of the Irish was so grievously either galled or scarred therewith, that (being strangers and in a manner neutralls) they had neither good heart to goe forward, nor good likeing to stand still, nor good assurance to run away. The Lord Gray perceiued this amazement, and conceiued thereby occasion to be ripe, wherevpon when the enimy was not [Page 32] about two flight shot from the English avantguard, suddainly and against direction with his men at armes, he charged them on head.

The Scots were then in a fallow field, where into the English could not enter, but ouer a crosse ditch and a slough, in passing whereof many of the English horse were plunged and some mired, when with some difficulty and much disorder they had passed this ditch, the ridges of the fallow field lay trauerse, so as the English must crosse them in presenting the charge. Two other disadvantages they had, the enimies pikes were longer then their staues, and their horses were naked without any barbs. For albeit many brought barbes out of England, yet because they expected not in the morning to fight that day, few regarded to put them on.

The Scots confident both in their number, order, and good appointment, did not only abide the English, but with some biteing termes provoked them to charge. They cloased and in a manner locked themselues together, shoulder to shoulder, so neere as possibly they could, their pikes they strained in both hands and therewith their buckler in the left, the one end of the pike against the right foote, the other breast high against the enimy. The fore ranke stooped so low as they seemed to kneele, the second ranke close at their backs, crossed their pikes ouer their shoulders, and so did the third and the rest in their order, so as they appeared like the thornie skinne of a hedghogge, and it might be thought impossible to breake them. Not withstanding the charge was giuen with so well gouerned fury, that the left corner of the Scots battaillon was enforced to giue in, But the Scots did so brauely recouer and acquit themselues, that diverse of the English horsemen were overthrowne, and the residue so disordered as they could not conueniently fight or fly, and not only justled and bare downe one another, but in their confused tumbling backe brake a part of the Avantguard on foote. In this encounter 26 of the [Page 33] English were slaine most part Gentlemen of the best esteem. Divers others lost their horses, and carried away markes that they had beene there. The Lord Gray was dangerously hurt with a pike in the mouth, which strucke two inches into his necke. The Lord Edward Seymer sonne to the Lord Generall lost his horse, and the English Standard was almost lost.

Assuredly albeit encounters betweene horsemen on the one side, and foot on the other are seildome with the extremity of danger, because as horsemen can hardly breake a battaile on foot, so men on foot cannot possibly chase horsemen. Yet hearevpon so great was the tumult and feare among the English, that, had not the commanders bin men both of approued courage and skill, or happely had the Scots beene well fournished with men at Armes the army had that day beene vtterly vndone. For an army is commonly like a flocke of fowles when some begine to flie all will follow. But the Lord Gray to repaire his error endevoured with all industrie to [r]allye[48] his horse: The Lord Generall also mounted on horsebacke and came amongst them both by his presence and aduice to reduce them into order. Sir Ralph Vane and Sir Ralph Sadler did memorable service. But especially the Earle of Warwicke who was in greatest danger declared his resolution and judgment to bee most present in reteyning his men both in order and in heart. And hauing cleered his foot from disturbance by the horsemen, hee sent forth before the front of his Avantgard Sir Peter Mewcas Captaine of all the Hackbutters on foot, and Sir Peter Gamboa, a Spaniard Captaine of 200 Hackbutters Spanish and Italians on horse. These brought their men to the slough mentioned before, who discharging liuely almost close to the face of the enimy did much amaze them, being also disordered by the late pursuit of the English horsemen, and by spoiling such as they had ouerthrowne. At the backes of these the Archers were placed, who before had marched on the right wing of the Avantguard, and then [they][49] sent such [Page 34] showers of shot ouer the Hackbutters heads, that many bodies of their enimies being but halfe armed, were beaten downe and buried therewith. And besides the Master of the Artillery did visit them sharply with murthering haileshot from the peeces mounted towards the top of the hill, also the Artillery which flanked the Arriere executed hotly. Lastly the ships were not idle, but especially the galley did play vpon them and plague them very sore.[50]

The Scots being thus applied with shot, and perceiuing the Avantguard of the English to be in good order, neerely to approach, and the men at armes to haue recouered their Array, turned their Avantguard somewhat towards the South, to win, as it was thought, some advantage of ground. By this meanes they fell directly on head on the English battaile, wherevpon the Earle of Warwicke addressed his men to take the flanke. The Avantguard of the Scots being thus [set]⁵¹ vpon, and beset with enimies, began a little to retire towards their great battaile, either to be in place to be relieued by them, or happely to draw the English more separate and apart. The Irish Archers espying this and surmising the danger to be greater then it was, suddenly brake vp and committed the saftie of their liues to their nimble footmanship. After whose example all the rest threw away their weapons, and in headlong hast abandoned the field, not one stroke hauing been giuen by the English on foot. But then the horsemen comming furiously forward had them very cheap.

The flight was made three waies, some running to Edenburgh, some along the sands towards Lieth, but the most towards Dakeith, which way by reason of the marish the English horse were least able to pursue. The chase was given from one of the clocke in the afternoone til almost six. It reached fiue miles in length, and foure in breadth, all which waies the Scots scattered in their flight Jackes, Swords, Bucklers, Daggers, or whatsoeuer was either cumbersome, or of weight to impeach their hast, yea some cast [Page 35] off their shooes and dublets and fled in their shirts. Divers other devises were practised to avoid or deferre the present danger. Some intreated and offered large ransomes, some being pursued only by one, sodainly turned head and made resistance, by whom many horses were disabled, and some of their horses⁵² either slaine or hurt. The Earle of Angus a man of assured both hardiness and vnderstanding, couched in a furrow and was passed ouer for dead vntill a horse was brought for his escape. 2000 others lying all the day as dead departed in the night. Divers others plunged into the river Eske and couered themselues vnder roots and branches of trees, many so streined themselues in their race that they fell downe breathlesse and dead, whereby they seemed in running from their deaths to runne vnto it.

The English discerned in their retreit that the execution had beene too cruell, and farre exceeding the bounds of ordinary hostility, which happely was a cause in the secret judgement of God, that they had no better fruit of their victory. The dead bodies lay all the way scattered so thicke as a man may see sheepe grazing in a well stored pasture, most slaine in the head or necke for that the horsemen could not well touch lower with their swords, and scarse credible it is how soone they were stripped and laid naked vpon the ground. But then againe the eyes of all men were fastned vpon them with pitty and admiration, to behold so many naked bodies, as for talness of stature, whitness of skinne, largeness and due proportion of limbes, could hardly be equalled in any one country. The ground where their severall battailons first brake, lay strewed with pikes so thicke as a floore is vsually strewed with rushes, whereby the places could hardly be passed ouer either by horse or by foote the riuer Eske ran red with blood, so as they who perished therein might almost bee said to bee drowned in their fellowes blood.

On the other side when they came to the place where the Englishmen at Armes had beene defeated, many of [Page 36] their horses were found grieuously gashed or goared to death. The English who there perished were so deeply wounded, especially on the head that not one could be discerned by his face. Braue Edward Shellie, who was the first man that charged, was knowne only by his beard, Little Preston for that both his hands were cut off being known to haue worne bracelets of gold about his wrests, others were brought to knowledge by some such particular marks. Hereby appeareth (as I said before) what blessing is growne to both nations by their late happy union when before they were like two rude encountring Rammes, whereof he that escapes best is sure of a blowe.[53]

Divers of the Nobilitie of Scotland were here slaine, and many Gentlemen both of worth and noble birth, of the inferior sort about 10,000, and as some say 14,000 lost their liues. Of the English were slaine 51 horsemen and one footman, but a farre greater number hurt. The Scottish prisoners accounted by the Marshals booke, were about 1500. The chiefe whereof were the Earle of Huntley, the Lords Yester, Hoblie, and Hamilton, the Master of Sampoole, and the Laird of Wimmes.[54] A Herault was also taken but discharged forthwith. The execution was much maintained by the Scots owne swords, scattered in every place. For no sooner had an English horseman brake his sword, but forthwith he might take vp another. Insomuch that many of them brake three of foure before their returne. So

apparant is the hand of God against violation of faith, that it is often
chastised by the meanes appointed to defend it.

Of all other the English men were least favourable to the Priests
and Monkes, by the Scots called Kirkmen, who had beene equally
troublesome in peace and vnprofitable in warre. To whom many as
well English as Scots imputed the calamity of that day, these made
a band of 3 or 4000, as it was said, but they were not altogether so
many, howbeit many Bishops and Abbots were amongst them, from
these divers Scots feared more harme by victory, then they [Page
37] found among their enimies by their ouerthrow. After the field
a banner was found of white sarcenet, whereon a woman was
painted, her haire about her shoulders kneeling before a crucifix,
on her right hand a church, and along the banner in faire letters
written Afflictae ecclesiae ne obliuiscaris. This was supposed to
haue beene the Kirkemens banner. But could this crucifix haue
spoken, as one is said to haue spoken to St Francis and another to
St Thomas, it might happely haue told them, that neither religious
persons are fit men for armes, nor armes fit meanes either to establish or advance Religion.

I must not forget the fidelity of a Scottish souldier towards the
Earle of Huntly. He finding the Earle assaulted by the English, and
without his helmet, tooke of his owne headpeece and put it on the
Earles head. The Earle was therewith taken prisoner but the souldier
for want thereof was presently stroke downe. This Earle was of great
courage and for this cause much loued of his souldiers, to whom he
was no lesse louing againe. This he manifested by his great care for
such Scottish prisoners as were either wounded or poore, providing
at his proper charge, cure for the one and releife for the other. This
Earle being asked whilst he was prisoner, how he stood affected to
the marriage, answered that he was well affected to fauour the marriage but he nothing liked that kinde of wooing.[55]

Certaine of those who escaped by flight excused their dishonor,
not without a sharpe jest against some of their leaders, affirming that
as they had followed them into the field, so it was good reason they
should follow them out. Those bitter jests the more truth they carry,
the more biting memory they leaue behinde.

The day of this fight being the 10th of September seemeth to be
a most disastrous day to the Scots, not only in regard of this
ouerthrow, but for that vpon the same day 34 yeares before they were

in like sort defeated by the English at Flodden field. The victory raised exceeding [Page 38] joy among the English partly because it came so cheape, and partly by reason of the great danger and greater terror that had bin cast vpon them by reason of the repulse and disarray of their men at Armes.

Now as seildome one accident either prosperous or adverse, cometh vnaccompanied with the like, so this calamity hapned not to the Scots alone. For whilst the English army had thus drawne both the preparations and intentions of the Scots wholly vpon them. The Lord Wharton and the Earle of Leuenoxe entred Scotland on the west marches with 5000 men, and hauing marched two miles they wonne the church of Anan, a strong place and alwaies much annoying the English, there they tooke 62 prisoners, fired most part of the spoyle, and ouerthrew the fort with powder, passing 16 miles further they tooke the castle of Milke, which they fortified strongly and planted a garrison therein, and after much spoile and wast of the country returned safely into England.

These successes did strike such a terror into many of the Scots that the Earle Bothwell and diuerse cheife gentlemen of Tiuedale and Meers supposing to finde more easy conditions by yeelding then by striuing, submitted themselues to the King of England, and were receiued by the Lord Generall into protection. But it is most certaine that the English made not their best improuements of these fortunate euents, and that especially by two miserable errors, cunctation in prosecuting, and haste in departure. But doubtlesse the vnion of these two realmes was a worke most proper to Gods omnipotent arme, which, afterwards effected the same, as by milder meanes, so in a more durable manner then they could haue bin vnited by Armes. This high appointment of God we must reuerence and admire, but not omit to obserue the errors committed.

First therefore after the retreit, the English lodged the same night in the place where the battaile had bin fought. Where and in the villages not farre distant they sojourned [Page 39] fiue daies, without doing anything, in the meane time the English [navie burnt diuerse townes on the north shore on the Frith][56] searched the riuers and hauens whether the Scottish ships were retyred, in such sort as they left few ships of war vnspoiled or vntaken, the army also gathered the spoile of the field, whereof 30,000 jacks and swords, and 30 pieces of great artillery were shipped for England.

The English hauing thus long breathed and thereby giuen breathing to their enimies fired Lieth tooke St Colmes: Broughticragge, Rockesborough, Humes castle, Aymouth, Fial castle, Dunglasse, Kilnecombe, and diuers other small pieces, whereof parte they ruined, parte they enlarged and fortified and furnished them with able souldiers, accustomed with often and prosperous successe. Herewith as if they had beene weary of their faire fortunes they suddainly brake off the enterprise and returned another way into England, hauing staid not aboue 25 daies in Scotland, and lost vnder 60 men. The pretence of their departure was worse then the departure it selfe, namely for that the yeare and their prouisions were far spent, and the country afforded little forrage. Assuredly as nature taketh least care for those things which she formeth in hast, so violent and stormlike fortunes how terrible so euer, are seldome durable.

Now the Lord Gouernor of Scotland being of great courage and sober judgement, as a man might well read in his face, as he had amply performed his duty both before the battaile and in the field, so especially after the fight he declared himselfe to be of a stout and vnbroken spirit. For first he assembled the dispersed forces of the Scottish army, albeit not in sufficient manner to giue a fresh battaile, by reason that much of their armor was lost, yet able to keepe the English from ranging at large. Then hee presented the English with diuers offers of treaty touching matters in difference, vntill the country was discharged of them, lastly knowing right well that counsels are commonly censured by euents, and that in matters of armes, albeit the praise of prosperous successe is shared amongst many, yet the blame [Page 40] of misaduentures is charged vpon one. And fearing hereby mutinies amongst his owne people, and contempt of others, hauing first assured the young Queene in place of good defence, he assembled the Scottish nobility and vsed words to this effect.

I assure my selfe that many of you my Lords and more of the vulger are much displeased with me for that I haue advised this warre whereof so sad euents haue followed, for this cause I haue assembled you together to reduce you to a better opinion, or to blame you deepely, either if you remaine offended, or if you cast downe your courage throw feare, the betrayer of all succors which reason can afforde, for tell me if you are discontented with me for aduising this warre, doe you not condemne your selues for following the aduice?

It is certaine that at the first you were all of my opinion, and that I did nothing without your approuement. If now vpon one misadventure you change your judgements, and charge the fault only vpon me, you doe me wrong and discouer your owne weaknesse, in being vnable to endure those things which you knew were casuall, and which you were resolued to endure. But I make no doubt but the same reasons which induced you to entertaine this warre, will induce you also to prosecute the same, howsoeuer sodaine and vnexpected euents dismay your judgements, for the present.

Touching my selfe I was alwaies of opinion, and shall never change, that it is better the kingdome should be in good estate, with particular losse to many of the people, then that all the people should be well and the state of the kingdome altogether lost or dishonourably impaired, euen as it is better that a ship should be preserued with some discommodity to the sailers, then that the sailers being in health the ship should perish, or as it is lesse dangerous when diuerse parts of a tower are decaied and the foundation firme, then when the foundation is ruinous, albeit the parts remaine entire. For the common estate is but weakened by calamities of particular persons, but the ruine of the state inuolueth all in a generall destruction. And therefore they are to be blamed alike, both who [Page 41] moue and who decline warre vpon particular respects, the com[mon][57] either honour or necessity must bee the true measure of both.

But the cause of this warre is no other then that wee will not incontinently submit our selues to doe what our neighbours require. That is because at the first word wee are not forward to thrust our necks vnder the girdles of our enimies, yea our old enimies, yea our only enimies of any accompt for many years, who in their gluttenous hope haue devoured our kingdome, who by the bloody execution of their late victories haue shewen what curtesie wee may expect at their hands. In doeing whereof wee shall abandon our ancient and approved friends, who as they neuer failed vs in our extremities, so are they now prepared with large aides to relieue vs, who will not feare or pause at the least, before he leap vpon this sodaine charger, who will forsake long tryed friends to rely vpon those, who alwaies haue beene ready by Armes to infest vs. Not at all times vpon desire either of revenge or spoile, but to bring us vnder their ambitious dominion, which of vs had not rather dye, this day then see our enimies in our

strongest castles and yoakes of garrisons cast vpon our necks? Who
will not preferre a death for libertie before a life without it?

Their promises are faire and large indeed I must say but of what
assurance? What assurance can we haue but that when we haue lifted
them into the chaire of state, wee shall not be compelled to be their
footemen? If our prince were a man and should marry an inheretrix
of England, wee should happily haue no cause to feare, but that he
would maintaine the liberty of his natiue country, but being a woman
and desired in marriage of a King of England, vnder whose power
and custody she must abide, how shall we be able against his minde
either to benefit or preserue vs, verily as men hate those that affect
that honour by ambition which pertaineth not to them, so are they
much more odious who either through negligence or through feare
will betray the glory and liberty which they haue.

[Page 42] Now my Lordes if any surmise either that this warre
will be long, or that we shall haue the worst in the end, his error is
great, for removing whereof, I must tell you, that which many of you
seeme either little to remember or never to haue knowen doe you
suppose the state of this realme, (of the valour whereof the enimy
hath often found wofull proofe) to be now so feeble that it cannot
beare off a greater blow then this? It hath often done it and is able
of it selfe to doe it againe, if our endeavours be answerable to our
meanes. Our Ancestors haue sustained many greater dangers, and
yet retaining their libertie haue left both it and their honour entire
to vs, what are wee of lesse heart then they? For of lesse ability we
are not, shall we shew our selues vnworthy of our succession from
them? Assuredly it is more shame for a man to loose that which he
holdeth, then to faile in getting that which he never had.

But suppose our forces to be neerer driven then they are our
ancient allies the French are vpon the seas and neere approaching
for our reliefe, also our friends in Italie and other partes haue sent
vs money to supply our wants, wherfore Lords it is meete that we
resume our ancient courage, and addresse our selues for new preparation not only vpon those hopes both from our selues and our
friends, but in contempt of our enimies. For often it hapneth that a
prosperity vnexpected maketh men carelesse and remisse if they be
not very wise, whereas they who haue receiued that wound become
more vigilant and collected, especially when they see not only the

common honour and liberty but their particular both seignories and safeties to be at the stake.

And albeit the enimy hath done that which it was to be belieued they would endeavour to doe, in case we would not yeeld vnto them, yet as those things must be endured vpon necessity, which happen by the hand of God. So those which come from enimies must be borne by vertue. And since it is a custome of our country so to doe, sith our people are famous for being nothing abashed at crosse events, take wee heed this vertue faile not in vs. If it doth? If we shew our selues [Page 43] heartlesse and faint, wee shall vtterly overthrow not only the glory but the memory, both of our ancestors and of our state.

As for those who haue yeelded to our enimies, let vs esteeme them as fugitiues and traitors, who endeavour to cast themselues and their country into subjection but let vs stand assured, that they who least shrinke at the stormes of fortune, whether in publique or private affaires are alwaies most vertuous and victorious in the end.

On the other side King Edward added to his glory, curtesie and liberality; shewing himselfe most gratious in countenance to all, and giuing rewards sutable to every mans performance or place. The Lord Protector he rewarded with lands of the yeerely value of £500 and certaine it is that these first fortunes raised vnto him a great respect both in other countries and among his owne people, and the rather because he was discerned to be much searching both into the Counsailes and after the events of all his affaires, and likewise into the condition and state both of his owne strength and of the countries neere vnto him.

But these prosperous proceedings were not only hindred, in their fairest course, but altogether stayd and in some measure turned backe by reason of the vnadvised forwardnesse of divers chiefe counsailors, in making both sodaine and vnseasonable alterations in matters of state, whose greedy desires of hauing their wills in all they liked bred both trouble to the realme and to themselues danger, for great and sodaine changes are never without danger, vnles the Prince be both well setled in government and able to beare out his actions by power, but whilest King Edward was both vnripe in yeers and new in government to attempt a change both sodaine and great, could not [but]⁵⁸ be accompanied with many mischiefs. The great matters wherein alteration was wrought were especially two, religion and enclosures.

Now for that Religion is of so high and noble a nature, of so absolute necessity in a commonwealth; that it is esteemed the foundation of Lawes, and the common band of humane [Page 44] society, no sodeyne alteration can almost be made therein, but many will be induced thereby to attempt some alteration in rule, whence (saith Dio)[59] conspiracies and seditions are often occasioned. For Religion being seated in the high throne of conscience is a most powerfull ruler of the soule and farre preferred before estimation of life, or any other worldly respect for this advanceth man to the highest happinesse. It leadeth him to his last end, all other things are but instruments, this is the hand, all other things are but accessaries this is the principall. And therefore as all men are naturally moued by religion, so when they are violently thrusted forward by those who (as Liuie speaketh) make it their purpose to possesse soules by superstition, then doe they breake all bands of reason and of rule, no persuasion of the one, no command of the other can then restraine them. Multitudo vbi religione capta est melius vatibus quam ducibus suis paret, Curt. lib. 4.

I will not deny but that some change in religion is often expedient and sometimes necessary because more in that then in any other thing, it is hard to containe men from running into one of these extreames either of vaine superstition or of carelesse contempt, but this must be done with a [soft][60] and tender hand, and as Cicero speaketh, vt quum minimo sonitu orbis in republica convertatur. Some respect should also haue been given to those greene times, to the monstrous multitude muffled with 2 great plagues and corruptions of judgement, custome and ignorance, whereto may be added griefe at their owne wants, and envy at the prosperity of others, especially for that many bold spirits were busied, not only to incense but to lead them into much variety of mischiefe. And if it be said that King Henry VIII had quietly passed the like change before, I answere the example was not then to be followed, [because][61] the kings were not equall either in spirit or in power. Euen as it is in the fable that albeit an Eagle did beare away a lamb in her talents with full flight, yet a raven endeavouring to doe the like was held entangled and fettered in the fleece.

Touching enclosures, I am not ignorant what a profitable [Page 45] purchase is made thereby, not only to particular persons, but generally to the whole Commonwealth, in case it bee without depopulation, because [champaine][62] lands inclosed, are therby improved in worth 2 or 3d[63] parts at the least, hereby two great commodities ensue, riches and multitude of people, because the more ritches are raised out of lands, the more people are thereby maintained. This doth plainely appeare by two shires almost, equall both in greatnesse and in goodness of soyle. Northampton much champion, and Somerset altogether enclosed, for if estimation may be made by musters, and by subsidies, tenths and fifteens enclosure hath made the one county more then double to exceed the other both in people and in wealth.

Notwithstanding the Lord Protector gaping after the fruitlesse breath of the multitude,[64] and more desirous to please the most then the best causing a proclamation to be set forth against enclosures, commanding that they who had inclosed any lands accustomed to lie open should vpon a certaine paine before a day assigned lay them open againe. This Proclamation whilst fewe were forward to obey gaue occasion to the mutinous multitude instable in judgement and tempestuous[65] when they are stirred all carried with a headlong rashnesse, and one following another as wiser then himselfe immoderately both in desire and hope to be easily drawn by others who had deeper reaches then themselues to matters which at the first they least intended.

And againe soone after the beginning of the young kings raigne, certaine injunctions were set forth for remouing images out of Churches which had beene highly, not onely esteemed but honoured before, and for abolishing or altering some other ancient observations in the Church. Herevpon commissioners were dispatched into all parts of the realme to see those injunctions to be executed, with those divers preachers were sent furnished with instructions to persvade the people from praying to Saints or for the dead, from adoring Images, from vse of beades, ashes and processions, from masse, dirges, [Page 46] praying in unknown languages, and from some other like things wherevnto long custome had wrought a religious observation and for defect of preachers, homilies were appointed to be publikely read in Churches, ayming to the very same end.

Some other offring to maintaine these ceremonies were either punished or forced to recant, Edmund Bonner Bishop of London was committed prisoner to the Fleet, for refusing to receiue these injunctions, Stephan Gardiner was likewise committed first to the Fleet, afterwards to the Tower, for that he had openly preached that it were well these changes in religion should be stayed, vntill the King were of yeares to governe by himselfe. This the people apprehending worse then it was either spoken or meant, a question began to bee raised among them, whether during the Kings minoritie such alterations might lawfully be made or no for the like causes Tonstall Bishop of Duresme, and Heath Bishop of Rochester, were in like committed to prison, all these being then and still continuing famous for learning and judgement were dispossessed of their Bishoppricks, but no man was touched in life.

Herevpon a Parliament was held in the first yeare of the King: and by prorogation in the second, wherein diverse Colleges, Chantries, free Chappells, Fraternities, Guildes, etc. with all their lands and goods were put into the actuall possession of the King: part of the goods and lands being sold at a low value, enriched many, and enobled[66] some, and thereby made them firme in maintaining the change, also that no man should speake against receauing the Eucharist vnder both kindes, which had beene restrained in times before, and that Bishops should be placed by collation of the King vnder his Letters Patents, without any precedent election or confirmation ensuing, and that all processes ecclesiasticall should be made in the Kings name, as in writs at the common Law, and that all persons exercising Ecclesiasticall jurisdiction should haue the kings armes in their seales of office, and further the Statute of the 6 Articles, and other statutes concerning punishment of Lollards were repealed, and so was another statute restreining [Page 47] the vse of Scriptures in the English tongue, and the Kings supremacy ouer the Church of England was confirmed. Herewith a booke was set forth for publike prayers by proclamation, and for administration of the Sacraments, and other rights and offices of the Church, and diuerse punishments were appointed by proclamation,[67] either for not vsing the formes prescribed in that booke, or for depraving anything therein contained.

I forbeare to rehearse other acts of this Parliament, albeit a noble writer in our time esteemes it to be a mayme in historie that the acts of Parliament should not bee recited, which I conceiue so farre to bee true as they occasion tumults or division, or some remarkable alteration in state, otherwise as I finde them not regarded by most imitable writers, so I account the relation of them both fruitlesse and improper for a true caryed history.

Now in this meane time the commissioners before mentioned were earnest in executing their authority. And either pulled downe or defaced all images in Churches, and that in such vnseasonable and vnseasoned fashion as if it had beene done in hostility against them, hereat many did expresse a sense of distast, some for religious respects, others in regard of the excellent artifice of some of their pieces, affirming that albeit religious reverence might happily haue beene either taken away or moderated, yet the civill regard which all men do not only afford but affect, in maintaining the memory of those whom they honour or loue, might be endured without offence.

Certainly albeit the religion of the Romans endured 170 yeeres according to a law of Numa Pompilius without any images, albeit the Persians had neither images nor temples nor altars, being of opinion that God could bee represented by no device that he had no temple but the world, no Altar but the heart of man, albeit Eusebius writeth that the people of Asia called Seres by expresse law forbad adoration of images, albeit that images were forbidden of [Page 48] Lycurgus as drawing men from the true worship of that which cannot be seene. Albeit the ancient Germans and from [them][68] the Brittaines, and the Gaules had neither Images nor Temples, albeit the Jewes, and in imitation of them, the Saracens and Turkes abhorre nothing more then Images, either in their temples, or in their houses, because the Lawe of God forbiddeth not onely to adore but to make any image. Albeit the Christians continued a long time without Images in their Churches, yet were they never entertained into any religion, but presently they tooke deepe root in the hearts and consciences of the common people. When Leo Isauricus surnamed Iconomadius assembled a counsell at Constantinople, wherein it was decreed that Images should be cast out of Churches and burnt, the West part of his Empire did therevpon first rebell, and afterwards revolt.

And yet while these proceedings were but in the bud, affaires of state without the Realme were maintained in good condition of honour, but seemed rather to stand at a stay, then either to advance or decline. In Scotland the warres were maintained by the Lord Gray

of Wilton, Lieutenant of the North, with variable successe, he fortified Haddington, fired Dawkeith, and wonne the Castle where
fourteene Scots were slaine, and 300 taken prisoners, hee spoiled
much of the country about Edenburgh, Lowthum, and Meers, fired
Muscleborough, and fortified Lowder, and tooke Yester, at the yeelding where of he granted life to all except to one who had vsed vild
speeches against King Edward. Those speeches were commonly cast
vpon one Newton but he charged them vpon one Hamilton. Herevpon Hamilton challenged Newton to the combate, which hee did
readily accept and the Lord Gray consented to the triall, to this
purpose Lists were erected in the market place at Haddington
whereinto at the time appointed, both the combatants entered, apparelled only in their doublets and hoses, and weapned with sword,
buckler, and dagger. At the first [Page 49] encounter Hamilton draue
Newton almost to the end of the lists which if he had fully done he
had thereby remained victorious, but Newton on the suddaine gaue
him such a gash on the legge that therewith he fell to the ground,
and Newton forthwith dispatched him with his dagger, certaine
gentlemen then present offered to haue fought with Newton vpon
the same point, but this was adjudged to be against the lawes of
combate, wherefore Newton was not only acquited but rewarded
with a chaine of gold, and with the gowne which the Lord Gray did
then weare, howbeit many were perswaded that he was faulty and
happily neither of them was free, but he enjoyed neither his escape
nor his honor long, for soone after he was hewen in pieces by Ham-
iltons friends.

On the other side the Scots came before Broughticragge with
8000 men and 8 pieces of Artillerie, but it was for that time well
defended by the English who by often sallies enforced their enimies
with losse of their Artillerie to abandon the attempt, after this
diverse other enterprises were made vpon that fort; at the last it was
taken where the Scots slue all except Sir John Latterel the captaine
who was taken prisoner.

And now Henry II of France having newly succeeded Francis I,
who dyed the last of March 1547 sent Mounsieur Dassie his Lieutenant into Scotland with an armie of about 10000 French and Almaines who joining with the Scots besieged Haddington and that
with so good earnest as six pieces of artillerie discharged 340 shot
in one day and in another 200 within 60 paces of the wall, they lodged

so neere within the very ditches that the English slue divers of them with plummets of lead tyed to a trunchion or staffe by a cord, the place was but weake and the [breaches][69] faire but the defendants by resolution supplyed all the defects, making divers sallies with such liuely spirit that the Assaylants were thereby discouraged from making assault. The English from Barwicke with about 1500 horse [Page 50] did often relieue the defendants by breaking through the the middest of their enemies, but at the last they were so strongly both encountred and encloased betweene the French Almaines and Scots, and that Sir Thomas Palmer the chiefe leader and about 400 were taken prisoners and divers slaine. Herevpon the Earle of Shrewsbury was sent with an army of about 15000 men whereof 3000 were Almanies, but vpon notice of his approach the French raised the field, retyred so farre as Muscleborough and there encamped, attributing much honour to the English for their valour in regard of the small strength of the place which they defended, when the Earle had victualled and reenforced the towne, he marched forth towards the enimies and encamped neere vnto them, and first a fewe of the English horse aproached neere the army of the French, who sent forth some troopes of their horse to encounter them, but the English retyred vntill they had drawn the French into an ambush laid for the purpose and then charging together they had them cheap, amongst which two captains of account were taken prisoners. The next day the Earle presented his army in plaine field before the enimies campe cloased in three bodies and ranged ready to abide battaile. The French had newly receiued supply of 14 or 15000 Scots but yet remained within their strength holding it no wisdome to venter on men resolud to fight, who being forthwith to depart the realme and could neither longe endanger nor indamage them much. So the Earle after that he had remained about an hower and perceiuing that the French intended not to forsake their strength, returned vnto his campe and afterwarde to England, destroying Donbarr and some other which stood neere his passage, the Army being dissolud, and the Scots thought secure, the Lord Gray with his horsemen entred Scotland did great wast in Tuedale and Liddesdale for the space of 20 miles, and returned without encounter. Also a navy was apoynted to coast along with the army before [Page 51] mentioned. This fleet coming to Brent Iland fired 4 ships then atempting vpon St. Minces[70] were repulsed by the Lord Dun, and so without either glory or gaine returned into Englande.

Not long after the departure of the English army Mr Dassie with his French and Almaines attempted sodenly to surprise Haddington, the enterprise was gouerned in so secret manner that the French had slaine the English escouts and entred the base courte and aproached the maine gates before any alarme was taken, but then the Townesmen came forth many in their shirts, who with the helpe of the watch susteined the assault, vntill the Souldiers in better apointment came to their aide. These issued into the base court, through a pryuie posterne, and sharpely visited the Assailants with Halbeards and swordes. Here the fight grew hot, the darkenes and danger terrifying some and animating others. Blowes flew at all adventures, woundes and deathes given and taken vnexpected, many scarce knowing their enimies from their friends: But shame wrought such life and courage in the English, as very few of the enimies who entered the court escaped aliue, leauing their fellowes bleeding in their deadly wounds, yet Mr Dassie not discouraged herewith gaue 3 liuely assaults more that morning, but was repelled with so great losse, that 16 Carts and Waggons were charged with carrying away their dead and dying bodies, besides 300 left in the base court.

After divers like adventures the English perceiving that the towne could not bee kept without danger, not lost without dishonour, the Earle of Rutland was sent with 3000 Almaines and as many borderers to demolish the towne and to bring the artillerie a way to Barwicke. The Earle not only accomplished his Charge but made wide wast in his passage by ruine and spoyle. Herewith the castle of Hame[71] was sodenly surprised by the Scots and all the English therein either taken or slaine. This was effected by [Page 52] meanes of certaine Scots who vsed to bring victualls to the English and were reputed their assured frindes, these both obseruing the weakenes of the place and orders of the garrison, discouered them to their fellowes and gaue entertainment for the surprise Giueing also warning to others never to trust either the curtesyes or services of those whom they haue provoked to be their enimies.

About these times Sir Edward Bellingham Lord Deputie of Ireland first with great diligence and care, then credite and reputation especially gained by that service, tooke Ocanor and Omor[72] and reduced the other seditious Lords to good subjection. Ocanor and Omor guided by overlate counsaile of necessity left their Lordships and had a yeerely pension of £100 assigned to either of them.

And now the French supposing that by reason partly of suspence of hostility betweene England and France, and partly of the English affaires in other places, matters with them would be neglected, determined to attempt a suddaine surprise of the fortresse of Bullingberge, to this end 7000 men were appointed vnder the conduct of Mr Chastilion furnished with ladders and other preparations for the surprise. They marched secretly in the dead time of the night, and when they approached within a quarter of a league. One Carter who had beene discharged of his pay by the English for takeing a French woman to wife, and then serued vnder the French ranne privily before, and gaue the Alarme to those in the Forte. The English drewe him vp the walles betweene two pikes and vnderstanding the danger addressed themselues to their defence by reason whereof the French at their approach had so warme a welcome, every of the English contending that his valour might be noted for some helpe in the fight, that at their departure they laded 15 wagons with their dead. Carter himselfe adventured brauely in places of greatest danger, and receiued two great hurts in his body. Sir Nicholas Arnault the captaine was likewise hurte with a pike in the face, diuers [Page 53] others were wounded and about 25 slaine. The assault continued with great obstinacy from midnight vntill somwhat after the breake of day.

Shortly after 300 English on foote and 25 horsemen were appointed to goe to a wood, about 2 leagues from Bullingberge, hauing carriages with them, for bringing certaine timber for mounting great Artillery, and some other vses when they approached neerer the edge of the woode, about 500 French horsemen issued forth and gaue three sharpe charges vpon them, the English empaled themselues with their pikes, and therewith bare off their enimies, and being lined with shot (the cruell plague of horsemen) the French were in such sort galled with arrowes that many were wounded Mr Cauret and diuers others slaine, 70 great horses lay dead in the field and one Cornet was taken. The English fearing greater forces began to retyre, and therewith appeared about 2000 French and Almaines on foote. But the English maintained an orderly retreat, vntill they came within favour of the shot of Bullingberge and then the enimy adventured no further, and in this manner the old wounds of warre began freshly to open and bleede betweene England and France.

But in this meane time such tempests of sedition tumbled in England more by default of governors then the peoples impatience to liue in subjection, that not only the honour but the safetie of the state was thereby endangered. For as the commissioners before mentioned passed to divers places for establishing of their new injunctions, many vnsavory scornes were cast vpon them, and the further they went from London as the people were more vnciuill so did they more rise into insolencie and contempt. At the last as one Mr Body a commissioner was pulling downe images in Cornwall, he was sodainely stabbed into the body by a Priest with a knife.

Herevpon the people more, regarding commotioners then commissioners, flocked together in diverse parts of [Page 54] the shire as clouds cluster against a storme, and albeit justice was afterwards done vpon the offenders, the Principall being hanged and quartered in Smithfield, and divers of his chiefe complices executed in divers parts of the Realme, albeit so ample a pardon was proclaimed for all others within that shire touching any action or speech tending to treason, yet could not the boldnesse be beaten down either with that severity or with this lenity be abated. For the mischiefe forthwith spread into Wiltshire and Somersetshire, where the people supposing that a common wealth could not stand without Commons, beat downe enclosures, laid parkes and fields champaine. But Sir William Herbert afterwardes Earle of Pembroke with a well armed and ordered company set sharpely vpon them, and oppressing some of the forwardest of them by death, suppressed all the residue by feare. But their duty depending vpon feare the one was of no greater continuance then the other.

The like motions followed in Sussex, Hampshire, Kent, Glocestershire, Warwickeshire, Essex, Hartfordshire, Leicestershire, Worcestershire, [Suffolk]73 and Rutlandshire. But being neither in numbers nor in courage great, partly by authority of Gentlemen, and partly by entreaty and advice of honest persons they were reduced to some good appeasement, as with people more guided by rage then by right, yet not altogether mad, it was not vneasy. But herein happely some error was committed, that being only brought to a countenance of quiet, regard was not had to [extinguish]74 the rebellion fully.75 For soone after they brake forth more dangerously then before for no part could content them who aimed at all. After this the people in Oxfordshire, Devonshire, Northfolke and Yorkeshire fell into the same madnes, incensed by such who being in themselues base and degenerate, and dangerous to the state had no hope but in troblesome times. To Oxfordshire the Lord Gray of Wilton, was sent with 1500 horse and foote, to whom the gentlmen of the country resorted, drawing many [Page 55] followers with them, the very name of the Lord Gray being knowne to be a man of great valour and fortune, so terrified the seditious, that vpon the very report of his approach, more then halfe fell away and dispersed, of the residue, who being either more desperate or more sottish did abide in the field, many were presently slaine, many taken, and forthwith executed. To Devonshire was sent John Lord Russell, Lord of the priuy seale, whose forces being indeed, or being by him distrusted to be inferior to the importance of the service, he sate downe at Honington,[76] whilest the seditious did almost what they would, vpon this heavines of the kings forces going forward interpreted to be feare and want of mettle, divers either of the most audacious or such as pouerty or feare of punishment might easily plunge into any mischiefe, resorted to the seditious daily from Cornwall and other parts, as bad humors gather to a bile, or as divers kennels flow to one sinke, so in short time their numbers encreased to 10000 tall and able bodies. They were chiefly guided by Humphery Arundell a man well esteemed for military seruices.[77] About 6 others of inferior note were bold actors with him. Many priests vnworthy to be named were also impetuous and importunate incensors of the rage, men of some academicall learning in discourse, but their minds not seasoned with any vertuous or religious thoughts.

Assuredly the vulgar multitude is not vnfairly termed a beast, with many heads not guided, I will not say with any proportion but portion of reason, violence and obstinacy like two vntamed horses, draw their desire in a blindefold Carriere. They intend most foolishly what they never put in action, and often act most madly what they never intended, all that they know to doe, is that they know not what to doe, all that they meane to determine proues a determination and meaning to doe nothing. They attribute more to others judgement then to their own, esteeming bold obstinacy for bravest courage and imprudent [Page 56] prating for soundest wisdome, and now being assembled into one company rather without a Lord then at liberty, to accomplish their misery they fall to division of all calamities the worst, and so broken in their desires that many could not learne either wherefore they came, or what they would haue done. Some were commonwealth mutiners, and some did mutiny for religion. They who were for the common wealth could agree vpon no certaine thing, but it was certaine they could agree vpon nothing, some would haue no justices, some no gentlemen, some no [lawyers][78] nor ordinary courts of justice, [some would haue counsailers of state changed, some taken away, some complained of imposts, some of one thing and some of another but][79] aboue all enclosures must downe, but whether all or which or how to be emploied none could tell, every man regarding what he followed but not what might follow thereof. All would haue the state transformed, but Whether reformed or deformed they neither cared nor knew. They concurred only in confused clamors, every man thinking it no lesse reasonable that his opinion should be heard, then that his body should be adventured.

The religious mutiners were not altogether so various in their voices, as hauing some few spirits among them by whom they were both stirred and guided, these in the name of the people hammered vp the Articles following, and sent them to the King, vpon granting of which they professed that both their bodies and their goods should be absolutely at the kings devotion.

1. That curats should administer baptisme at all times of necessity aswell on weekedaies as on holidaies.
2. That their children might be confirmed by the Bishop whensoeuer they should within the dioces resort vnto him.
3. For asmuch as they believed that after the words of consecration noe substance of bread remaining but the reall body and blood of Christ, that the masse should be celebrated without any man communicating with the priest, for that many put noe difference betweene the Lords body and other meat, some saying that it is bread before and after, some saying [Page 57] that is profitable to none except he receiues it.
4. That they might haue reseruation of the Lords body in their Churches.
5. That they might haue holy bread and holy water in remembrance of Christs precious body and blood.

6. That Gods service might be said or sang with an audible voice in the Quire and not forth like a Christmas play.
7. That Priests liue chast (as St Paul did) without marriage, who said to all honest Priests, be yee followers of me.
8. That the 6 Articles set forth by King Henry VIII, be so used as they were in his time, at least vntill the King should accomplish his full age.

Now albeit the King knewe right well that no reasons would serue for deniall, and that the yeelding to them in anything would profit him nothing, but rather make them rise to more insolent demands, yet hee returned an answere in writing and therewith his generall pardon, in case they would desist and open their eyes to discerne how their vncircumspect simplicity had beene abused especially in matters of religion, for that as some vertues resemble some vices so neere, as the one is often taken for the other, so religion and super-stition doe so neerely resemble, that it was easie for men to disguise the one vnder the maske of the other. First therefore hee reproued them fairely for their disorderly assemblies, against the peaceable people of the Realme and against the honour of his estate, fearing much that by reason of their disobedience, his lenitie should appeare to be lesse then he would haue it, also for that they vsed his name in all their writings, not only without his authoritie but even against himselfe, abusing thereby the weaknesse of many, and drawing them into societie of their evill. Then he pitied their ignorance and the errors thence arising, whereby they were allured to new hopes by some, who could not thriue so well by their honest endeavours, as by rapine and spoile, who stopped all course of law and discourse of reason to open the full [Page 58] floudgate of their vnmeasurable madnesse, who to overthrowe the state pretend libertie, but if they should ouerthrowe it all libertie were lost.

For saith he who hath borne you in hand that children even in case of necessitie cannot be baptised but vpon holidaies, whereas there is no day nor houre wherein the Minister is not only permitted but commanded to baptise. By like abuse you are perswaded that many hold that the blessed Sacrament of Christs body doth nothing differ from common bread, whereas lawes, Statutes, Proclamations, common practise agree, that common bread is only to sustaine the body but this blessed bread is food for the soule. Touching confirmation, doth any beleeue that a child baptised is damned vnlesse it be confirmed? If it be baptised and also confirmed, is it saued only by confirmation, and not by baptisme? Or is it the more saued by confirmation? Children are confirmed at the age of discretion to teach them what they receaued in their infancie, they are taught by confirmation to continue in that whereto they were baptised, oh how much doe they need who will never bee content? What may satisfie those who haue no limits to their desires.

As for the order of service and vse thereof in the English tongue, which you esteeme new it is no other then the old, that same words in English which were in Latine, except a few things omitted so fond, that it had bin a shame to haue heard them in English, and how can any reasonable man be offended to vnderstand what God by his word speaketh vnto them, what they by their prayers speake vnto God: If the service were good in Latine, it remaines so in English, for nothing is altered but to make you vnderstand what is said. In like sort the masse with great judgment and care was reduced to the same manner as Christ left it, as the Apostles vsed it, as the ancient Fathers receaued, practised and left it.

But you would in sober earnest haue the six Articles againe reuiued. Doe you vnderstand what you would haue, [Page 59] or are you masters of your owne judgment. If you vnderstand them and yet desire them, it is not long since they were enacted, and haue since drawne much blood from the subjects. [And][80] would you haue bloody lawes againe in life, or would they any long time be endured? Vpon pitty they were taken away, vpon ignorance they are againe demanded. Verily that in the Gospell may truly bee said of you, yee aske yee knowe not what, for you neither know what good you shall haue by receiuing them, nor what evill you haue lost by their abolishing, our intention is to haue our lawes written with milke, but you would haue them written with blood. They were established by law and so observed, although with much expence of blood, they are abolished by law with sparing of blood, and that also must be obserued, for unlesse lawes be duly obserued, neither the authority of the Prince, nor safetie[81] of the people can be preserved.

And whereas you would haue them remaine in force vntill our full age, if you had knowne what you speake, you never would haue giuen breath to such an vnseasoned thought, for what is our authoritie the lesse for our age, or shall we be more King hereafter then now?

or are you lesse subjects now then in future times you shall be? Verily as a naturall man we haue now youth, and by Gods sufferance expect age; but as a King we haue no difference in yeares, we are rightfull king by Gods ordinance, and by descent from our roiall ancestors, and not by any set number of yeares, and much it is to bee feared, that they who moued you to require this suspence of time, would absolutely denie our royall power, if they durst so plainely expresse themselues.

The seditious as men alwaies dangerous when they haue once broken awe, interpreted this or any other milde dealing to proceed from some faining or fainting disposition either doubting or daring most when they are most fairely entreated, and the more to enflame the popular rage, [Page 60] fresh rumors were devised and divulged, that the people should be constrained to pay a ratable taxe for their sheep and other cattle,[82] and an excise for every thing which they should eat or drinke, by which and other like reports the simple were blinded, the malitious edged, all hardned from applying to any peaceable perswasion.

And now vnable to support themselues either with their own estate or by wast of villages, they aspired to the spoile and subjection of citties, and first they came to Exeter and demanded entrance, but the citizens as they were both civill and rich, so were they better advised, and therefore closed their gates, and refused to haue any entercourse with the seditious, but either by common obedience, or else by hostility and armes; the popular fury being thus stopped, swelled the more. Wherevpon they resolued to apply their endeauours for taking the citty, and either by destroying it to increase terror, or else by sparing it to winne an opinion of moderation, they had no great artillery to open a breach, and yet without reason they gaue an assault, and vsed divers meanes to mount the walls, but the more madnesse they shewed in their attempt, with the greater losse they were driuen backe, then they fired the gates at two severall times, but the citizens at both times by casting in wood maintained the fire, vntill they had cast vp a halfe moone within, vpon which when the seditious attempted to enter they were slaine from the corners like dogges. After this they mined the walls, laid the powder and rammed the mouth [intending to blowe vp a breach][83] but the citizens made a countermine, whereinto they powred such plentie of water, that the wet powder could not be fired.

In the meane time the Lord Privy Seale lay at Hunnington expecting more strength, and knowing right well that as the multitude
are slow to danger, so are they most desperate when they are stirred,
but whilst he expected more companie, many of those he had slipped
away from him. Herevpon he resolued for retaining the rest to entertaine some [Page 61] present enterprise, and first he [assayed][84]
by a by way to enter and relieue the citty, but the seditious for
prevention hereof had felled all the trees betweene St. Mary Outry[85]
and Exeter, and laid them crosse the waie in such sort as they
impeached his passage, herevpon firing such places as hee thought
might serue either for vse or ease to the seditious, he determined to
returne to Hunnington. But the seditious forelaied a bridge, over
which hee should passe, called Fennington bridge, and in a great
faire meddow behinde the bridge placed a great number vnder
banners displaid. The Lord privy seale had but a small company in
regard of the seditious. Yet with good order and courage hee attempted the bridge but could not force it, at the last finding the riuer
to be fordeable at the foot of the bridge, he there set ouer his horse,
wherevpon the guardes appointed to defend the bridge forsooke
their charge, and retyred to their strength in the meddow. Then the
kings forces charged liuely vpon them, and they againe as stoutly
receiued the charge, but being an vntrained multitude without either
souldier or guide, they were soone broken and put to flight, yet they
[rallyed][86] themselues and tumultuously charged vpon the kings
forces, but were presently rowted and cast out of the field, the chase
was not far pursued for feare of fresh succours from before the citty.
Notwithstanding the seditious lost 600 of their men, and the Lord
Privy seale returned without losse to Hunnington.

At this time the seditious liued by rapine and ruine of all the
country, omitting nothing of that which savages enraged in the height
of their vnruly behaviour doe commit, but the Cittizens driven to
great distresse for want of victuales, bread they made of coursest
branne moulded in cloathes, for that otherwise it would not cleaue
together. Their finest flesh was of their owne horses, [which was
indifferently distributed to all][87] especially for 12 daies they endured
most extreame famine. During this time they were much encouraged
by an aged cittizen, who brought forth all his provisions and said,
that as hee did [Page 62] communicate vnto them his store, so would
he participate of their wants. And that for his part he would feed on

the one arme and fight with the other before he would consent to put the citty into the seditious hands. Herewith the lord privy Seale for want of power to performe any services, was about to rise and returne to London. But in good time the Lord Gray came to him with supply of forces most Almane horsemen, and with him came Spinola with his band of Italians consisting of 300 shot, purposed for Scotland, also 200 men were sent vnto him from Reading, so being in all not much aboue 1000 strong, he made head against the seditious. So departing from Honington he came to a little village from whence lay 2 waies towards Exeter, both which were blocked vp with 2 bulwarkes of earth, made by the seditious, hither they had driuen 2000[88] men from before Exeter whom they divided into 4 companies. In either of the Bulwarkes they lodged one, at the bridge neere the backe of one of the fortes, a third company was placed, the 4th was laid in ambush behinde a hedge on the high way, at the backe of the other fortresse, the Arriere of the kings forces led by captaine Wauers[89] set vpon one of the fortes, the vaward and battaile vpon the other, Spinola with his shot did beare vpon those within, who offered to appeare vpon the walls. At length Captaine Wavers wonn the fort which he assailed, and draue the defendands to the bridge where one of their companies made stand. Herewith the other two companies did forthwith resort vnto them, one from the second fort, the other from the ambush. These casting a strong guard vpon the bridge, marshalled the residue vpon a plaine ground behinde the bridge. The kings forces coming forward draue the guard from the bridge, and making profit of the fresh terror set vpon those who were vpon the plaine. The kings footmen were firmely ranked, the troopes of horse in good array, whereas the seditious had neither weapons, order nor counsaile, but being in all things vnprovided were slaine [Page 63] like beasts. They tooke their fight towards St Mary Cliffe[90] but the souldiers vpon disdaine of their vnworthy actions filled themselues with revenge and blood, and slue of them aboue 900 not sparing one.

This sad blow abated much the courage and hope of the seditious, and yet the next day about 2000 of them affronted the Kings forces at the entrance of a high way, whom when they found both ready and resolute to fight, they desired enterparlance, and in the meane time began to fortify. But vnderstanding that their intention was vnderstood more like slaues then souldiers they furiously ran away.

The same night the seditious before Exeter raised their seige, and therewith discharged the citty from many miseries and dispaires. The King afterwards enlarged the constant obedience of the citty with enlargement both of liberties and of revenews, hee gaue vnto them the mannor of [Exeland][91] for a perpetuall remembrance both of their loialty and of his loue.

Now the seditious driven almost to a dead dispaire and supported only by the vehemency of desire, brought forth their forces to Clifton heath,[92] to whom many of the most vile vulgars resorted hourely, which much enlarged their numbers but nothing their strength, but what measure haue men in the encrease of madnes, if they keepe not themselues from falling into it, they brought with them a crucifix vpon a carte couered with a canopie, and beset with crosses, tapers, banners, holy bread and holy water as a representation of those things for which they fought. The Lord Gray encouraged his men to set sharpely vpon the [vayne][93] villaines good neither to liue peaceably nor to fight, and to win at once both quiet to the Realme and to themselues glory, so he brought the Kings forces vpon them rather as to a carnage then to a fight, insomuch as without any great either losse or danger to themselues, the greatest part of the seditious were slaine, divers also were taken, of whom the common sort were forthwith executed by [Page 64] martiall law, the chiefest leaders were sent to receiue justice at London. Some escaped and sailed to Bridgewater, who taking dangers to be the only remedy against dangers, endeavoured to set vp the sedition againe, but they were speedily repressed, and thereby the sedition suppressed wholly.

The sedition thus broken and beaten downe Sir Anthony Kingston prouost marshall of the kings army was deemed by many not only cruell but vncivill, and inhumane in his executions. One Boyer maior of Bodmin in Cornwall was obserued to haue beene among the seditious, but by absolute enforcement as many others were. The Martiall wrote to him a letter that he would dine at his house vpon a day which he appointed, the maior seemed glad, and made for him the best provision that he could, vpon the day he came and large company with him, and was receiued with many ceremonies of entertainment. A little before dinner he tooke the maior aside and whispered him in the eare, that execution must that day be done in the towne, and therefore required him that a paire of gallowes should be framed and erected against the time that dinner should end; the maior was diligent to accomplish his demand, and no sooner was dinner ended, but he demanded of the Maior whether the worke were finished; the Maior answered that all was ready, I pray you said the provost bring me to the place, and therewith he tooke him friendly by the hand, here beholding the gallowes he asked the Maior whether he thought them to be strong enough, yes said the Maior doubtlesse they are, well then said the provost get you vp speedily for they are prepared for you, I hope answered the Maior you meane not as you speake, in faith said the provost there is no remedy, for you haue beene a busie rebell, and so without respite or defence hee strangled to death.

Neere the said place dwelled a Miller who had beene a busy actor in that rebellion, and fearing the approach of [Page 65] the provost martiall, told a sturdy tall fellow his servant that he had occasion to goe from home, and therefore gaue directions that if any one should enquire after the miller, he should not speake of him but affirme that himselfe was the miller, and that so he had bin for three yeares before. So the provost came and called for the miller, his seruant came forth and said he was the man. The provost demanded how long he had kept the mill, these three years answered the seruant, then the provost commanded his men to lay hold on him, and to hang him on the neerest tree, then the fellow cried out that the was not the miller but the millers man, nay Sir answered the provost I will take thee at thy word, and if thou beest the miller thou art a busy knaue, if thou beest not, thou art a false lying knaue, whatsoeuer thou art thou shalt be hanged, when others also told him that the fellow was but the millers man, and what then said he? Could he ever haue done his master a better service then to hang for him, and so without more to doe he was dispatched. Assuredly this might haue passed for a tollerable jest if it had not beene in a case of life.

Divers others were executed by martiall law, and a great part of the country was abandoned to the spoile of the souldiers, who not troubling themselues to discerne betweene a subject and a rebell, whilest their liberty lasted made indifferently profit of both.

The seditious in Northfolke were somewhat dangerous, both because their strength was greater, as also because the citty of Norwich was a friend vnto them, or at least wished them no great harme, and being faithfull to neither side, was alwaies ready to entertaine the stronger, their first attempt was made at Attleborough where they

threw downe the fences of one Greene of Wilbie, who was supposed
to haue enclosed a parte of Attleborough common adjoining to the
common pasture of Harsham. Afterward they assembled at a play
accustomed yeerely to be kept at Wimondham, and from thence
went to Morley a [Page 66] mile distant, and there cast downe the
ditches of one Hubbarde, next by incitement of John Flowerdew of
Netheset,[94] a gentleman of good estate, but neuer expressing desire
of quiet, they did the like to certaine enclosures of Robert Ket a
tanner in Wimondham, [a man of some wealth][95] and receiued of
him [3s 4d][96] for their labour, this Ket who hath made his obscure
beginning well knowen by his mishievous attempts to [requite][97]
Flowerdew carried them to Netheset, where they cast down all the
enclosed pasture of Flowerdew, and not staying there he led them
indifferently to divers other places, laying all enclosures where hee
came rather wast then open.

And the rather to traine them to his allure, he told them both often
and with vehement voice, how they were over topped and trodden
downe by gentlemen, and other their good masters, and put out of
possibility ever to recover foote, how whilest rivers of riches ran into
their landlords coffers, they were pared to the quicke, and fed vpon
pease and oats like beasts, how being fleeced by these for privat
benefit, they were flayed by publique burthens of state, wherein
whilest the richer sort favoured themselues, they were gnawen to
the very bones, how the more to terrify and torture them to their
minds, and winde their necks more surely vnder their arme, their
tyrannous masters did often implead arrest, cast them into prison,
and thereby consume them to worse then nothing, how they did
palliat these pillaries with the faire pretence of authority and of law,
fine workemen I warrant you, who can so closely carry their dealings,
that then men only [can then discern] them [when it is beyond their
powers to prevent them][98] how harmelesse counsailes were fit for
tame fooles, but for them who had already stirred there was no hope
but in adventuring boldly.

The likenes of affection and the masking of vices vnder pleasant
tearmes, procured not only assent, but applause to all that he said,
and so by often and earnest repeating of these and the like speeches,
and by bearing a confident [Page 67] countenance in all his actions,
the vulgars tooke him to be both valiant and wise, and a fit man to
be their commander, being glad they had found any captaine to follow.

Their numbers encreased daily, and therewith their boldnesse and power to doe harme, they were largely supplied at the first both with victualls and armes, albeit not with open consent of the places adjoining, yet with much private goodwill, for many did not only secretly favour but openly approue their designes. Generally every good man was much grieued, many vpon some dislikes before rejoiced in their greater harmes, and not regarding in what liberty they stood, were ready to runne into any bondage. The Sheriffe of Northfolke resorted vnto them, and made proclamation in the Kings name, that forthwith they should peaceably depart, and had he not beene ready and his horse swift to depart in time, hee should hardly haue departed from them aliue.

After this they drew towards Norwich and seated themselues at Monshold[99] neere Mount Surrey and vpon St. Leonhards which hangeth ouer Norwich, another company seated at Rising neere Lynne, but they were dislodged by the gentlemen of the countrey, and forced to draw to their fellowes at Monsholde. Here the maine body encamped and sent divers light companies forth to terrifie and roue. To this place many resorted out of Suffolke, and from all places of Northfolke, many for want, but most vpon a turbulent minde, and in all places thereabout beacons were fired and bells rung, as a roaring furtherance to his vproare, so as in short time the multitude encreased to 16,000, and yet rather to be esteemed a number then an army.

Their actions were couered and disguised with [two][100] mantles very vsuall in time of disorder of religion and justice,[101] for they had one Coniers for their chaplaine, a man brought vp in idle and dead studies, who both morning and evening read solemne prayers, many sermons they also had either by entreatie or enforcement. But Dr Parker afterwards [Page 68] Archbishop of Canterbury in his sermon before them touched them for their liuing so neere, that they went neere to touch him for his life, as for Justice they had a bench vnder a tree where Ket vsually sate, and with him two of euery hundred whence their companies had beene raised, here complaints were exhibited and examined aswell against those of their owne company, who receiued judgement for their offences as against any gentleman or other in the country, by commandment from hence many were very violently pulled from their houses, of whom some were enforced to follow them, others were cast into prison and happily fettered with irons, and not a few rudely and dangerously entreated, from hence also warrants were sent forth in the kings name, whereby ordinance, powder and shot were commanded out of ships and any other furniture of warre out of houses where it could be found. This tree was ever since termed the oake of reformation.

And now the seditious being advanced vnto the height both of their power and of their pride, presented certaine complaints to the King, and desired that a herald or some other messenger of credite may be sent vnto them to receiue articles of all those matters wherewith they [did conceive][102] themselues to be grieued. The King tooke it for a great indignity that base traitors and theeues should offer to capitulate with him as enimies lawfully holding the field, and yet knowing right well, that as good counsailes gather strength by time, so vpon a little respite evill advices either vanish or grow weaker to winne some advantage of time, returned an answere. That seeing he was ready alwaies to receiue and relieue the quiet complaints of any of his subiects, he marvailed much either vpon what opinion of necessity in themselues or of injustice in him, they should first put themselues into armes, as a partie against him, and then present him with their bold petitions, especially at such a time when hauing fully reformed many other matters, he had lately set forth a proclamation against [Page 69] excessiue prices of victualls, and had also appointed commissioners with ample authority for [reformation of enclosurers, of depopulations, of taking away commons and of][103] divers other things, whereof many doubtlesse had beene by that time redressed, had not these disorders giuen impediment to his designes, generally when they might well discerne both his care and endeavours to set all matters in a right frame of reformation, as might best stand both with his honour and their sureties,[104] and with justice and providence towards all. Touching their particular complaint for reducing lands and farmes to their ancient rents although it could not be done by his ordinary power without a parliament, yet he would so farre extend his authority roiall and absolute as to giue charge to his commissioners to trauaile with all persons within their counties, to reduce lands to their former rents whereat they were farmed 40 yeares before, and that rents should be paid at Michelmas then next ensuing according to that rate and that such as would not presently yeeld to his commissioners for that redresse, should at the parliament which he would forthwith summon be overruled.

Concerning their complaint for price of wolles hee would forthwith giue order that his commissioners should cause clothiers take
wolles paying only two partes of the price, whereat they were commonly sold the yeare next before, and for the other third part, the
owner and the buyer should stand to such order as the parliament
should appoint. At which time also he would giue order that landed
men to a certaine proportion should be neither clothiers nor farmers,
and farther that one man should not vse divers occupations, nor haue
plurality of benefices, nor of farmes and generally that he would the
giue order for all the residue of their requests, in such sort as they
should haue good cause not only to remaine quiet, but to pray for
him, and to adventure their liues in his service.

This parliament he promised should beginne in the beginning of
October then next ensuing, against which time they should appoint
4 or 6 of their countey, to present bills [Page 70] of their desires, and
in the meane season apply themselues to their harvest and other
peaceable businesse at home, and not to driue him to necessity
(whereof he would be sorry) by sharper meanes to maintaine both
his owne dignity and the common quiet.

These letters carrying the Kings name in the front, and the protectors with the kings signature at the foote, were sent by a heralde
to Monsholde, a place guarded with great, but confused and disordered strength of the seditious, herewith also the King sent his
generall pardon, in case they would quietly desist and dissolue. But
the seditious were so farre from accepting these or any other offers
of accord that herevpon they discharged the first shot against the
citty, and because their Artillery being planted on a hill could little
or nothing endammage the walls, they remoued their batterie to a
lower ground, but because their citty was weake, and the cittizens
but weakely disposed against them, with no danger and little travaile
they made themselues masters thereof. Here they imprisoned the
Maior and many other of the chiefe cittizens, and ordered all things
at their pleasure, but maintained the chiefe seat at Mansholde, where
it was before. The Maior of Norwitch and some other gentlemen of
credite they constrained to be present at all their counsells, with
intention to countenance their actions with some authority, but in
no sort to be guided by them. All this time the Kings forces advanced
but slowly, being imploied in appeasing the like disorders more neere
the heart of the kingdome. So that it is most certaine, that had these

seditious beene so mischievously bent as in number they were great, they might haue proued more dangerous then they were, but they aimed not at ambitious ends, their rude earthly spirits were neuer seasoned with any manly adventurous thought, and therefore they were content with a licentious and idle life wherein they might fill their bellies by spoile rather then by labour, to this [end][105] their companies ranged in all parts [Page 71] thereabouts, and tooke away for their vse much housholdstuffe and goods, especially they brought to their stations many droues of cattle, for besides deere out of parkes, besides beeues, besides fowles of all kinds within a few daies were brought out of the country [20,000][106] muttons, such numbers of sheepe were daily brought in, that a fat weather was sold for 4d. This was interpreted for a present plentie but it made such scarcitie afterwards, as could not in many yeares be repaired, Sir Edmond Kneuet Knight with such company as he could assemble, charged vpon one of their watches by night, but he was so farre inferior vnto them, that it was esteemed a great fortune that he departed from them with his life.

But soone after the Lord William Parre Marquis of Northampton was sent against them with 1500 horsemen, and a small band of Italians vnder a Captaine named Malatesta, he was accompanied with the Lord Sheffield, the Lord Wentworth with divers knights and gentlemen of principall estimation, when he approached within a mile of the citty, the magistrates and chiefe cittizens vpon summons, resorted to his standard, yeelded vnto him the citty sword, and professed their owne loialty, and excused others of inferior force, who [had either][107] by ignorance fauoured the seditious, or through feare durst not declare against them; with these the Lord Marquis entred the citty at St. Stephens gate, the citty sword being borne before him, and therewith caused the chiefe citizens to assemble in the market place, both to giue aduice and to take direction how the citty might best be defended.

In the meane time the strangers who came with him whether by appointment or by adventure, issued forth of the citty, to view both the numbers and orders of the seditious. They againe first put forth their Archers, then their horsemen, lastly a company ran furiously forth without either direction of others or judgement in themselues, intending to haue enclosed the Italians, but here might haue [Page 72] beene a great difference betweene men practised to fight, and men accustomed only to spoile. For the Italians in so well advised order receiued the seditious coming rashly vpon them without either feare or skill, that divers of the tumultuous numbers were slaine, at the last the Italians perceiuing themselues almost inuironed, cast themselues into a ring and retired backe into the citty. But they left one gentleman of their company behinde, who being overthrowne from his horse fell into the hands of the seditious, who like sauages spoiled him of his armour and of his apparell, and hanged him ouer the walls of Mount Surrey.

This caused the seditious to remaine the first part of the night within their station, which by reason of the nastines of the beastly multitude, might more fitly be termed a kennell then a campe. Within the citty diligent watch was kept, which was often visited and relieued. The souldiers remained in their armor all night, and kept so great a fire in the market place that all parts of the citty were lighted therewith. The seditious about midnight began to shoote off their great artillerie very liuely and thicke, hereupon the Lord Marquis directed part of his forces to rampart the gates and ruinous places of the walls, which the seditious espying, with a hideous roaring and rage they powred themselues vpon the citty, some endeauoured to fire the gates, some to mount ouer the walls, and some to passe the riuer, the fight continued three houres, and it is almost incredible with what rude rage the seditious maintained their assault, some being almost disable to hold vp their weapons would striue what they could to strike their enimies, others being thrust through the body with a speare, would runne themselues further to reach those who gaue them that deadly wounde, at the last their obstinacy was overcome, and they returned to their cabbines with losse of 300 of their company.

The residue of the night which was not much, the [Page 73] souldiers within the citty applied in refreshing themselues, but the next morning the seditious both with greater strength and better order entered the citty by the hospitall and began a most desperate surprise, the forces of the Marques albeit inferior in numbers, yet by reason of the freshnes[108] of the place might haue beene sufficient, if they had charged in order, and together, but being scattered in the streets, they were not able to make resistance, herewith they were much endammaged by the cittizens from their houses, so as 100 of them perished, many were hurt, and the residue driven to forsake the citty, the Lord Shiffields horse fell with him into a ditch, wereby hee fell into the power of the seditious, and as he pulled off his helmet to shew them who he was, a butcher slew him with the stroak of a club. Divers gentlemen to the number of 30 were taken and committed to streight prison, where they were vexed alike with scarcity and scorne. The seditious lost about seauen schoore of their company, and yet much fleshed with this successe, they spoiled many parts of the citty, and fired the houses of those whom they esteemed not to bee their friends, but the rage of the fire was at first hindred and then appeased by fall of a suddaine shower of raine, wherevpon many presaged that the flames of this sedition should neither spread farre nor long endure. The report of this repulse flying to London, the most made of that which was true, and many falsities added thereto. The Earle of Warwicke was sent with such forces both English and strangers, wherewith hee had appointed for seruice in Scotland. When he came to Cambridge the Lord Marquis resorted unto him, and also the Lord Willoughby, Powes and Bray,[109] his two sonnes Ambrose and Robert and many knights and gentlemen of name, with these hee marched somewhat leasurely because the importance of the danger might make the service the more esteemed, At length hee presented his forces consisting of 6000 foote and 1500 horse before the citty vpon the plaine, and forthwith sent [Page 74] to summon the seditious and to offer pardon if it would be accepted, but neither summons nor pardon was any thing regarded. Insomuch as when the Kings pardon was offred by a herault, a lewd boy turned towards him his naked britch, and vsed words sutable to that gesture, one standing by and moued with this barbarous behaviour discharged a harquebur vpon the boy, and stroke him with the shot a little aboue the reines. Hereat those seditious that seemed moderate before became desperate, and those who were desperate seemed starke mad, whence such tumults, such confused hollowings and howlings ensued, that heralde was glad to withdraw himselfe.

Then the Earle planted his cannon against St. Stephens gate, and set pioners to worke against the brazen gate. The cannon against St. Stephens gate executed so well, that in short time the Portcullis and gate were broken, and entry opened into the city. Others entered at the brazen gate but in that entrance some were slaine. Also the Maiors deputy opened Westwicke gate where the Earle himselfe entred without resistance and possessed himselfe of the market place, at these entrances 130 of the seditious were slaine 60 were taken and forthwith executed by martiall law. As the Earles carriages were brought into the citty neither garded nor regarded as they should, divers of them were surprised by the seditious and driuen to Monsholde. At this bootie they were more joyfull then grieued at the losse, either of the cittie or of their companions especially for that they were supplied thereby with good store of powder and shot, wherein their want did most consist.

The Earle being in possession of the citty rampared all the gates except those who opened towards Monsholde, wherein he planted good artillerie. But the seditious the more terrible by reason of their more desperate fury fell vpon those gates albeit without order, yet with such rude and carelesse courage and cries, that they beat backe the guardes, slew the principall gunners, carried away their [Page 75] artillerie and therewith certaine carts laden with munition, here were boies obserued to be so desperatly resolued as to pull arrowes out of their owne flesh, and deliuer them to be shot againe by the archers on their side, herevpon the Earle was enforced to blocke vp those gates as hee had done the rest, but the city was so weake that it could hardly be defended.

For the seditious being now furnished with artillerie powder and shot battered Bishopsgate, and cast downe a great part of the walls vpon that side of the citty. They afterwards passed the riuer likewise and assailed the Earles men vpon advantage in the streets, of whom many they slew and fired divers places prostrating two parishes almost entirely, so they did mischiefe they little cared what they did or to what end, and in such sort the danger encreased that many perswaded the Earle to submit courage to rage, and for a time to abandon the citty. But he not easily vincible in spirit, and well assured that hauing stopped all passages for reliefe, shortnesse of provision would in very short time draw the obstinacy of the seditious to shorter limits, drew his sword and caused others to doe the like, and (according to a souldiery custome in cases of extremity by enterchange of a kisse by every of them vpon the swords of others, sealed a resolution to maintaine the place.

Assuredly as it is advantageable to a physition to be called to the cure of a declining disease, so it is for a commander to suppresse a sedition which hath passed the height, for in both alike the noxious humor doth first weaken and afterwards wast and weare to nothing, and besides it is scarse possible that a rude and ruinous miltitude should continue long together, if any preuention be applied but they will fall into irreparable wants, and so it hapned to these seditious, who after three daies, finding their provision to faile, fired their cabbines built of timber and couered with bushes, and with a broken noise betweene [vn]certaine[110] questions and doubtfull answeres dislodged from [Page 76] their hill, and entrenched them at the foote thereof in a valley called Dussendale where they invited the Earle to a present encounter, and as there hath seldome hapned any sedition within this realme, but the chiefe actors therein haue beene abused with some prophecies of doubtfull construction, so the seditious were moued to remoue to this place vpon a prophecy much credited among them, that they should fill it with slaughtered bodies, but whether of their enimies or of their owne it was left vncertaine, the words of the prophecy were these.

> The country Knuffes Hob, Dicke and Hick,
>   with clubbes and clouted shoone:
> Shall fill vp Dussendale,
>   with slaughtered bodies soone.

The Earle being newly supplied with 1400 horse was glad that the seditious had forsaked their hill, for that his horsemen in whom consisted his greatest strength, could there performe but little service, so the next morning he sent forth all his horsemen of whom 1000 were Almaines, as accustomed so aduentrous in armes, his foote hee retained within the towne. The seditious ranged themselues for the fight, placing all the gentlemen whom they had taken in front every two coupled together to make them sure from starting away. The Earle before he would charge sent to them an offer of a generall pardon, one or two of the principall excepted. But this more [caused][111] the rage of those who were resolued either to liue or dye together and what cared they for pardon, who haue nothing but a vile and servile life to loose. For no more could be gotten from their estates, then from the shauing of an egge, wherefore in a proud scorne they answered this offer with a great shot, that stroke the kings standard bearer on the thigh, and his horse on the shoulder. Herevpon the Earle commanded his artillery to be applied, the

Almaines also and Captaine Drury with his troopes gaue a resolute
charge, and yet with such discretion that most of the captiue [Page
77] gentlemen who were placed in the front escaped without harme,
these were so well seconded by the light horse, that in short time
they brake the seditious, chased them aboue three miles, and filled
themselnes with blood vntill night, there dyed of them 2000 as King
Edward tooke the number, but our histories report more then 3500.

In the meane time they who guarded the artillerie and baggage,
encloased themselues with carriage[s, made][112] a trench, and pitched
stakes to beare of the approach of horses, determining to stand stifly
vpon their defence. The Earle returning from the execution, did
certifie them by message, that because the King his master was
desirous to establish peace rather by benignity then by blood,[113] hee
did assure them their pardon if they would submit, otherwise they
might expect nothing but death. Answere was made that they expected nothing but death, and that they respected nothing at all, but
it was by the sword if they stood vpon defence, and by the halter if
they should yeelde, wherefore they made choice to dye rather as
souldiers then as dogges. The Earle sent againe to know if they
would entertaine their pardon in case he should come in person and
assure it, they answered, they did conceiue him to be so honourable,
that from himselfe they would most thankfully embrace it. So hee
roade and caused their pardon to be read to them, and engaged his
honour that it should be performed. Then seeming to respect life
more then any other thing, threw away their weapons and disloialty
together, and with voices so lowd as before they were lewd wished
all joy and prosperity to the King.

The commander Ket hauing a good horse fled away with the first,
and the next day was taken with his brother William in a barne, and
brought with a guard of 20 horsemen to Norwich both of them
hauing made good proofe that they were no lesse peaceable to guide
an army in war, then they were to gouerne themselues in peace.
Nine of the principall were hanged vpon the tree of Reformation,
of [Page 78] whom two were seducing prophets, a third was a most
excellent cannonier, whose good skill euelly imploied did much
endammage the forces of the King. Robert Ket and his brother were
sent to London, and from thence returned to be executed in
Northfolke. Robert Ket was hanged in chaines vpon Norwich castle,
his brother William was in like sort executed vpon Wimondham

steeple, but not without some murmuring. For that church dedicated to the seruice of God, and which is polluted by violent deathe,
should be made a place of publique execution. The day of this
defate of the seditious was a long time after yearely obserued for a
festivail day by the inhabitants of Norwitch, as well by cessation
from labour, as by resorting to Church to giue publique thankes for
their deliuerance.[114]

About the same time another sedition was raised at Semor in the
Northriding of Yorkeshire where of the chiefe mouers were William
Ombler a gentleman,[115] Thomas Dale a parish clarke, and Steuenson
a post. They tooke encouragement from a darke and deceivable
prophecy, a common law [barator][116] both of obedience and peace,
which did foretell that the time should arriue when there should be
no King, when the nobility and gentry should be destroied, when
the Realme should be ruled by foure gouernors elected by the
commons holding a parliament in commotion, which should beginne
at the South and North seas of England, and that [they vnderstood
to be the time present],[117] and that the rebellions in Devonshire
Norfolke and Yorkeshire should draw together to accomplish this
prophecy. The pretences were to restore the church to her ancient
Rights (for that was alwaies one note in their musique) to relieue the
poore, to abate the rich, and generally to disburthen the Realme of
all grieuances, a seemely taske for such vndertakers.

And now for execution hereof, first by firing of beacons and
ringing of bells (as if the coast had beene assailed by enimies) they
assembled about 3000 in armes, whom they [Page 79] drew to be
appliable to their purpose. Then to beginne their great worke of
refomation they slew one White a Gentleman, Sauage a Merchant
and two others of meaner quality, and left their bodies naked vpon
the [weild][118] neere Semor. After this they passed to the Eastriding
in Yorkeshire, their company daily increasing like a snowball in
rowling, and many they tooke with them much against their mindes.
But no sooner was the kings pardon presented, but most of them fell
off and dispersed, leauing Ombler and Dale almost alone. These as
they were riding like mad men from towne to towne charging people
in the Kings name to assemble at Hummanby were apprehended,
and with foure others of the most tumultuous, soone after executed
at Yorke whose speedie punishment staid others who were thought
to wauer betweene obedience and revolt.

Now the French king supposing to make his hand by these rude rauages in England brake of his treaty of peace proclaimed hostilitie and denounced the same by his Embassador to the King. Hereupon all French men in England not Denizens were taken prisoners, and all their goods seized for the Kinge. The French King vnderstandinge that certaine English ships lay at Jersey set forth a fleete of gallies and ships intending to surprise them as they lay at Anchore. But the English being both vigilant and well appointed in such sort did entertaine them, that their ships departed terribly torn with losse of 1000 men at the least. The French King fearing least that the bad successe of this first enterprise, might both discourage his people and bring disreputation to himselfe, forbad any report to be made not only of the euent, but of the journey.

After this the French King leuied an army by lande wherewith marching towards Bulloine, he tooke Blacknesse and Newhauen two fortes of the English neere vnto Bulloine. This he did effect chiefly by the treason of one Sturton a bastard sonne of Lord Sturtons, and by reuolt of [Page 80] diuers Almaines, who serued in the garrisons, who being meerely mercenaries did easily encline to the strongest.

From whence the French King marched towardes Bullaine vpon whose approach Sir Nicholas Arnault captaine of Bullingberge holding the place not of strength to be held withdrew all the ordinance and matters of worth into high Boullaine and with gunpowder blew vp the Forte. So the French Kinge brought his armie before Boulline, but because the plague raged amongst his souldiers and the weather was vnseasonable by reason of much fall of raine, he departed from his army and left Chastilion gouernor in his steed.

Chastilion bent his siege against the Pierre, which was erected in Boulline haven and after batterie of 20000 shot or more the breach was thought reasonable and therevpon the assault was giuen. But the same was so well encountred by the valour of the defendants, helped with advantage of place, that the obstinacy of the assailants did nothing but increase their losse, so as the first fury being broken and spent. The French resolued to attempt the [Pierre][119] no more by assault, notwithstanding they continued the seige, presented diuers skermishes and false attempts, but they spent both their labour and shot without putting the defendants in any feare. Then they planted their artillery against the mouth of the hauen, to empeach supply of victualls to the towne. Yet the English victualers surceased not at the Kings adventure to bring all things necessary, vntill the end the souldiers of the towne set vpon the French suddainly by night, slue many of them and dismounted their pieces.

Then the French applied their batterie againe, wherein they sometimes spent 1500 shot in one day. But finding this to be a fruitlesse fury they afterwards vsed it more sparingly and rather vpon a shew of hostility then vpon any hope thereby to prevaile. In the meane season they charged a galley with grauel and stones, and prepared to sinke it in the middest of the hauen. But the English tooke the [Page 81] galley before it sunke and drew it to the shoare, and vsed the stones to reenforce the Pierre. After this they made faggots of light matter, mixed with pitch, tarre, tallow, rosin, powder, and wildfire, with intention to fire the ships in the hauen, but that enterprise was defeated by the Bullenois, and their fagots taken from the French. During these enterfeits diverse skirmishes passed betweene the English and the French about the frontires of Calleis, which as they were but light, so most of them ended with disadvantage to the French.

And now if all these troubles had not beene sufficient to trauaile the realme of England, at once a great diuision fell among the nobility, so much the more dangerous, by how much the spirits were more actiue and high. And albeit the heat thereof was much appeased for a time by the great judgement and moderation of the King, yet did it breake forth in the end to tragicall euents, not vpon particular persons only, but did much ouerflow and almost ouerwhelme the whole realme with disquiet, and hereof the most apparent originall was this.

The King had two vnkles brothers to Queene Jane his deceased mother, Edward Duke of Somerset Lord Protector, and Thomas Lord Seymer Baron of Sudley, high Admirall of England, as the Duke was elder in yeares, so was hee more staied in behauiour. The Lord Sudley[120] was fierce in courage, courtly in fashion, in personage stately, in voice magnificent, but somewhat empty of matter, both were so faithfully affected to the King that the one might well bee termed his sword, the other his target. The Duke was greatest in fauour with the people, the Lord Sudley most respected by the nobility, both highly esteemed by the King both fortunate alike in their advancements, both ruined alike by their owne vanity and folly, whilest these two brothers held in amity, they were like two armes, the one defending the other, and both of them the King, but many things did moue together to dissolue their loue and bring [Page 82] them to ruine. First their contrary disposition, the one being tractable and milde, the other stiffe and impatient of a superior, whereby they liued but in cunning concord as brothers glued together but not vnited in graine, then much secret enuy was borne against them, for that their new lustre did dimme the light of men honoured with ancient nobility. Lastly they were openly minded, as hasty and soone moued, so vncircumspect and easy to be minded.[121] By these the knot not only of loue but of nature between them was dissolued, so much the more [pitied][122] for that the first cause proceeded from the pride, the haughty ha[r]te,[123] the vnquiet vanity of a mannish or rather of a diuelish woman.

For the Lord Sudley had taken to wife Katharine Parre Queene Dowager last wife to King Henry VIII, a woman beautified with many excellent vertues, especially with humility the beauty of all other vertues. The Duke had taken to wife Anne Stanhope a woman for many imperfections intollerable, but for pride monstrous, [a vice since her time familiare to some others of her familie and name][124] she was exceeding both subtle and violent in accomplishing her ends, for which she spurned ouer all respects both of conscience and of shame. This woman did beare such invincible hate, first against the Queene Dowager for light causes and womans quarrells, especially for that she had precedency of place before her, being wife to the greatest Peere in the land, then to the Lord Sudley for her sake. That albeit the Queene Dowager dyed by childbirth, yet would not her malice either dye or decrease. But continually she rubbed into the Dukes dull capacity, that the Lord Sudley dissenting from him in opinion of religion, sought nothing more then to take away his life, as well in regard of the common cause of Religion, as thereby happely to attaine his place. Many other things she boldly fained being assured of easie beliefe in her heedlesse hearer, alwaies fearfull and suspitious (as of feeble spirit) but then more then euer by reason of some late opposition against him. Her perswasions she [Page 83] cunningly intermixed with teares, affirming that she would depart from him, as willing rather to heare both of his disgraces and dangers, then either to see the one or participate of the other.

The Duke embracing this womans counsaile (a womans counsaile indeede and nothing the better) yeelded himselfe both to aduise and deuise for destruction of his brother. The Earle of Warwicke had his finger in the businesse and drew others also to giue either furtherance or way to her violent desires. Being well content she should haue her minde, so as the Duke might thereby incurre infamy and hate. Herevpon the Lord Sudley was arrested and sent to the tower, and in very short time after condemned by act of parliament. And within few daies after his condemnation a warrant was sent vnder the hande of his brother the Duke, whereby his head was deliuered to the Axe. His owne fierce courage hastened his death, because equally ballanced betweene doubt and disdaine, he was desirous rather to dye at once, then to linger long vpon curtesie and in feare.

The accusations against him contained much friuolous matter, or terme them pittifull if you please. The act of parliament expresseth these causes of his attaindor. For attempting to get into his custody the person of the King,[125] and gouernment of the realme [for obteining manie offices and reteining manie men in his seruice],[126] for making much prouision of mony and of victualls, for endeauouring to marry the Lady Elizabeth the Kings sister, for persuadinge the Kinge in his tender age to take vpon him the Rule and order of himselfe: The proofes might easily be made because he was neuer called to his answeare. [His courage and libertie of speech being some what feared][127] But aswell the protestations at the point of his death, as the open course and carriage of his life cleered him in opinion of many. So doubtfull are all weighty matters whilest some take all they heare for certaine, others making question of any truths, posterity enlarging both. Dr Latymer pretending all the grauity and sincerity of a professed diuine, yet content to be seruiceable. [Page 84] to great mens ends, declared in a sermon before the King that whilest the Lord Sudley was a prisoner in the Tower he wrote to the Lady Mary and the Lady Elizabeth the Kings sisters, that they should reuenge his death, which indeed the Lady Mary afterwards more truely did by executing the Earle of Warwicke, then either shee was or at that time could in particular be required.[128] Many other imputations he cast forth, besides most doubted many knowne to be vntrue, and so whereas Papinian a ciuill lawyer but a heathen chose rather to dye then to defend the murther which the Emperor Caracalla had done vpon his brother Geta, some theologians haue beene imploied to defile places erected only for religion and truth by defending[129] oppressions and factions, desteining their professions, and the good artes which they had learned by publishing odious vntruths vpon report and credite of others.

O wiues! The most sweete poison, the most desired evill in the world. Certainly as it is true as Syracides saith, that[130] there is no malice to the malice of a woman, so no mischiefe wanteth where a malitious woman beareth sway, a woman was first giuen to man for a comforter but not for a counsailor, much lesse a controler and directer, and therefore in the first sentence against man this cause is expressed because thou obeyedst the voice of thy wife.[131] And doubtlesse the protector by being thus ruled to the death of his brother seemed with his left hand to haue cut off his right. For herevpon many of the nobility cryed out vpon him that hee was a bloodsucker, a murtherer, a parricide, a villaine, and that it was not fit the King should be vnder the protection of such a rauenous wolfe. Soone after it was giuen forth and belieued by many that the King was dead, wherevpon he passed in great estate through the cittie of London to manifest that he was both aliue and in good health, whether this speech were spread either by aduenture or by arte, it is vncertaine, certain it is it did something shake the strength [Page 85] of the Kings affection towards the Protector.

Besides many well disposed mindes conceiued a hard opinion of him, for that a church by Strand-bridge and two Bishops houses were pulled downe to make a seat for his new building in digging the foundation whereof, the bones of many who had beene there buried were cast vp and carried into the fields, and because the stones of those houses and the church did nothing suffice for his work, the steeple and most part of the church of St. John of Jerusalem neere Smithfield most beautifully erected and adorned not long before by Docray Priour of that church was mined and ouerthrowne with powder, and the stones applied to this spatious building. And because the worke could not be therewith finished, the cloister of Paules on the north side of the church in a place called Pardonne church yearde and the dance of death, very curiously wrought about the cloister, and a chappell that stood in the midst of the church yeard, also the charnell house that stood vpon the south side of Paules (now a carpenters yeard) with the chappell tombes and monuments therein were beaten downe, the bones of the dead carried into Finsbury fields and the stones conuerted to his building. It is constantly affirmed that for the same purpose hee intended to pull downe the church of St. Margaret in Westminster, and that the standing thereof was preserued only by his fall, assuredly as these actions were in a high degree impious, so did they draw with them both open dislike from men and much secret reuenge from God.

And now hath the Lord Protector played the first act of the tragedie of his life, namely his high and prosperous estate, he is now stepping into the second act, wherein he beginneth mainly to decline.

For the Earle of Warwicke espying opportunity shewing himselfe and knowing that in troublesome times the obedience of great persons is most easily shaken, drew about 18 of the priuy counsaile to knit with him against the Lord [Page 86] Protector. These he did so winde vp to his purpose that they withdrew from the courte, fell to secret consultations, and walked in the citty with many seruants weaponed and in new liueries, the causes thereof many conjectured but few knew.[132] They were all desirous that the Protectors greatnesse should be taken lower, but none conceiued that the Earles malice did extend vnto death. But the Lord Protector as humble then as he had beene haughty before sent secretary Peeter[133] to them in the Kings name to vnderstand the causes of their assembly, and to declare vnto them that he would thanke them for hating him in case they did it in loue to the King, intreating them for the Kings sake if not for his safetie yet for his quiet, that they would forbeare open shew of hostility and resort vnto him peaceably that they might commune together as friends. In the meane time he armed 500 men parte of the kings and parte his owne, the court gates were rampard and people raised both by letters and proclamation to aide the King, and the more to encrease the present terror he remoued the king by night from Hampton courte to Windesor with a company more resembling an army then a traine.

On the other side the Lords at London[134] first taking possession of the tower sent for the Maior and Aldermen of the citty to the Earle of Warwicks lodging at Ely house in Holborne, here they presented themselues secretly armed, and the Lord Rich then Lord Chancellor of England, a man of quicke and liuely deliuery of speech, but as of meane[135] birth so prone to thrust forwards the ruine of great persons, in this manner spake vnto them.

I am not ignorant into what aduenture I now plunge my selfe in speaking against a man both high in honour and great in fauour both with the King and many of the [common][136] people. But my duty prevailing against respect of danger, I will plainly declare the discontentments of the Lords of his Maiesties counsaile, haue already conceiued against the actions past of the Lorde Protector, as also their fears touching matters to [Page 87] ensue, that with your aide they may in good time happily remedy the one and remoue the other, assuring you all that as I will not vtter any thing falsly, so will I forbeare to tell many truths.

And first to touch vpon his open ambition, with what good reason or purpose thinke wee did he being a man of many imperfections, as want of eloquence, personage, learning, or good wit aspire to the great offices of gouerning all affaires of state, fit for none but whom God hath fauoured with fitting graces. And albeit these defects might haue beene well supplied by sufficiency of others of the counsaile, yet was hee so peeuishly opiniatiue and proud, that he would neither aske nor heare the advice of any, but was absolutely ruled by the obstinate and imperous woman his wife, whose ambitious and mischieuous will so guided him in the most weighty affaires of the realme, that albeit he was counsailed by others what was best, yet would he doe quite contrary, least he should seeme to need their aduice, And yet this was not enough, as auarice and ambition haue neuer enough, but to adde dignity to authority, and to make sure that as no man should as in power so in title surmount him, he would be aduanced to the Degree of duke of Somerset, which hath alwaies beene a title for one of the kings sonns inheritable to the crowne.

And albeit it may seeme a light matter to speake of bribery and extortion against him, yet his robberies and oppressions haue beene such, that no man would willingly haue adventured to commit them, vnlesse he thought by treason[137] so to assure himselfe as he could not be called to answere for them. For he hath laid his rauenous hands vpon the Kings treasure and Jewels left by his Father, which were knowne to be of [inestimable riches; but he appointed not commissioners to view them vntill two moneths after King Henries death which were then found of so small valew as][138] it might well be said euen as he had giuen forth, that King Henry died a very poore prince, and had beene vtterly shamed in case he had liued one quarter of a yeare longer.

Then also what hauocke hath he made of the Kings lands and inheritance? What sales and exchanges vpon pretence of [Page 88] necessity? And yet what a high deale hath he transported to himselfe? Without regard of others who haue emploied their trauailes and estates in seruice of the King and of his deceased Father? What artes hath he vsed to spend those and spare himself against the time of his mischievous purpose. How greedily, how insatiably hath he neuer ceased the whilest to rake and gleane mony together? What shamefull sale of offices and preferments hath he made, nothing regarding the worthinesse of the person, but the worth and weight of the gift. Betraying thereby the administration of the realme into the hands both of worthlesse and corrupt men. To speake nothing the whilest of his minte at Duresme[139] place erected and vsed for his priuate profit. To speake nothing of the great Boutisale[140] of colledges and chantries, to speak nothing of all his other particular pillages, all which were so farre from satisfying his bottomles desires that he proceeded to fleece the whole Commonwealth, to cut and pare it to the very quicke.

For vnder colour of warre, which either his negligence drew on or his false practices procured, he leuied such a subsidie vpon the whole realme as neuer was asked a greater at once, which should not haue needed, albeit the warres had beene just, in case he had not [imbezeled][141] the Kings treasure as he did, for besides he extorted money by way of loane from all men who were supposed to haue it, and yet left the Kings souldiers and servants vnpaid. But in all these pretended necessities, how profuse was he in his priuate expences? Carrying himselfe rather as fitting his owne greatnesse then the common good? How did he riot [and][142] surfeit vpon vaine hopes, as if new supply for wast would neuer want? What treasures did he bury in his sumptuous buildings? And how foolish and fancifull were they? A fit man forsooth to gouerne a realme, who had so goodly gouernment in his owne estate. All these things as there are but few but know, so we may be assured that hee neuer durst haue committed halfe of them with a minde to haue remained a subject vnder the law, and to be answerable for his actions afterwards, but did manifestly intend to [Page 89] heape his mischiefs with so high a treason as he might climbe aboue his soveraigne and stand sure beyond reach of law.

And for inducement to this his traiterous designe he suborned his seruants and certaine preachers to spread abroad the praises of his government, with as much abasing the noble King Henry as without impudence they could deuise. Following therein the practises of King Richard the tyrant, by deprauing the Father to honour the sonne, to extinguish the loue of the people to the young King, by remembring some imperfections of his Father; which example both traiterous and vnnaturall who doubts but his heart was ready to follow, whose heart was ready to defame his father, and set nought by his mother (as it is well knowne) and to procure, yea labour the death of his brother, whom albeit the law and consent of many had condemned vpon his owne speeches yet his earnest endeauor therein did well declare what thoughts can sinke into his vnnaturall breast, and what foule shifts he would haue made, rather then that his brother should haue escaped death, to that end that he might remoue at once both an impeachment to his poysenous purposes and a surety to the Kings life and estate. To this ende he also practised to dispatch such of the nobility as were like to oppose against his mischeiuous drift, and in such sort either to encumber and weaken the rest, that they should be noe impediments to him. In the meane time he endeauored to winne the common people both by strayned curtesy and by loosenes of life, whereto he gaue not only licence, but encouragement and meanes.

And the better to advance his intents he deviseth to intangle the realme not only with outward warre that with rumor thereof his dangerous diuices might be obscured, but with inward sedition by stirring and nourishing discontentments among the nobility gentry and commons of the realme. This he did vnder pretence of such matters as all men desired might be redressed more gladly then hee, but in a more quiet and setled time. But the time seemed most convenient for him when vnder the sweete pretence of release and [Page 90] libertie to the people might haue destroied the Nobility and gentry, who are the defence and safety of the people, and so at pleasure haue reduced all vnder his tyrannous subjection.

Which how insupportable it would haue beene may well be conjectured by his actions already past, what pride and insolency of his men made vp of naught? What instruments had he in euery shire to worke his purposes, to spread his rumors, to harken and to carry tales? And those what flatterers? [What parasites?][143] What lyers? How greedily gaping for other mens liuings? How vigilant to grope mens thoughts, and to picke out somewhat whereof they might complaine?

And such vile vermine how deere were they to him? And namely
John Bonham his one hand in Wiltshire, Sir Gyles Partridge his other
hand in Glocestershire, his customer in Wells, Piers Cou[rtney],[144]
his minister in Deuonshire, besides many his bad conditioned min-
ions in courte, what monsters were they? How esteemed they his
fauour aboue all mortall respects.

And further to accomplish his ambitious ends, he devised to make
the French king his friend, by betraying vnto him the Kings
fortresses beyond the seas, which the late noble King Henry with
great charge courage and glory, had brought vnder his power, which
practise was so caryed, that no man but such as discerned nothing
but did perceiue it. And that aswell by his often private conference
with the French Embassadors and their secretaries, as by failing to
furnish those pieces with necessarie supplies, as also by the speeches
which himselfe and his servants cast abroad, that Bulloine and the
fortresses about it were an vnprofitable burthen to the realme. But
for the charge no man will conceiue that he wanted money to keepe
them, who vndertooke so great a charge as the conquest of Scotland,
and wasted euery day a £100 vpon his phantasticall building.

Besides it hath beene often heard from his owne communication,
how he intended to procure a resignation of the rights of the Kings
Majesties sisters, and others who are entitled to the possession of
the Crowne, and to haue entailed the same [Page 91] vpon his owne
issue, which when he had effected, and hauing the Kings person in
his power, the chaine of soueraignty could not long haue tied him
short, he might haue atchieued all his ambitious intentions at will.

Wherefore surely he hath thus put on the person not only of a
robber, and of a murtherer, but of a traitor to the state, since we haue
euidently discouered both his lofty and bloody minde. It behoueth
you to joyne in aide with the Lords of his Majesties privy counsaile,
as in extinguishing a raging fire, as in repelling a cruell enimie, for
assuredly wee must either weakly yeelde to his rule and commande,
or else the ambitious author must be taken away.

In the afternoone of the same day the Lord Maior assembled a
common counsaile[145] in Guildhall, where two letters arriued almost
in one instant, one from the King and the Lord Protector for 1000
men to be armed for defence of the Kings person, another from the
Lords at London for 2000 men to aide them in defence of the Kings
person, both parties pretending alike, but both intending nothing

lesse. The Recorder whose voice accordeth commonly with the Lord Chancellor did so well set forth the complaints of the Lords against the Protector, that many were inclinable to fauour their side. But one named George Stadlowe somewhat better aduised stept vp and spake vnto them as followeth.

The businesse (right Honorable Lord Maior and the residue of this court) as it is a very high passage of state, so it is worthy of serious consideration, and that vpon sodeine aduice nothing be done or determined [therein],[146] least happely by being serviceable to the designes of other men whose purposes we know not, we cast our selues into the throat of danger which hitherto wee doe not see, two things I much feare in case wee afford present aide to the Lords, either of which should cast vpon vs a bridle rather for stopping a while, then for stepping or stirring too soone or too fast at their incitement. One is the certaine dangers of the citty, the other the vncertaine aduenture [Page 92] of all the realme.

First then if wee adjoine to the Lords, whether they prevaile or not wee engulph our selues into assured danger, an example whereof I finde in Fabian whose report I entreat you all to obserue. In the time of King Henry III, the Lords in a good cause for maintenance of divers beneficall lawes desired aid of the citty against the King. Ayde was granted and the quarrell brought to the arbitrement of the sword. In this battaile the King and his sonne were taken prisoners, and vpon their enlargement free pardon was granted not only to the Lords but the cittizens of London which was afterwards confirmed both by oath and by act of Parliament. But what followed? Was the displeasure forgotten? Noe verily, nor euer forgotten during that Kings life, for afterwards the liberties of the Citty were taken away, strangers were appointed governors, and the cittizens perpetually vexed, both in their persons and in their estates. So heauy and durable is the wrath of Kings. That Solomon faith: The indignation of the King is death. For it is naturall for princes to vphold their soueraignty, and to holde it in highest esteeme, in no case to endure their supreame authority to be forceably either oppressed or [depressed][147] by their subjects. Insomuch as they mortally hate such subjects as haue once attempted either to ouerrule them by power, or to cast any terror vpon them. And howsoeuer they may be either constrained or content to beare saile for a time, yet are they so sure paymasters in the end, that few haue held out their liues, I will not say prosperously but safely, who haue offered enforcements against their King.

Now touching my feare for the commonwealth, I much suspect these considerations. I alwaies expect from them some lurking mischiefe, which the more cunningly it be kept in, the more dangerously it will breake forth. For albeit there be many hands in this action, yet one is the head who doubtlesse hath skille to play his owne game, and albeit the pretences giuen forth are alwaies faire, and for the publique good, yet are the secret intentions commonly ambitious, and only aime at [Page 93] priuate ends, yea many times the end is worse then the first intent. Because when a subject hath obtained the hand against his prince, I will not say he will be loath, but doubtlesse it is not safe for him to giue ouer his advantage, wherefore I am of opinion, that for the present if wee will not be so vncurteous as to delay, and suspend our giuing aide to the Lords for a time.

Vpon this aduice the courte resolued to arme 100 horsemen and 400 foote for defence of the Citty. To the King they returned answere that they would be ready vpon any necessity to apply all their forces either for his defence or for his honour. But they intreated him to bee pleased to heare such complaints as were objected against the Lord Protector before he assembled forces in the field, which in those tempestuous times as it could not be done without great danger, so without great cause it should not: To the Lords they answered that they were ready to joyne with them in any dutifull petition to the King, but to joyne with them in armes, they could not vpon the sodaine resolue.

The next day the Lordes at London dispatched a letter to the Lords at Windesore, wherein they charged the protector with many disorders both in his priuate actions, and in his manner of gouernment, requiring that hee would disperse the forces which he had raised, and withdraw himselfe from the King, and be content to be ordered by justice and reason. That this done they would gladly commune with the rest of the counsaile for the surety of the Kings person, and for ordering of his estate, otherwise they would make no other accompt of them then they might trust to finde cause, and would assuredly charge them according to their demerits.

The King all this time was so farre from gouerning his Lords, that he was scarce at his owne liberty, and considering that the late rebellions had but newly wear[i]ed[148] themselues into quiet, and fearing new rages among the vnstable [Page 94] people daily threatned, and vpon such occasion not vnlike to take flame, conceiuing[149] also that the confederacy trenched no deeper, or that the only remedy was to seeme so to conceiue, dissolued his companies except only his guarde, but charged them vpon warning to be ready, so it is most certaine that the troublesome times were a great aduantage to the Lords. Had the people beene well setled in subjection, or the Protector a man of spirit or witt,[150] they had beene in danger to haue beene vndone, but the protector instead of vsing his authority sent secretary Peter (who vnder pretence of gravity couered much vntrustinesse of heart) to the Lords at London, with some secret instructions sent especially to perswade them that for a publique benefit, all either priuate [grudges][151] or vnkindnesses might be laid aside. But neither did hee returne to Windesor, neither was any answere returned from the Lordes. After this he wrote two letters, one in his owne name to the Earle of Warwicke, the other in the name of the Lords at Windesore to the Lords at London, in both which he so weakly complained, expostulated, intreated, yeelded vnder their hande, as it was sufficient to haue breathed courage into any enimy once declared against him.

And indeed herevpon the Lords forthwith published a proclamation vnder the hands of 17 persons, either for nobility or authority of office well regarded, wherein the causes of such calamities and losses as had lately before happened, not only by inward diuisions which had cost the liues of many thousands of the Kings subjects, and threatned more, but also by the losse of diuers pieces beyond the seas, which had beene wonn by great adventure of the late Kings person and consumption of his treasure. They perceiued that the only roote from whence those mischiefes sprung, was the evill gouernment of the Lord Protector, whose pride, couetousnes and ambition couered only his priuate ends, and therefore he was deepely busied in [Page 95] his spatious and specious buildings in the hottest times of warre against France and Scotland whilest the poore souldiers and seruitors of the King were vnpaide, and laboured to make himselfe strong in all countries, whilest within the realme lawes, justice, and good order peruerted, prouisions for the forts beyond the seas neglected, and the Kings subjects by most dangerous diuisions (by his means either raised or occasioned) much disquiet. That hereupon the Lords of the counsaile for preuenting aswell present dangers to the Kings person, as the vtter subuersion of the state of the realme, concluded to haue talked to him quietly, without disturbance to the King, or to the people, for reducing him to liue within reasonable limits, and for putting order for safety of the kings person, and preseruation of the commonwealth of the realme, and so to haue passed ouer his most vnnaturall and traiterous deseruings without further extremities. But he knowing that he was vnable to answere for any part of his demeanour,[152] began forthwith to spread false rumors, that certaine Lords had conspired against the Kings person, vnder pretence whereof hee leuied forces in a disordered vproare, albeit the treason rested in him and some other his complices, wherefore seeing he troubled the whole realme for accomplishing his traiterous ends, and vsed the King in his tender age for an instrument against himselfe, causing him to put his hand to many of his owne deuises, and to speake things tending to the destruction of himselfe they desired and in the Kings name charged all subjects not to obey any precepts, licenses or proclamations, whereunto the Protectors hand should be set, albeit he should abuse the Kings hand and seale vnto them, but to quit[153] themselues vpon such proclamation as should proceede from the body of the coun-saile, protesting therewith their faithfull hearts to the King and their loialty towards the people.

Instantly after the publishing of this proclamation the Lords di-rected their[154] letters to Windesore, [one][155] addressed to [Page 96] the King, another to the Protector, the third to the houshold which was openly read. The letter to the Protector was guilded ouer with many smooth words intimating faire promises and full of hope, but the other two did fully and fowly set forth his obstinacie, his auarice his ambition, his rash engagements into warres, in the Kings vnsetled, both age and estate, his negligences, his deceits, and all other insufficiences mentioned before. Herewith Sir Robert Wingfield captaine of the guarde was sent from the Lords to Windesore who so well persuaded the King both of the loyall affec-tion of the Lordes towardes him and of their moderate desires against the protector (who then was in presence) that partly thereby but chiefly in regard of the turbulent times the Protector was remoued from the Kings person, and a guard set vpon him vntill the next day, when the Lords at London were appointed to be there.

So the next day diuers of the counsell rode from London to
Windsore, but the Earle of Warwick rode not with them, for he was
a perfect Master of his craft: he had well learned to put others before
him in dangerous actions, and in matters of mischiefe to be seene to
doe least, when in very deed all moued from him. He had well
learned of the ape to take nuts out of the fire with the pawe of the
cat. These Lords comming before the King did againe runne ouer
their complaints against the Protector, and also vnder colour of loue
and duty aduiseth the King to beware of such as were both powerfull,
ambitious, mischieuous and rich. Affirming that it would be better
surety vnto him, if this great authority should be committed to many,
who cannot so readily knit in will or in action, as when the whole
mannage resideth in one. In the end the Duke of Somerset (for
hereafter he must be no otherwise called) was committed into their
power and committed to custody in Beauchampe tower within the
castle.

The next day he was brought to London as if he had bin a captaine
caried in triumph. He rode through Holborne [Page 97] betweene
the Earles of Southhampton and of Huntington, and was followed
with Lords and Gentlemen to the number of 300 mounted on
horsebacke. At Holborne bridge certaine Aldermen attended on
horsebacke, and the cittisens housholders stood with halberds on all
sides of the streets, through which he passed. At Soper Lane he was
receiued by the Maior, Sheriffes, Recorder and diuers Knights of
especiall note, who with a great traine of officers and attendants
bearing halbeards carryed him forthwith to the Tower, all this was
to beare in shew, both that the Duke was a dangerous man and that
the common both aide and applause concurred in his restraint.

Forthwith the King was brought to Hampton courte, where all
things being borne as done well, because nothing was ill taken,
seauen of the Lords of the counsaile and 4 Knights were appointed
by turnes to attend the Kings person. The Lords were the Marquis
of Northampton the Earles of Warwicke and Arundell, the Lordes
Russell, St John, and Wentworth, the knights were these Sir Andrew
Dudley, Sir Edward Rogers, Sir Thomas Darcy, and Sir Thomas
Worth. As for affaires of state the gouernment of them was referred
to the whole body of the counsaile. Soone after the King rode to his
house in Southwarke, (then called Suffolke place) and there dined
all. After dinner he rode in great estate through the citty to West-

minster, as if the people should be giuen to vnderstand, that nothing was deminished either from the safety or glory of the King by imprisonment of the Duke.

And now when the Duke had breathed a small time in the tower, certaine Lords of the counsaile were sent vnto him, who after a shorte preface in such termes as hate and dissimulation could temper together, remembring how great the amity had beene betweene them, and of what continuance. Then acknowledging what offices and seruices he had done for the commonwealth, and yet enterlacing some errors and defects, wherewith they seemed to reproach [Page 98] him. Lastly they presented him certaine articles as from the residue of the priuy counsaile, [the articles which had been published against him][156] desiring his present answere, whether hee would acknowledge them to be true, or else stand vpon his justification. The articles objected against him were these.

1. That he tooke vpon him the office of Protector vpon expresse condition, that he should doe nothing in the Kings affaires, but by assent of the late Kings executors, or the greatest part of them.

2. That contrary to this condition he did hinder justice, and subuert Lawes of his owne Authority, aswell by letters, as by other commande.

3. That he caused diuers persons arrested and imprisoned for treason, murther, manslaughter, and fellony to be discharged against the lawes and statutes of the realme.

4. That he appointed Lieuetenants for Armies and other officers for the weighty affaires of the king vnder his own writing and seale.

5. That he communed with Embassadors of other realmes alone of the weighty matters of the realme.

6. That he would taunt and reproue diuers of the kings most honourable counsailors for declaring their aduice in the Kings weighty affairs against his opinion, sometimes telling them that they were not worthy to sit in counsaile, and sometimes that he needed not to open weighty matters to them, and that if they were not agreeable to his opinion, he would discharge them.

7. That against law he held a court of request in his house and did enforce diuers to answere there for their freeholde and goods, and did determine of the same.

8. That being no officer without the aduice of the counsaile, or most part of them, he did dispose offices of the Kings guift for money,

grant leases, and wards, and presentations of Benefices pertaining to the King, gaue Bishoprickes, and made sales of the Kings lands.

9. That he commanded Alchimie, and multiplication to [Page 99] be practised, thereby to abase the Kings coine.

10. That diuers times he openly said that the nobility and gentry were the only cause of dearth. Whereupon the people rose to reforme matters of themselues.

11. That against the minde of the whole counsaile he caused proclamation to be made concerning enclosures, wherevpon the people made diuers insurrections and destroied many of the Kings subjects.

12. That he sent forth a commission with Articles annexed, concerning enclosures, commons, highwaies, cottages, and such like matters giuing the commishioners authority to heare and determine those causes whereby the lawes and statutes of the realme were subuerted and much rebellion raised.

13. That he suffered rebells to assemble and lie armed in campe against the nobility and gentry of the realme without speedie repressing of them.

14. That he did comfort and encourage diuers rebells by giuing them money, and by promising them fees, rewards and seruices.

15. That he caused a proclamation to be made against law, and in fauour of the rebells, that none of them should be vexed or sued by any for their offences in their rebellion.

16. That in time of rebellion he said that he liked well the actions of the rebells, and that the auarice of gentlemen gaue occasion for the people to rise, and that it was better for them to dye then to perish for want.

17. That he said, the Lords of the Parliament were loath to reforme enclosures and other things, therefore the people had a good cause to reforme them themselues.

18. That after declaration of the defaults of Bouline and the pieces there by such as did surview[157] them, he would neuer amend the same.

19. That he would not suffer the Kings pieces of Newhauen, and Blacknesse to be furnished with men and prouision, albeit he was aduertised of the defaults and advised thereto by the Kings counsaile, whereby the French King was [Page 100] emboldened to attempt vpon them.

20. That he would neither giue authority nor suffer noble men, and gentlemen to suppresse rebells in time conuenient, but wrote to them to speake the rebells faire, and vse them gently.

21. That vpon the fifth of October the present yeere at Hampton courte for defence of his owne priuate causes, hee procured seditious bills to be written in counterfeit hands, and secretly to be dispersed into diuerse parts of the realme beginning thus, Good people, intending thereby to raise the Kings subiects to rebellion and open warre.

22. That the Kings priuy counsaile did consult at London to come to him, and moue him to reforme his gouernment, but he hearing of their assembly declared by his letters in diuers places, that they were high traitors to the King.

23. That he declared vntruly aswell to the King as to other yong Lords attending his person, that the Lords at London intended to destroy the King, and desired the King neuer to forget, but to reuenge it, and required the yong Lords to put the King in remembrance thereof with intent to make sedition, and discorde betweene the King and his Nobles.

24. That at diuers times and places he said, the Lords of the counsell at London intend to kill mee, but if I dye the King shall dye, and if they famish mee, they shall famish him.

25. That of his owne head he remoued the King so sodainly from Hampton courte to Windsore, without any prouision there made, that he was thereby not only in great feare but cast into a dangerous disease.

26. That by his letters he caused the Kings people to assemble in great numbers in Armor after the manner of warre to his aide and defence.

27. That he caused his seruants and friends at Hampton court and Windesore to be apparelled in the Kings armor, when the Kings seruants and guarde went vnarmed.

28. That he intended to fly to Iernsey[158] and Wales and laid posthorses, and men, and a boat to that purpose.

[Page 101] Now albeit there is little doubt but that some of these articles were meerely deuised, others enlarged, or wrested, or otherwise inforced by odious interpretation, yet the Duke being of base golde and fearing the touch,[159] subscribed with his owne hand, that he did acknowledge his offences contained in them, and humbly vpon his knees submitted himselfe to the Kings mercy. That in like manner he entreated the Lords to be a meanes to the King that he would conceiue that his offences did proceede rather from negligence, rashnes, or other indescretion, then from any malitious thought tending to treason, and also that he would take some gratious way with him, his wife and children, not according to extremity of lawes, but after his great clemency and mercy. Written with my owne hand 23 December Anno 3 Edw. Regis.

To this I make no other defence, but intreat the reader not to condemne him for perishing so weakly, and for that he who should haue lost his life to preserue his honour, cast away both his life and honour together. Assuredly he was a man of a feeble stomacke, vnable to concoct any great fortune prosperous or aduerse. But as the judgement of God, and malice of a man concurre often in one act, although it be easie to discerne betweene them; so is it little to be maruailed, that he who thirsted after his brothers blood, should finde others to thirst after his; Notwithstanding for that present his blood was respited but hee was stripped of his great offices of being Protector, Treasurer and Marshall, lost all his goods and neere £2000 lande, in which estate if he had continued, the longer he had liued the more punishment he should endure, herewith it was scoffingly said that he had eaten the kings goose and did then regorge the feathers.

After this he sent letters to the Lords of the counsaile wherein he acknowledged himselfe much fauoured by them in that they had brought his cause to be fineable which although it was to him importable, yet as hee did [Page 102] neuer intend to contend with them or any action to justifie himselfe, as well for that he was none of the wisest and might easily erre; as for that it is scarce possible for any man in great place so to beare himself, that all his actions in the eye of justice shall be blamelesse; so hee did then submit himselfe wholly to the Kings mercy, and their discretions for some moderation; desiring them to conceiue that what he did amisse was rather through rudenes, and for want of judgement, then from any malitious meaning, and that he was therefore ready both to doe and suffer what they would appoint. Finally hee did againe most humbly vpon his knees entreat pardon, and fauour, and they should euer finde him so lowly to their honours, and obedient to their orders, as hee would thereby make amends for his former follies.

These subjections, objections, dejections of the Duke made a heauenly harmony in his enimies eares. But they wrought such compassion with the King, that forthwith he was released out of the Tower, his fines discharged, his goods and lands restored, except such as had beene giuen away, either the malice of the Lords being somewhat appeased, or their credit not of sufficient strength to resist, [the kings pleasure][160] within a short time after he was entertained and feasted by the King with great shew of fauour, and sworne againe of the priuy counsaile, at which time betweene him and the Lords perfect amity was made, or else a dissembling hate. And that all might appeare to be knit vp in a comicall conclusion, the Dukes daughter was afterwards joined in marriage to the Lord Lisle sonne and heire to the Earle of Warwick, and the Earle also was made Lord Admirall of England, yet many doubted whether the Earle retained not some secret offence against the Duke, which if hee did, it was most cunningly suppressed, doubtlesse of all his vertues he made best [use][161] of dissimulation. And as this friendship was drawen together by feare on both sides so it was not like to be more durable then was the feare.

[Page 103] And thus the second act ended of the tragedie of the Duke, the third shall follow in the proper place.[162]

In the meane time the Earle of Warwicke for what mischeiuous contriuance it was not certainly knowne, but conceiued to be against the Duke joined to him the Earle of Arundell late Lord Chamberlaine, and the Earle of Southhampton sometimes Lord Chancellor, men of their owne nature circumspect and slow, but at the time discountenanced and discontent, whom therefore the Earle of Warwicke singled as fittest for his purpose. Many secret conferences they had at their seuerall houses, which often held the greatest part of the night. But they accustomed to afford at other times either silence, or [shout][163] assent to what he did propose, did then fall off and forsake him, procuring thereby danger to themselues without doing good to any other. For when the Earle of Warwicke could by no meanes draw them to his desires, hee found means that both of them were discharged from the counsell, and commanded to their houses. Against the Earle of Arundell objections were framed that he tooke away bolts and locks at Westminster, and gaue away the Kings stuffe. Hee was fined at £12000 to be paid £1000 yeerely. But doubtlesse the Earle of Warwicke had good reason to suspect, that they who had the honesty not to approue his purpose, would not want the heart to oppose against it.

During these combats among the nobility many popular insurrections were assayled. One Bell was put to death at Tyborne for mouing a new rebellion in Suffolke and in Essex, hee was a man nittily needy and therefore aduentrous, esteemed but an idle fellow, vntill he found opportunity to shew his rashnesse. Diuers like attempts were made in other places, but the authors were not so readily followed by the people as others had done before. Partly because multitudes doe not easily moue, but chifly because misaduentures of others in like attempts had taught them to be more warily aduised. About this time a Parliament [Page 104] was held at Westminster wherein one Act was made against spreading of Prophecies the first motiue of rebellions, and another against vnlawfull assemblies, the first apparant acting of them. But for feare of new tumults, the Parliament was vntimely dissolued and gentlemen charged to retyre to their country habitations, being furnished with such forces and commissions as were held sufficient to hold in bridle either the malice or rage of reasonlesse people, yea so great grew the doubt of new insurrections that [in the yeare 1550][164] Trinity terme did not holde least gentlemen should by that occasion be drawen out of the country where they were esteemed to doe good seruice by keeping the Commons from commotions. All these mouements seemed to be pretended by mouing of the earth in diuerse places of Sussex.

The affaires of England beyond the seas all this time were caried with variable successe, Sir Thomas Cheynie was sent to the Emperour to treat with him, that his forces might joine with the forces of England against the common enimies of them both according to the Articles formerly concluded. These articles had bin well obserued for a time especially against the French. But afterwards the emperour being diuerted about other preparations, and therewith much solicited by the Scots, not to be a helpe to ruine their kingdome fell by degrees from the King of England, filling his Embassadors with emptie hopes at the first, wherein also he daily fainted and failed in the end.

In France the King placed the Rhenegraue with diuers Regiments of Almaine, Lancequenots, and certaine ensignes of French to the number of 4 or 5000 at the towne of Morguison midway betweene Bouline and Calais to empeach all entercourse betweene those two places, wherevpon the King of England caused all the strangers that had serued the yeere against the rebells to the number of 2000 to be transported to Calais, to them were adjoined 3000[165] English, vnder the command of Francis Earle of Huntingdon, and Sir Edward Hastings his brother to [Page 105] dislodge the French, or otherwise to annoy them.   But the French perceiuing that the troubles in England were perfectly appeased; and that the King thereby was much strengthened in his estate, for that the vicious humors against him were either corrected or spent, finding also that he daily grew rather into admiration then loue, aswell for that it was apparant, that hee had so well improued that little stocke which his father left, as he was like to proue a thriuer in the end, also weary in maintaining warres with Scotland, as well in regard of the charge, as for that his people were nothing desirous of seruice in that distant country. Lastly hauing tried aswell the strength as curtesy of the English nation, and doubtfull of the estates of the empire and of Spaine, by whom not only the wings of his Kingdome had beene clipped on euery side, but the whole body thereof dangerously attempted, he resolued to fasten peace with England if he could.

Herevpon he dispatched to the English court Guidolti an Italion borne in Florence who made many ouertures to the Lords of the counsaile, but all as from the Cunstable of France, and espying with a nimble eye that matters of counsaile were chiefly swayed by the Earle of Warwicke by great gifts and gretter hopes he wrought him to be appliable to his desires.   In the end it was concluded that foure Embassadors should be sent from the King of England into France, and foure from the French King to treat with them that the English commissioners should come to Guisnes and the French to Arde, and that their meeting should be chiefly at Guisnes.   The English yeelding to all with sincerity of minde, the French accepting all but with intentions reserued to themselues.   The Lords appointed by the English were John Earle of Bedforde, William Lord Paget, Sir William Peeter, and Sir John Mason. Secretaries of State, on the French side were appointed Mounsier Rochpott, Mounsier Chastilion, Guilliant de Mortier, and Rochetele de Dassie, in short time after the Earle of [Page 106] Warwicke was made Lord great Master another feather to his mounting minde.

The day wherein the English Embassadors arriued at Calais, Guidolti resorted vnto them with a letter from Mounsier Rochpot whereby he signified that the French intended not to come to Arde, but desired that the English would goe to Bouline, and that the meeting might be besides the Towne. For this he alleadged that he was so weakly disposed in health that he could not trauaile farre, and that he being Gouernor of Picardie and Chastlion of Newhauen they might not depart such distance from their charge, and further that there must be much wast of time if the English should lye at Guisnes and the French at Ardes, and that the equality would be more, and the dishonour to one of the sides lesse, if the enterview should be vpon the Frontires, then if one part should be drawen into the territory of the other.

Vpon this rubbe the English Embassadors thought fit to demurre, and so sent into England to receiue directions from the Lords of the counsaile. They againe referred the matter wholly to the judgement of the Embassadors affirming that it was a circumstance not much to bee stood vpon in case it were not vpon some finenesse,[166] but for ease and commodity of them and their traine, which indeed they might better finde neere Bouline then at Ardes, in case also they could discerne no deepe inconuenience which might hinder the good issue of the good busines in hande, which they esteemed sufficient if in substance it might be effected, albeit in all points they had not so much of their mindes, as they then desired, and as at another time they would expect, and so the English Commissioners went to Bouline, and the French came to one of their forts neerest to Bouline.

Not long before the Emperour had beene assailed by the King of England to aide him in defence of Bouline against the French, which he expresly refused, alleaging [Page 107] that he was not bound so to doe by conditions of the league. For that Bouline was a piece of new conquest acquired by the English since the league was made, then the King offered to yeelde the Towne absolutely into his hands in case he would maintaine it against the French, which offer also he refused to accept. At the arriuall of the English embassadors the souldiers were sharply assailed with wants. There was not one drop of beere in the Towne. The bread and breadcorne sufficed not for six daies. Herevpon the souldiers entred into proportion, and to giue them example the Lord Clinton being Lord Deputie limited himselfe to a loafe a day. The King was indebted in those parts aboue £14,000 besides for the Earle of Huntingdons numbers which were about 1300 foote, besides also the increases daily rising, for the monethly pay of English and strangers amounted to £6000 besides allowance for officers. Hereof the band of horsemen out of Germany tooke little lesse then £800[167] the moneth, and the Almains on foote £4000 accounting the gulden at 3s 4d, but accounting it more, as without a higher valuation little seruice and happily some mischiefe might be expected, the monethly pay to strangers amounted higher. Hereby a great error was discouered, in that the strangers for defence of Boulaine were of greater strength then were the English.

Now the English commissioners hauing first procured some releife both for victualls and pay, prepared a tent without the towne for meeting with the French. But they erected a house on the further side of the water within their owne territory, in a manner halfe way betweene their forte and the towne. The English perswaded the French to surcease their building, pretending but for their fantasies it was not necessarie, because neither their treaty was like to continue long, neither was it by solemne meeting that the businesse in hand must be effected. But in truth they feared least if peace should not follow, the French might in short time either with filling or massing the house, or else by [Page 108] fortifying make such a piece as might annoy the hauen or the towne. Not withstanding the French not only proceeded [to finish their work] but refused any other place of enteruiew.[wherto the councell out of England gaue allowance.][168]

At their first meeting much time was spent in ceremony of salutation. Then the commissions were read, then Mr de Mortier in a sharpe speech declared that the French King their Master had vpon just grounds entred the warre for recouery of his right, and defence of his allies, yet was he well minded for an honourable peace, so as the things for which the warre began, might be brought to some reasonable appointment; and hearing of the like disposition of the King of England he had sent them to treat of those affaires, nothing doubting but that the English would accord to the restitution of Bouline, and other pieces of their late conquest, which so long as they should keepe, so long they may be assured the warre would continue. He further added that Bouline was but a bare ruinous Towne, without territory or any other commodity to ballance the charge of defending it against the power of France. Lastly he said there should want no good will in them to bring matters to good appointment, hopeing to finde the like affection in the English.

After that the English commissioners had conferred a while, the Lord Paget answered that the causes of the warre both with them and their Allies (whom he tooke to be the Scots) being just and honourable. The towne of Bouline and other pieces subdued aswell by their late great master against them, as by the King their then Master against their Allies were acquired by just title of victory, and therefore in keeping of them no injury was offered, either to the French King, or to the Scots. But the further declaration hee left off vntill their next meeting, because both the time was spent and the tide summoned them to departe. Touching the good inclination of the King their Master hee had declared it well by sending them thither, in whom they should finde such good conformity, that if good [Page 109] successe ensued not, the fault should be (which they expected not) in the French. Nothing else was done sauing a sur-cease of hostility concluded for 15[169] daies, which was proclaimed in both the frontires.

At the next meeting the Lord Paget spent much speech in setting forth the King of Englands title to Bulloine and to his debts and pension from the French king, with all arrerages; together with the justice of his warre against the Scots. The French were as earnest in maintaining the contrary, wanting no words whatsoeuer their reasons were. For betweene great Princes, the greatest strength carrieth the greatest reason. At the last Mr de Mortier roundly said that to cut off all contentions of words, he would propose two means for peace. [One] that for [all old][170] matters of pensions, debts and arrerages, the English should make white books and neuer mention them more, but for Bullione to set the higher value, (or else said he) let old quarrells remaine, so as your right may be reserved to [clayme],[171] and ours to defende. And let vs speak frankly of some recompence for Boulloine. As for the Scottish Queene. (For this had beene also mentioned before) our King is resolued to keepe her for his sonne and therefore we desire you to speake thereof no more, but of what other points you please, so as we may draw shortly to an end.

The Lord Paget answered for the other commissioners that they had greatest reason to desire a speedy end, but the matters where upon they stood were of greater importance then to be determined vpon the sodaine. For said he you may make doubts as you please. But if the debt to our King be not just, being confessed, judged, sworne, and by many treaties confirmed, wee know not what may be deemed just, neither is it a summe to be slenderly regarded being 2,000,000[172] crowns cleere debt, besides 12,000[173] crowns resting in dispute. The justice of the warres against Scotland he maintained aswell in regarde of breach of [treaties][174] with themselues as for that contrarie to their [Page 110] comprehension in the last treaty [with][175] France they had inuaded England in these entercourses, the whole afternoone being spent, it was agreed that both parties should advise vpon such matters as had beene propounded vntill the next meeting.

But the French either hauing or supposing that they had aduantage ouer the English partly by reason of their firme intelligence in the English court, and partly because they found the English commissioners much yeelding to their desires, as first in cumming into France, then to Bouline, lastly to a house of their owne erecting began to be stiffe and almost intractable, sharpely pressing both for speedie resolution and short times for meetings. But Guidolti continually trauailed to draw both parties to conformity, the French being willing to be entreated by their friend to their most dissembled desires. Guidolty in steed of the Queene of Scots propounded that the French kings daughter should bee joyned in marriage to the King of England, affirming that if it were a drie peace, it would hardly be durable, but hereto the English gaue no inclinable eare. Then he deliuered 17 reasons in writing, for which he said it was necessarie for the English to conclude a peace. The English demanded how many reasons he had for the French; he answered that he had also his reasons for them, which he intended likewise to deliuer in writing.

At the next meeting the French shewed themselues as before peremptory and precise, standing stifly vpon their owne ouertures, which they had they said no commission to exceede, and therefore they refused to treat either of the pension or debt demanded by the English, and declared themselues rather desirous then willing to breake off the treaty. The English answered that before their comming Guidolti had declared from the French King that so as Bulloine might be rendred, all that was owing from him to the King of England should be paid, which Guidolti being present affirmed to be true; well said they [Page 111] what our King told Guidolti we know not, but to vs hee hath giuen no other commission then you haue heard, which in no case wee must exceede. As for the pension whereof you speake, thinke you that a King of France will be tributary to any? No, No, assure you he will not, and touching the debt because the King of England gaue occasion to the warres wasted the French Kings countrey, and thereby caused him to expend such summes of mony as exceeded the debt, he tooke himselfe to be acquitted thereof.

Hereto the English[176] answered that the French King might take matters as he pleased, but in honour justice, and conscience no debt was more due, and the warres being made for deniall thereof, he could not be for that cause acquitted. That the pension was also granted vpon diuers causes both weighty and just, and amongst other by reason of the King of Englands vncontrouleable title to Normandie Gascoine and other parts of France. Here they were interrupted by Mr Rotchpot, who brake forth into warme words, and was againe as warmely answered, but the French would nothing moue from their owne ouertures which they stood vpon by way of conclusions.

At the last the English said that they might doe well to report these differences to their Masters on both sides and that their pleasures might therein be knowne. Hereto the French answered that they knew their Kings pleasures so well, that if they should send to him againe, he would and might thinke them of small discretion and herewith they offered to breake. The English told them that if they would breake they might, but they intended to conclude nothing vntill they had further instructions from England; which they would procure as soone as they could. To this the French did easily incline.

These matters aduertised into England much troubled the counsaile, and the rather for that the Earle of Warwicke was at that time retired, pretending much infirmity in his health. Hereupon many sinister surmises began to [Page 112] spring vp among some of the counsaile, partly probable and parte happely deuised, for as they knew not whether hee were more dangerous present or away; so as the nature of all feare is they suspected that which happened to be the worst. From hence diuerse of the counsaile began in this manner to murmure against him.

What said they is he neuer sicke, but when affaires of greatest weight are in debating? Or wherefore else doth hee withdraw himselfe from the company of those who are not well assured of his loue? Wherefore doth he not now come forth and openly ouerrule, as in other matters hee is accustomed? Would he haue vs imagine by his absence that he acteth nothing? Or knowing that all moueth from him, shall wee not thinke that he seeketh to enjoy his owne ends, which bearing blame for any euent? Goe to then; let him come forth and declare himselfe, for it is better that [he][177] should finde fault with all things whilest they are doing, then condemne all things when they are done; with those and the like speeches he came to counsaile more ordinary then before, and at last partly by his reasons and partly by his authority, peace with France was esteemed so necessarie, that new instructions were sent to the English Embassadors, according whereto peace was concluded vpon these articles.

1. That all titles and climes on the one side and defences on the other should remaine to either party as they were before.

2. That the faulte of one man (except he were vnpunished) should not breake the peace.

3. That prisoners should be deliuered on both sides.

4. That Bouline and other pieces of the new conquest, with all the ordinance except such as had beene brought in by the English should be deliuered to the French within 6 moneths after the peace proclaimed.

5. That ships of merchandise might safely passe and ships of warre be called in.

6. That the French should pay for the same 200,000 crownes of the summe, euery crowne valued at six shillings 8d [Page 113] within three daies after the deliuery of the towne, and 200,000[178] like crownes more vpon the fifth day of August then next ensuing.

7. That the English should make no new warres vpon Scotland, vnlesse new occasions should be giuen.

8. That if the Scots rased Lords[179] and Dunglasse, the English should rase Roxborough and Aymouth, and no fortification to be afterwards made in any of those places.

To these articles the French King was sworne at Amiens, the King of England at London; Commissioners being especially appointed to take their oaths, and for further assurance 6 Hostages were deliuered for the French at Ards and 6 for the English at Guisnes, and it was agreed that at the deliuery of Bulloine the English hostages should be discharged, and that vpon the paiment of the first 200,000 crownes 3 of the French hostages should be discharged, and other 3 vpon paiment of the last 200,000 crownes. In the peace the Emperor was comprised in case he would consent, and further to cut off future contentions, commissioners were appointed both by the English and French to make certaine the limits betweene both territories. Other commissioners were appointed summarily to expedite and determine all matters of piracie and depredations betweene the subjects of both kingdoms, whereby many had not only liued but thriued many years before.

So the Lord Clinton gouernor of Bulloine hauing receiued his warrant, discharged all his men except 1800 and with them issued out of the towne, and deliuered it to Mr Chastilion hauing first receiued of him the 6 English hostages, and an acquittance for deliuery of the towne, and safe conduct for his passage to Calais. These 1800 men were afterwards placed vpon the frontires betweene the Emperor and the English. Soone after the first paiment of money was made by the French to certaine English commissioners wherevpon 3 of their hostages were discharged, the other three namely count de Anguien next heire [Page 114] to the crowne of France after the Kings children, the Marquis de Meaux brother to the Scottish Queene, and Montmorencie the constables sonne who at that time chiefly guided the affaires of France, came into England. They were honourably accompanied and with great estate brought to London, where euery of them kept house by himselfe.[180]

Of the monies of the first paiment £10,000 was appointed for Calais £8000 for Ireland, £10,000 for the North, and £2000 for the Nauie, the residue was carefully laid vp in the Tower. Likewise of the second paiment (wherevpon the hostages aforenamed returned into France) £8000 was appointed for Calais £5000 for the North, £10,000 was emploied for encrease towards outward paiments, certaine persons vndertaking that the mony should bee doubled euery*[181] moneth, the residue was safely lodged in the tower.

And now it remained that the chiefe actors in this peace (whatsoeuer their aimes were) must be both honoured and enriched with great rewards, and first Guidolti the first mouer of the treaty was recompenced with knighthood, 1000 crownes rewards, 1000 crownes pension and 250 crownes pension to his sonne. The Earle of Warwicke was made generall warden of the North, had 1000 markes land granted to him and 100 horsemen of the Kings charge. Mr Herbert his chiefe instrument was made president of Wales and had a grant of £500 land, and thus whether immoderate fauours breed first vnthankfulnesse and afterwards hate, and therewith ambitious desires, or whether God so punisheth immoderate affections, it often happeneth that men are prone to raise those most who worke their ruine in the end. Also the Lord Clinton who had beene deputie of Bulloine was made Lord Admirall of England. The captains and officers were rewarded with lands, leases, offices and annuities, the ordinary souldiers hauing all their pay, and a moneths pay ouer were sent into their countries, and great [Page 115] charge giuen that they should be well obserued, vntill they were quietly setled at home. The light horsemen and men at armes were put vnder the Marquis of Northhampton captaine of the Pensioners. All the guarde of Bulloine were committed to the Lord Admirall. The chiefe captaines with 600 ordinaries were sent to strengthen the Frontires of Scotland. Lastly strangers were dispatched out of the realme, who after some idle expence of their monies and time were likest to be forward either in beginning or in maintaining disorders.

Presently after this agreement of peace. The Duke of Brunswicke sent to the King of England to offer his seruice in the Kings warres with 10,000 men of his [l]ande,[182] and to entreat a marriage with the Lady Mary the Kings eldest sister. Answere was made touching his offer of aide, that the Kings warres were ended. And touching marriage with the Lady Mary that the King was in speech for her marriage with the Infanta of Portugall, which being determined without effect, he should fauourably be heard.

Vpon this also the Emperors Embassadors did expostulate with the King that he had broken his league with the Emperor. To this the King answered that because the Emperor failed in his performances the King was enforced to prouide for himselfe. The Embassador desirous as it seemed to make a breach, demanded boldly that the Lady Mary should haue the free exercise of the masse. This did the King not only constantly deny, but herevpon sermons were encreased at court and order taken that no man should haue any benefice from the King but first he should preach before him, and in short time after vnder pretence of preparing for sea matters £5000 were sent to relieue Protestants beyond the seas, and further because the Emperor made diuers streight lawes against those of the religion. Merchants were charged to forbeare their trade into Flanders so much as they could. So as it appeares, had some of the English nobility beene either lesse powerfull or more [Page 116] faithfull then they were [had they not more respected their own then the common good, the King had heart][183] enough and hands enough aswell at home as among good friends abroad, either to haue maintained warres against the French or to haue reduced them to a more honourable peace.

Warres being thus at good appointment, peaceable busenes was more seriously regarded, and whereas an Embassador arriued from Gostaue King of Sweden to knit amity with the King for entercourse of merchants. At last these articles were concluded.

1. That if the King of Sweden sent Bullion into England he might carry away English commodities without custome.

2. That he should carry Bullion to no other Prince.

3. That if he sent Ozimus,[184] steele, copper, etc. he should pay custome for English commodities as an English man.

4. That if he sent other merchandise he should haue free entercourse paying custome as a stranger.

The mint was set to worke so as it gained £24,000 yearly to the King, which should beare his charges in Ireland and bring £10,000 to the treasur[ie].[185] 400 men were sent into Ireland and charge giuen that the lawes of England should there be administred, and the mutinous be seuerely suppressed. Verily it may seeme strange that among all the horrible hurries in England, Ireland was then almost quiet. But besides that the King drew much people from thence for seruice in his warres, who happely would not haue remained quiet at home, the gouernors at that time were men of such choice, that neither the nobility disdained to endure their commande, nor the inferior sort were suppressed to supply their wants.

Further £20,000 weight was appointed to be made so much baser as the King might gaine thereby £160,000. Agreement was also made with Yorke Master of one of the mints, that he should receiue the profit of all the Bullion which himselfe should bring, and pay the Kings debts to the value of £120,000 and remaine accountable for the rest, paying six shillings 8d[186] the ounce vntill the exchange were [Page 117] equall in Flanders and afterwards six shillings 8d[187] and further that he should declare his bargaine to any that should be appointed to ouersee him, and leaue off when the King should please that for this the King should giue him £15,000 in prest, and license to transport £8000 beyond the seas to abase the exchange. Herewith the base monies formerly coined were cried downe.

Now it is certaine that by reason of the long hostility which England held against Scotland and France, peace was not so hardly concluded as kept. But albeit occasions of breach were often offered, yet the judgement and moderation of both parts sufficed either to auoide or apease them. The Bishop of Glasco comming into England without safe conduct was taken prisoner. The French Embassador made means to the King for his discharge, but answere was made that the Scots had no such peace with the English that they might passe without safe conduct. This was not denied by the Master of Erskine, whereupon the Archbishop was retained prisoner, but after a short time remitted to his liberty. After this the Queene Dowager of Scotland going from France to her countrey, passed through England but the French Embassador first obtained her safe conduct, she arriued at Portsmouth and was there encountered by diuers of the English nobility of highest quality and estimation as well for doing her honour as for that hauing such pledges she neede not feare, at London she sojourned 4 daies being lodged in the Bishops pallace, and defraied at the charge of the Citty, in which time she was roially feasted by the King at Whitehall. At her departure she was attended out of the Citty with all ceremonies pretending to state, the Sheriffes of euery shire through which she passed receiued her accompanied with the chiefe gentlemen of the countrey, as also they conveied her from one shire to another (making alwaies prouision for her entertainment) vntill shee came into the borders of Scotland.

The Earle of Maxwell came with a strong hand to the [Page 118] borders of England, against certaine families of Scots who had yeelded to the King of England, and the Lord Dacre brought his forces to their aide, in which seruice his valour and discretion did equally appeare. For albeit the gentlemen of those families did often skirmish with the Earles men, and slew many of them, yet were they neuer therein aided by the English, neither would they assaile him vpon any aduantage. But when any of these gentlemen were distressed by the Earle the English did then encounter him by armes. Generally the English would not offer to offend the Scots, but only in defending their friends.

About this time the French king sent Mounsier Lansat to request of the King of England, that the fishing of Tweede, Edrington, the debatable ground, and the Scottish Hostages which had beene sent into England in the time of King Henry VIII might be restored to the Scots, and that[188] the English prisoners who were bound to pay their ransomes, before the peace should not be comprised in the conditions therof. The King sent Sir William Pickering to declare to the French King, that to the last demand he agreed without exception, and albeit he had to the places required, yet he was content as well for them as for other demands, to performe whatsoeuer should be agreed on by commissioners on both sides, so commissioners were appointed and the matters setled in quiet agreement.

In the meane time the King sent new supply of forces and other prouisions into the North parts of the Realme, wherevpon the French King sent a nauie of 160 saile into Scotland, laden with graine, powder, and ordinance, of these 16 of the greatest perished vpon the coast of Ireland, two charged with Artillery and 14 with graine, the residue so shaken and torne, that it gaue a maine checke to their further designes, but because many saued themselues in the harbors of Ireland. The King sent thither 4 ships 4 barkes, 4 pinnaces, and 12 victualers. These possessed themselues [Page 119] of three hauens, two on the south side toward France and one towards Scotland. The Lord Cobham was appointed Generall lieuetenant, who fortified those hauens and drew downe the chiefest forces of the country towards the south parts thereof, and thus euen in peace either of the Kings so vigilantly obserued euery motion of the other, as if they had liued vpon the Alarme. The will of friends is best assured when they haue no power to doe hurt.

In France a difference did rise about a place called Fineswood, whether it pertained to the English or to the French. On the French part 800 men assembled at armes vpon this quarrell, on the English 1000. But the readines of the English to fight moued the French to abstaine from blowes, and to permit the English to enjoy their ground. Herevpon the King fortified Calais and his other pieces in France, in such sort as they had neuer beene in like condition of defence. And whereas one Styward a Scot was apprehended in England and imprisoned in the Tower, for intending to poison the young Queene of Scots, the King as well to manifest his justice as his loue and respect towards the young Queene, deliuered him to the French King vpon the frontires of Calais to be justiced by him at his pleasure.

And yet this aduice was not approued by many, for albeit it be both honourable and just, that they who offend against their proper prince, should be deliuered to him to be punished, yet is it growne out of common vse. And for this cause the condition is often expressed in leagues, that the subjects of one Prince should be deliuered by the other in case they be required, the contrary custome may happely holde reasonable in ordinary offences, in which case the Scripture forbiddeth to deliuer a slaue to his angrie Lord, but in grieuous and inhumane crimes, in such as ouerthrow the foundation of state, in such as shake the surety of humane society, I conceiue it more fit that offenders should be remitted to their Prince to be punished in the place where they haue offended.

[Page 120] But of all other the Kings amity with the Emperor was least assured, being as fullest both of practise and distrust, so in danger euery houre to dissolue. Certaine ships were appointed in the Lowe Countreys with men and furniture sutable to the attempts to transport the Lady Mary either by violence or by stealth out of England to Antwerpe. Diuerse of her gentlemen departed thither before, and certaine shipheres as they are termed, were discouered to view the English coast. Hereupon Sir John Gates was sent with forces into Essex where the Lady then lay, and besides the Duke of Somerset was sent with 200 men, the Lord Priuy seale with other 200, and Mr Sentlegier[189] with 400 men more to seuerall coasts vpon the sea; diuerse of the Kings ships were addressed to be in readines for the sea. Mr. Chamberlaine Embassador for the Queene of Hungarie in the Lowe Countries aduertised by his letters, that it was intended by this means to raise an outward warre to joine with some sedition within dores, and that the Queene of Hungarie had openly saide, that the Shipheres were [cowards][190]; who for feare of one gentleman durst not proceede in their attempt. Vpon these either dangers or feares the Lord Chancellor and Secretary Peeter were sent to the Lady Mary, who after some conference brought her to the Lord Chancellors house at Lyes in Essex and from thence to Hunsdon and from thence to the King at Westminster. Here the counsell declared vnto her how long he had permitted her the vse of the Masse, and perceiuing by her letters how vnmoueable she was, he was resolued no longer to endure it, vnlesse she would put [him][191] in hope of some conformity within short time. To this she answered that her soule was Gods, and touching her faith as shee could not change so she would not dissemble it. Reply was made that the King intended not to constraine her faith, but to restraine the outward profession thereof, in regard of the danger the example might draw. After some other like enterchange of speeches the Ladie was appointed to remaine [Page 121] with the King, but Dr Mallet her chaplaine was committed prisoner to the fleete, and almost herewith arriued an Embassador from the Emperor, with a menacing message of warre, in case his cozen the Lady Mary should not be admitted the free exercise of the masse. The King presently aduised with the Archbishop of Canterburie, and with the Bishops of London and Rochester who gaue their opinion that to giue license to sinne was sinne, but to conniue at sinne might be allowed in case it were neither to long nor without hope of reformation. Then was answere giuen to the Embassador that the King would send to the Emperor within a moneth or two to giue him what satisfaction should be fit.

In the meane time the counsaile considering how prejudiciall it would be to the realme if the subjects should loose their trade in Flanders, that the Flemmings had cloath for a yeere in their hands, that the King had 500 quintals of powder and much armor in Flanders, and the merchants much goods at the woll fleete, they aduised the King to send an Embassador legier for the Emperor, as well to satisfie him for other matters by him required, as to winne time, thereby both to prepare a mart in England and to withdraw their goods out of Flanders. So Mr Wotton was dispatched with particuler instructions to desire the Emperor to be lesse violent in his requests. And to aduertise him that the Lady Mary as she was his cozen, so was she the Kings sister, and which is more his subject, that seeing the King was a soueraigne Prince without dependancy vpon any but God, it was not reason[able][192] that the Emperor should entermeddle either with ordering his subjects, or with directing the affaires of his realme. Thus much hee offered that what fauour the Kings subjects had in the Emperors dominions for their religion, the same should the Emperors subjects receiue in England. The Emperor perceiuing that his threats were little regarded, regarded little to threaten any more. [Assuredly besides that the king was firme in his religion, it concerneth anie Prince, that great personages in his estate bee of the same religion which hee professeth: because as for noe other cause more readily men fall to bee treacherous; soe for noe other cause doe they more obstinately maintaine their treacherie.[193]]

[Page 122] About the time that the Lady Mary should haue beene transported vnto Antwerp, a rebellion was attempted in Essex where she then lay. For furtherance whereof speeches were cast forth, that strangers were arriued in England, either to rule or to spoile the naturall inhabitants, vpon this surmise many appointed to assemble at Chelmsforde, and from thence to make pillage as their wants or wanton appetites should leade, but the Principall being put to death and the residue pardoned, all remained quiet. Many Londoners also hunting after riot and ease, contriued to tumult vpon May day, pretending grieuances and fears from strangers, but because where many are of counsaile counsell is hardly kept, the enterprise was discouered and defeated before it was ripe, herewith Lyon, Gorran and Ireland persons of meane condition but desperate and discontent, endeauoured to raise a rebellion in Kent. They often met and had conferences both priuate and long. They seemed highly busied in minde, and their heads trauailing with troubled thoughts, which they often dissembled with impertinent speeches, this was first discouered by one of their seruants, doubtfull whether before knowing the mischiefe, and vntill then secret or ignorant before, and then first apprehending suspitions. So they were apprehended and after conuiction the danger determined by their deaths. Herewith rumors were raised of great discord and practices among the nobility, for this cause the Lords assembled at London, and feasted diuers daies together, giuing order to apprehend the reporters of these surmises, albeit happely not altogether vntrue. For this cause gentlemen were newly commanded to remaine in the countrey, to gouerne the people easy to be dealt with whilest they stand in feare. [All these motions seemed to bee portended by a motion of the earth in diuers partes of Sussex.[194]]

The King being thus vncertaine of the faith both of his subjects and of his confederats, intended by aliance to strengthen himselfe. To this purpose one Bortwicke[195] was sent to the King of Denmarke with priuate instructions to [Page 123] treat of a marriage betweene the Lady Elizabeth the Kings sister and the King of Denmarks eldest sonne. [And this was a secrett messinger, soe the matter was soe secretly caried, as the intention neuer come to vulgare notice. And doubtlesse there was some secrett eyther cause or conceit.[196]] But this Lady albeit she was furnished with many excellent endowments both of nature and education, yet could shee neuer be induced to entertaine Marriage with any.

After this the Lord Marquis of Northampton was directed with a solemne embassage to the French King, aswell to present him with the order of the garter, as to treat with him of other secret affaires, with him were joyned in commission the Bishop of Elie, Sir Phillip Hobbie, Sir William Pickering, Sir John Mason knights, and Mr Smith secretary of state. The Earles of Worcester, Rutland, and Ormond were appointed to accompany them, and likewise the Lordes Lisle, Fitswater, Bray, Abergauennie, and Yuers, with other knights and gentlemen of note to the number of 26[197] and for auoiding immoderate and burthensome traine, order was giuen that euery Earle should haue foure attendants, euery Lord three, euery Knight and Gentleman two. The commissioners were not limited to any number.

They arriued at Nants and were there receiued by Mounsier Chastilion and by him conducted to Chasteau Bryan where the French King then lodged, they were twice banquetted by the way, and the neerer they approached to the castle, the more encreased the resort of the French nobility to doe them honour, being come to the court they were forthwith brought to the King abiding then in his bedchamber. Here the Marquis presented vnto him the order of the garter, wherewith he was presently inuested, and thereupon gaue for the garter a chaine worth £200 and his gowne addressed with aglets esteemed worth £25.

Then the Bishop of Ely in a short speech declared how desirous the King of England was not only to continue but to encrease amity with the French King. That to this purpose he had sent the order of the garter to be both a testimony and tye of loue betweene them, to which [Page 124] purpose chiefly societies of honour were first deuised. He further declared that they had commission to make ouerture of some other matters, which was like to make the concord betweene the Kinges and their realmes not only more durable, but in all expectation perpetuall desiring the King to appoint some persons enabled with authority to treat with them.

To this speech the Cardinall of Lorraine answered that the French King was ready to apprehend and embrace all offers tending to encrease of amity, and the rather for that long hostility had made

their new friendship both more weake in it selfe, and more obnoxious to jelosies and distrusts, and therefore he promised on the Kings
behalfe that commissioners should be appointed to treat with them
about any matters which they had in charge, praying to God that it
might be a means not only to assure but to enlarge their late setled
loue, so a commission went forth to the Cardinall of Lorraine and
Chastilion the Constable, the Duke of Guise and certaine others;
at the first the English demanded that the young Queene of Scots
might be sent into England for perfection of marriage betweene
King Edward and her, but hereto the French answered that they
had taken too much aduenture, and spent too many liues vpon any
conditions to let her goe, and that conclusion had beene made long
before for her marriage with the Dolphine of France. Then the
English proposed a marriage between their King and the Lady
Elizabeth the French Kings eldest daughter, to which the French
did cheerefully encline.

So after agreement that neither partie should be bound either in
conscience or in honour vntill the Ladie should accomplish 12
yeares of age, they fell to treat of the portion which should be giuen
with her in marriage. The English first demanded [1,500,000][198]
crownes, and offered that her dowrie should be so great as King
Henry VIII had giuen with any of his wiues. The offer of dower
was not [Page 125] disliked, but for the portion some of the French
wondred, others smiled, that so great a summe should be demanded.
The English descended to 1,400,000 crownes and after by degrees
fell so low as 800,000, but the French as they held the first summe
to be vnreasonable, so all the other they esteemed excessiue. Then
the English demanded what the French would giue, first they
offered 100,000 crownes, afterwards 200,000, which they said was
the most and more then euer had bin giuen with a daughter of
France, the[n][199] followed a stiffe contention both by reasons and
precedents, but the French in no case would rise any higher, only
they agreed that the French King at his proper charge should send
her to the King of England 3 moneths before she should accomplish
her age for marriage, sufficiently appointed with jewells, apparell,
and furniture for house, and that bands for the performances should
then be deliuered at London by the King of England and at Paris
by the French King, and that in case the Lady should not consent
after she should be of the said age for marriage, the penalty should

be 150,000 crownes, the French set downe these offers in writing, and sent them to the King of England.

Soone after Mounsier le Marshall and other commissioners were sent by the French King into England, where they arriued at such time as the sweating sicknesse was most furious, a new strange and violent disease; for if a man were attached therewith he dyed or escaped within 9 houres, or 10 at the most. If he tooke cold he dyed within 3 houres. If he slept within 6 hours (as he should be desirous to doe) he dyed rauing, albeit in other burning diseases that distemper is commonly appeased with sleepe. It raged cheifly among men of strongest constitution and yeares, of whom 120 perished in some one day within the liberties of London few aged men or children or women died thereof. Two of Charles Brandons sonnes, both Dukes of Suffolke, one of the Kings Gentlemen and one of his groomes died of this disease. For which cause [Page 126] the King remoued to Hampton court with very few followers.

The same day the Marshall and other French commissioners were brought by the Lord Clinton Lord Admirall of England from Grauesend to London. They were saluted by the way with all the shot of more then 50 of the Kings great ships, and with a faire peale of Artillery from the Tower, and lastly were lodged in Suffolke pallace in Southwarke, and albeit they had more then 400 gentlemen in their traine, yet was not one of them nor any other stranger in England touched with the sweating disease, and yet the English were chased therewith not only in England, but in other countries abroad, which made them like tirants both feared and auoided wheresoeuer they came.

The next day the French were remoued to Richmond whence euery day they resorted to Hampton court, where the King remained, the first day after they had performed the Ceremonies of court, and deliuered to the King their letters of credence, they were led to a chamber richly furnished for their repose, the same day they dined with the King, and after dinner being brought into an inner chamber, the Marshall declared that they were come not only to deliuer vnto him the order of St Michaell, but therewith to manifest the entire loue which the King his Master beare him, which he desired him to conceiue to be no lesse then a father can beare to his naturall sonne. That albeit diuers persons either witlesse or malitious raise diuers vaine rumors to draw the King as it is thought from his Masters friendship, yet he trusted that the King would not listen vnto them. That it much concerned the common quiet, that good officers be placed vpon the Frontires, for as good may doe good in moderating things amisse, so euill will doe euill albeit no bad occasion be offered. Lastly he desired in case any new controuersie should arrise it might be determined by commissioners on both sides and not by conflicts the parent of warre.

[Page 127] To this the King both suddenly and shortly answered, that he much thanked the French King for his order, as for the large expression of his loue, which he would be ready in all points to requite. Touching rumours they are not always to be credited, nor alwayes to be contemned, it being no lesse vaine to feare all things, than dangerous to doubt of nothing, and in case at any time hee listned to them, it was only to prouide against the worst, and neuer to breake into hostilitie: concerning officers, he appointed such as hee esteemed good, and yet preferred the ouer-doubtfull before the ouer-credulous and secure, new controuersies he would alwaies be readie to determine by reason rather than by force, so farre as his honour should not thereby be diminished.

The French after this returne[d][200] to their lodging at Richmond, and the next day resorted againe to the King, inuested him with garments of the order, and accompanied him to the Chappell the King going betweene the Marshall and de Guise, both which after the Communion kissing his cheek. The residue of that day and a few dayes following were passed ouer with pastimes and feasts. At the last the Lord Marquis of Northampton and the residue, who had beene formerly sent with commission from the King into France, were appointed to treat with the French Commissioners touching the great matters of their Embassage. And because the French could be serued no higher that their offer of 200,000 crownes it was accepted. The one moitie to be paid vpon the day of marriage, and the other six moneths after, the Dote was agreed to be 10000 markes of English money, and not to be paid in case the King should die before marriage. This agreement was re-duced into writing, and deliuered vnder Seale on both sides: at the same time an Embassador arriued out of Scotland, to demand an exemplification of the articles of peace betweene England and France, vnder the great Seale of England, which without any difficulties they obtained.

[Page 128] The Marshall, at his taking leaue, declared to the King how kindly his Master did conceiue of the Kings readinesse to conclude this treaty, and also commended his Masters great inclination to the agreements thereof. Then he presented Mounsier Boys to be Embassador Legier for the French, and the Marquis presented Mr Pickering to be Embassador for the King of England in France. The reward of the Marshall was three thousand pound in gold, besides a Diamond taken from the Kings finger, esteemed worth an hundred and fifty pound: Mounsier de Guy[se][201] had £1000 Mounsier Chenault £1000 Mr Mortuillier £500 the secretary £500 and the Bishop of Periguer £500. The feastings were exceding sumptuous, and at their returne they were wafted ouer the seas by certaine of the Kings ships, by reason of the wars betweene the Emperour and the French King. The Lord Marquis reward was afterwards deliuered at Paris, worth £500 the Bishop of Ely £200 Sir Philip Hobbies £150 and so were the rewards of the rest.

Now the King supposing his estate to be most safe, when indeed it was most vnsure. In testimony both of his joy and of his loue aduanced many to new titles of Honour. The Lord Marquis Dorset, a man for his harmelesse simplicitie,[202] neither misliked nor much regarded, was created Duke of Suffolke, the Earle of Warwick was created Duke of Northumberland, the Earle of Wiltshire was created Marquis of Winchester, Sir William Herbert, Lord of Cardiffe, was created Earle of Pembroke, Sir Thomas Darcie, Vice-chamberlaine, and Captaine of the Guard was created Lord Darcie; William Cecil [to whose ensuing fortunes nothing wanted but moderation to vse them][203] was made one of the chiefe Secretaries; Master John Cheeke, the Kings Schoole-master, and one of the guides of his industrie and hope, and with him Mr Henry Dudley, and Mr Henry Neuill of the Priuie Chamber, were made Knights, and which was the accomplishment of mischiefe, Sir Robert Dudley one of the Duke of Northumberlands sonnes, a true heire both of his hate against persons of Nobility and his [Page 129] cunning to dissemble the same, was sworne one of the six ordinary Gentlemen, he was afterwards for lust and cruelty a monster of the court, as apt to hate, so a most sure executioner of his hate, yet rather by practise then by open dealing, as wanting rather courage then wit. After his entertainment into a place of so neere seruice the King enjoyed his health[204] not long.

The Duke of Northumberland being now inferior vnto none of the nobility in title of honour, and superior to all in authority and power could not restraine his haughty hopes from aspiring to an absolute command. But before he would directly leuill at his marke, the Duke of Somerset was thought fit to be taken away, whose credit was so great with the common people, that although it sufficed not to beare out any bad attempt of his owne, yet was it of force to crosse the euill purposes of others.

And now to begin the third act of his tragedie, speeches were cast that he caused himselfe to be proclaimed King in diuers countries, which albeit they were knowne to be false, insomuch as the millers seruant at Battlebridge in Southwarke lost both his [eares][205] vpon a pillory for so reporting, yet the very naming of him to be King, either as desired by himselfe or by others esteemed worthy, brought with it a distastfull rellish apt to apprehend suspition to be true.

After this he was charged to haue persuaded diuers of the nobility to choose him Protector at the next parliament. The Duke being questioned, neither held silence as he might nor constantly deni[ed][206] it, but entangled himselfe in his doubtfull tale. One Whaly[207] a busy headed man, and desirous to be set on worke gaue first light to this appeachment, but the Earle of Rutland did stoutly auouch it.

Herewith Sir Thomas Palmer a man neither louing the Duke of Somerset nor beloued of him, was brought by the Duke of Northumberland to the King, being in his garden. [Page 130] Heere he declared that vpon St George day last before, the Duke of Somerset being vpon a journey towards the North, in case Sir William Herbert Master of the horse had not assured him that he should receiue no harme, would haue raised the people, and that he had sent the Lord Gray before to know who would be his friends, also that the Duke of Northumberland, the Marques of Northampton, the Earle of Pembrooke, and other Lords should be inuited to a banquet, and if they came with a bare company to be set vpon by the way, if strongly, their heads should haue beene cut off at the place of their feasting, he declared further that Sir Ralph Vane had 2000 men in a readinesse, that Sir Thomas Arundell had assured the tower, that Seymor and Hamond would waite vpon him, and that all the horse of the Gendarmorie should be slaine. To this Mr Secretary Cecill added, that the Duke had sent for him and said that he suspected some ill meaning against him, whereto Mr Secretary answered, that if he were not in fault, hee might trust to his innocencie, [and weake suspitions were not to bee feared; but[208]] if he were, he had nothing to say but to lament him.

The Duke being aduertised of these informations against him by some who had some regard of honestie did forthwith defie the Secretary by his letters. Then he sent for Sir Thomas Palmer, to vnderstand what he had reported of him, who denied all that he had said, but by this hot and humorous striuing he did but draw the knots more fast.

A few daies being passed the Duke either ignorant of what was intended, or fearing if he seemed to perceiue it, came to the court, but somewhat later then he accustomed, and as too mindes possessed with feare, all things vnvsuall seeme to menace danger, so this late coming of the Duke was enforced as a suspition against him, and so after dinner he was apprehended. Sir Thomas Palmer, Sir Thomas Arundell, Hamonde Nudigates: John Seymor and Dauid Seymor were also made prisoners, the Lord Gray being newly come out of the country was attached. Sir Ralph Vane [Page 131] being twice sent for fled, vpon the first message it was reported that he said that his Lord was not stout, and that if he could get home he cared not for any, but vpon pursuit he was found in his seruants stable at Lambeth couered with straw, he was a man of a fierce spirit both sodaine and bold, of no euill disposition sauing that he thought scantnesse of estate too great an euill. All these were the same night sent to the tower except Palmer, Arundell, and Vane, who were kept in the court well guarded in chambers apart. The day following the Dutches of Somerset was sent to the Tower, no man grieuing thereat because her pride and basenesse of life ouerballanced all pitty, and doubtlesse if any mischiefe were then contriued, whereof many were doubtfull (euery one giuing forth as he belieued) it was first hammered in the forge of her wicked working braine, for shee had alwaies wicked instruments about her, whom the more she found appliable to her purposes, the more fauors she bestowed vpon them, who being engaged by her into dangers held it dangerous to fall from her, also with her were committed one Crane and his wife, and her own chamberwoman. After these followed Sir Thomas Holdcroft, Sir Miles Partridge, Sir Michaell Stanhope, Wingfield, Banister, Vaughan, and some others. In diuers of these was then neither any cause knowne or afterwardes discouered, but the number raised the greater terror, and doubled the conceit of the danger.

Sir Thomas Palmer being againe examined added to his former [confession][209], that the Gendarmorie vpon the muster day should be assaulted by 2000 foote vnder Sir Ralph Vane, and by 100 horses of the Duke of Somersets, besides his friends which should stand by, and besides the idle people which were thought inclineable to take his part, that this done he would runne throw the cittie and proclaime liberty, and in case his attempt did not succeed hee would goe to the Ile of Wight or to Poole. [which being most sencelesse and absurd, descreadited all that which might haue bin true.][210]

Crane confessed for the most part as Palmer had done [Page 132] and further added that the Lord Pagets house was the place, where the nobility being inuited to a banquet should haue lost their heads, and that the Earle of Arundell was made acquainted with the practise by Sir Michaell Stanhope, and that it had bin done but that the greatnesse of the enterprise caused delaies and sometimes diuersity of aduice, and further said that the Duke of Somerset once faining himselfe to be sicke, went to London to assay what friends he could procure. This Crane was a man who hauing consumed his owne estate had armed himselfe to any mischiefe.

Hamonde confessed that the Duke of Somersets chamber had beene strongly watched at Greenwich by night.

All these were sworne before the counsaile, and the greatest part of the nobility of the realme, that their confessions were true and as fauourably set downe in behalfe of the Duke, as with a safe con-science they could, and forthwith vpon the information of Crane the Earle of Arundell and the Lord Paget were sent to the Tower, so were Stradley, and St Albones seruants to the Earle of Arundell, the Lord Strange voluntarily enformed, how the Duke desired him to moue the King to take to wife his third daughter the Ladie Jane, and that he would be his esp[yall][211] about the King to aduertise him, when any of the counsaile spake priuatly with him, and to acquaint him what they said.

Herevpon to giue some publique satisfaction to the people, the Lord Chancellor who had words at will and wit enough to apply them, declared openly in the starre chamber all these accusations against the Duke of Somerset, letters were allso published to all

Emperors, Kings, Embassadors, and chiefemen in any state, wherein these matters were comprised. By other letters the muster of the Gendarmorie was deferred for certaine moneths, other letters were directed to Sir Arthur Darcy to take charge of the tower, and to discharge Sir Arthur Markham. For that without [Page 133] acquainting any of the Lords of the counsaile, he suffered the Duke of Somerset to walke abroad and permit entercourses of letters betweene Dauid Seymor and Mrs Poynes.

Whilest these matters were in trauerse, messengers arriued from Duke Maurise of Saxony, the Duke of Mickleburge, and John Marques of Brandenburge, Princes of the religion in Germanie, to vnderstand the Kings minde whether he would agree to aide them with 400,000 dollars in case any necessity should assaile them, they consenting to doe the like to him in case he should be ouercharged with warre, the King gaue them an vncertaine answere, but gentle and full of faire hopes, that because their message was only to know the Kings inclination, and not to conclude he could giue them no other answere then this, that he was well inclined to joyne in amity with them whom he knew to agree with him in religion, but first he was desirous to know whether they could procure such aide from other Princes as might enable them to maintaine their warres, and to assist him if need should require, and therefore he willed them to breake this matter to the Duke of Prussia and other Princes about them, and to procure the good will of Hamborough, Lubecke, and Breme, then he desired that the matter of religion should be plainly set downe, least vnder pretence thereof warres should be made for other quarrells, lastly he willed that they should furnish themselues with more ample instructions from their Lords to commune and conclude of all circumstances pertaining to that businesse.

The Kings answere was framed with these vncertainties and delaies, least if the King had assured his consent at the first, it might haue beene taken as breach of league with the Emperor, afterwards they and other Princes of Germany made a league offensiue and defensiue with the French King against the Emperor, into the which the French King desired the King of England to come, but because the French King was the chiefe of the league, the King did [Page 134] plainly perceiue that the warre was not for the cause of religion, wherefore he answered that he could not doe it with[out][212] breach of his league with the Emperor, against whom hauing no pretence of hostility, he was not so desirous of warres as without just cause of his owne to pull them vpon him.

About the same time the Lord admirall was sent into France as the Kings deputie to be Godfather at the baptisme of the French Kings sonne, also a French man who had committed a murther at Diepe, and fled into England was remitted into France and deliuered vpon the borders to receiue justice by the same lawes against which he had offended.

And now the Duke of Northumberland being impatient of long working wickednesse, the 4th act of the Duke of Somersets tragedie must not be delaied, least thereby feare abating, (as being false it could not be durable) either the Kings gentle disposition, or the loue which he had formerly borne to his vnkle might happily returne to their naturall working. So the Duke of Somerset after a short aboad in the tower was brought to his triall at Westminster. The Lord William Paulet Marques of Winchester and Lord treasurer sate as high Steward of England, vnder a cloath of estate on a bench mounted three degrees, the Peeres to the number of 27 sate on a bench one step lower. These were the Duke of Suffolke and of Northumberland, the Marques of Northampton, the Earles of Darby, Bedforde, Huntington, Rutland, Bath, Sussex, Worcester, Pembrooke, and Hereford. The Barons, Abergauenny, Audely, Wharton, Euers, Latimer, Borough, Zouch, Stafford, Wentworth, Darcie, Sturton, Windesore, Cromwell, Cobham, and Bray.

First the inditements were read in number 5 containing a charge of raising men in the north parts of the realme, and at his house, of assembling men to kill the Duke of Northumberland, of resisting his attachment, of killing the [Page 135] Gendarmorie, of raising London, of assaulting the Lords, and deuising their deaths, when the prisoner had pleaded not guilty and put himselfe vpon triall of his Peeres, the examinations before mentioned were read, and by the Kings learned counsaile pressed against him. [but without any rude or inhumane insulting][213] Hereto albeit he was both vnskilfull and much appalled (causes sufficient to driue him out of matters) yet after a short entreaty, that words either idly or angerly spoken might not be enforced to any high cr[ime],[214] to the points objected he answered.

That he neuer intended to raise the north parts of the realme, but vpon some brutes he apprehended a feare, which moued him to send to Sir William Herbert to remaine his friend. That he determined not to kill the Duke of Northumberland or any other Lord, but spake of it only and determined the contrary. That it had beene a mad enterprise with his 100 men to assaile the Gendarmory consisting of 900, when in case he had preuailed, it would nothing haue auailed the pretended purpose, and therefore this being senselesse and absurd, must needs discredid other matters, which otherwise might haue beene belieued. That at London he neuer projected any stirre but euer held it a good place for his surety. That for hauing men in his chamber at Greenwich it was manifest he meant no harme, because when he might haue done it he did not, and further against the persons of them, whose examinations had beene read against him he objected many things, desiring they might be brought to his face, which in regard he was a person of dignity and estate he claimed to be reasonable, especially against Sir Thomas Palmer he spake much euill, and yet in opinion of many farre short of the truth. Hereto no answere was made but that the worse they were, the fitter they were to be his instruments, fit instruments indeed (said he) but rather for others then for me.

The fa[c]t²¹⁵ being made the Kings learned counsaile auouched the law to be to assemble men with intent to kill the [Page 136] Duke of Northumberland was treason, by a statute of the 3 and 4th of King Edward then raigning, made against vnlawfull assemblies, that to raise London or the North parts of the realme was treason, that to minde resisting his attachment was felony, that to assault the Lords, and to devise their deaths was felony. But vnder fauour of their judgement the statute alleaged bears no such sense, either for treason or for felony, indeed by a statute of King Henry VII²¹⁶ it is felony for inferior persons to contriue the death of a Lord of the counsaile, but Lordes are therein expresly excepted. [Other statute or lawe to that purpose I could neuer yet eyther find or enquire.]²¹⁷

The Lordes went together and first the Duke of Suffolke nobly said that he held it not reasonable, that this being but a contention betweene priuate subject, vnder pretention thereof, any meane action should to draw to intention of treason. The Duke of Northumberland (in countenance bearing shew of sadnesse but in truth stifly obstinate) denyed that he would euer consent that any practise against him should be either imputed or reputed to be treason, yet this was not taken to proceede from modesty as he expected, but for that he could not with his honour or with reason so enforce it.

The Marques of Northampton was crosse and contentious with many, but neuer replied to any answere a manifest marke of no strong spirit. Some of the rest plainly brake forth that they held it vnfit that the Duke of Northumberland, the Marques of Northampton, and the Earle of Pembrooke should be of the triall, because the prisoner was chiefly charged with practises intended against them. But hereto answere was made that a Peere of the Realme might not be challenged. After much variation of opinions the prisoner at the barre was acquit of treason, but by most voices (most fauouring the Duke of Northumberland) he was found guilty of felony. Hereupon judgement followed that he should be hanged, but this would neuer haue gone so hard, had they not prosecuted all vnder pretence of treason.

[Page 137] The Duke of Somerset might haue craued his clerge, but he suffered judgement to passe, thanked the Lords for his gentle triall, craued pardon of the Duke of Northumberland, the Marques of Northampton, and the Earle of Pembrooke, for his ill meaning against them, and made suit for his life, in pitty to his wife, children, and seruants, and in regard of paiment of his debts. As he departed because he was acquit of treason, the axe of the tower was not openly carried, whereupon the people supposing that he was altogether acquit, shouted halfe a dozen times so loud that they were heard beyond Charing Crosse. It is certaine the people fauoured him the more because they saw that there was much secret hate borne against him. But as this immoderate fauour of the multitude did him no good, so will it vndoe so many as shall trust vnto it. It was told the King that after the Dukes returne to the tower, he acknowledged to certaine Lords, that he had hired Bartuile to make them away, that Bartuile[218] confessed so much, and that Hamond was not ignorant thereof, which whether it were true, or whether deuised to make the King more estranged from him, [men][219] of judgement could not hold themselues assured.

About this time Cuthbert Tonstall Bishop of Durham a man famous in those times[220] for learning, and integrity of life, was sent to the tower for concealement of (I know not what) treason, written to him I know not by whom, and not discouered vntill (what shall I call) the party did reueale it. But the Lord Chaucellor Rich hauing built a faire estate, and perceiuing what nimble ears were borne to listen after treason, also for that a parliament was towards wherein he was doubtfull what questions might arise, made suit to the King that in regard of the infirmities of his body, he might be discharged of his office, giuing good example to men sometimes by their owne moderation to auoid disgrace. So he deliuered the seale at his house in great St Bartholomewes to the Duke of Northumberland and [Page 138] the Earle of Pembrooke sent by the King with commission to receiue it. The same seale was forthwith deliuered to Dr Godricke Bishop of Ely, a man if happily able to discharg the place, assuredly no more. It was first deliuered vnto him only during the sicknesse of the Lord Rich, but in short time after he was sworne Lord Chancellor, because as keeper of the seale he could not then execute such matters as were to be dispatched in parliament.

And now after judgement against Somerset the Lords were not negligent to entertaine the King with all delights they could deuise, partly to winne his fauour, but especially to [di]uert[221] his thoughts from his condemned Vnkle, to this end they often presented him with stately masques, braue challenges at [tilt][222] and at barriers, and whatsoeuer exercises or disports they could conjecture to be best pleasing to him, then also he first began to keepe hall, and the Christmas time was passed ouer with banquetings, masques, plaies, and much other variety of mirth. Often they would call him to serious affaires wherein he tooke especiall pleasure. Sometimes they would remember him how dangerous the Duke of Somerset was, who hauing made away his only brother, contriued the death of the chiefe of the nobility. And where (say they) would his mischiefe haue rested? Would it haue raged against all and left the King only vntouched? Verily hauing beene alwaies both cruell and false,[223] there would haue beene no end of his mischiefe, and all his submissions must now be taken for counterfeit and dissembled. But his auarice and ambition once remoued, the way will be laid open to vertue and merit.

So about two moneths after his judgement the 5th and last act of his tragedie was brought vpon the stage. When being so often exposed to fortunes mercy before he was placed by a strong guard vpon a scaffold at tower hill, about eight of the clocke in the morning to suffer death, and albeit straight charge had beene giuen the day before to euery [Page 139] housholder in the citty, not to permit any to depart out of their houses before ten of the clocke that day, yet the people the more vnruly by this restraint,[224] by such thick throngs swarmed to the place, that before seauen of the clocke the hill was couered and all the chambers which opened toward the scaffold were taken vp.

Here the Duke first aduowed to the people, that his intentions had beene not only harmelesse in regard of particuler persons, but driuing to the common benefit both of the King and of the Realme. Then he exhorted them vnto obedience, assuring them that no persons could justly auouch their faith to God, who were not faithfull to their King.

But herewith behold certaine persons of a hamlet neere who had beene warned by the Lieuetenant of the tower to attend that morning about seauen of the clocke, comming after their hower through the posterne, and perceiuing the prisoner to be mounted vpon the scaffold, began to runne and to call to their fellowes to come away. The sodain[nes][225] of their coming, the hast that they made, the weapons they carried, but especially the word, come away, being often doubled, moued many of the neerest to surmise that a power was come to receiue the Duke, whereupon many cried with a high voice. Away, Away, the cry of those and the coming on of the other cast amazement vpon the rest, so much the more terrible because no man knew what he feared or wherefore, euery man conceiuing that which his astonished fancie did cast in his minde, some imagined that it thundred, others that it was an earthquake, others that the powder in the armorie had taken fire, others that troopes of horsemen approached. In which medly of conceits they bare downe one another, and jostled many into the tower ditch, and long it was before the vaine tumult could be appeased.

No sooner was the people setled in quiet, and the Duke beginning to finish his speech, but vpon another idle [Page 140] apprehension they fell to be no lesse riotous in joy then they had beene in feare. For Sir Anthony Browne coming on horsebacke vpon the spurre gaue occasion, whereby many entertained hope that he brought a pardon, whereupon a great shout was raised, A pardon, A pardon, God saue the King. But the Duke expressed great constancy at both these times, often desiring the people to remaine quiet that he might quietly end his life. For said he I haue often looked death in the face vpon great aduentures in the field, he is now no stranger to me, and among all the vaine mockeries of this world I repent me of nothing more then in esteeming life more deare then I should. I haue endured the hate of great persons, so much the more dangerous because vnjust. I haue incurred displeasure from inferiors, not alwaies for any great faults of mine owne, (albeit I was neuer free) but for giuing way to the faults of others, and now being constantly resolued, I neither feare to dy nor desire to liue, and hauing mastered all griefe in my selfe. I desire no man to sorrow for me, so hauing testified his faith to God, and his faithfulnesse to the King, he yeelded his body into the executioners hand, who with one stroake of the axe cut off all his confused cogitations and cares, the more pitied by the people for the knowne hate of Northumberland against him.

Assuredly he was a man harmelesse and faithfull, and one who neuer hatched any hopes prejudiciall to the King, but alwaies intended his safety and honour, but hard it is for greatnesse to stand when it is not sustained by the proper strength. The people whose property it is by excessiue fauour to bring great men to miserie, and then to be excessiue in pitty departed away grieued and afraid, and yet feared to seeme to be afraid, and for this cause chiefly did neuer beare good minde to Northumberland afterwards although in shew they dissemble the contrary, for nothing is more easie then to discerne when people obserue great men from the heart, or when [Page 141] they doe it for fashion or for feare, and as it often happeneth that men oppressed worke reuenge after their deaths. So the remembrance of Somerset much moued the people to fall from Northumberland in his greatest attempt and to leaue him to his fatall fall, whereat they openly rejoyced and presented to him handkerchiefes dipped in the blood of Somerset, for whom they thought he [receiued][226] rather late then vndeserued punishment. So certaine it is that the debts both of cruelty and mercy goe neuer vnpaied, I omit the meane scourges of conscience. For assuredly a body cannot be so torne with stripes, as a minde is with remembrance of wicked actions, but of him more hereafter shall be said, and how his greatnesse turned to be fortunes scorne.

But outwardly and for the present he gained a great hand ouer the nobility, who soone obseruing that he was able to endanger the estate of the greatest, and that the more respect they did beare to him, the more safely they liued and the more easily aduanced to honour, they all contended to creepe into his humor, to watch his wordes, his gestures, his lookes, and to doe that as of themselues which they conceiued he had a desire they should doe.

But the King albeit at the first he gaue no token of any ill tempered passion as taking it not agreeable to majesty, openly to declare himselfe, and albeit the Lordes did much helpe [him eyther to forgett his vncle or]²²⁷ to dispell any dampie thoughts which the remembrance of his vnkle might raise, by applying him with great variety of exercises and disportes, yet vpon speech of him afterwards he would often sigh and let fall teares, sometimes he was of opinion that he had done nothing that deserued death, or if he had, that it was very small, and proceeded rather from his wife then from himselfe. And where then said he was the good nature of a nephew? Where was the elemency of a Prince? Ah how vnfortunate haue I beene to those of my blood? My mother I slew at my very birth, and since haue made away two of her [Page 142] brothers, and happily to make away for the purposes of others against my selfe. Was it euer knowen before that a Kinges vnkle, a Lord Protector, one whose fortunes had much aduanced the honour of the realme, did loose his head for felony, for a felony neither cleere in law and in fact weakly proued? A lasse how falsely haue I beene abused? How weakly caried? How little was I master ouer my owne judgement? That both his death and the enuy thereof must be charged vpon mee?

Not long after the death of Somerset, because it was not thought fit that such a person should be executed alone, who could hardly be thought to offend alone. Sir Ralph Vane and Sir Miles Partridge were hanged on towerhill, Sir Michaell Stanhope, and Sir Thomas Arundell were there also beheaded. All these tooke it vpon their last charge that they neuer offended against the King, nor against any of his counsaile, God knowes whether obstinatly secret, or whether innocent, and in the opinion of all men Somerset was much cleered by the death of those who were executed to make him appeare faulty.

Sir Ralph Vane was charged with conspiring with Somerset, but his bold answeres termed rude and ruffianlike, falling into [ears]²²⁸ apt to take offence, either only caused or much furthered his condemnation. For besides his naturall fiercenesse enflamed by his present disgrace, he was the more free by reason of his great seruices in the field. The time hath beene, said he, when I was of some esteeme, but now we are in peace which reputeth the coward and couragious alike, and so with an obstinate resolution he made choice rather not to regard death then by any submission to entreat for life, indeed it was well knowne that he had beene famous for seruice, but therewith it was well knowen by whose fauour he had beene famous.

Sir Thomas Arundell was with some difficulty condemned, for his cause was brought to triall about seauen of the clocke in the morning, about noone the Jurors went [Page 143] together and because they could not agree, they were shut in a house [without meat or drinke]²²⁹ all the residue of that day, and all the night following, the next morning they found him guilty, vnhappy man, who found the doing of any thing or of nothing dangerous alike.

Sir Miles Partridge, and Sir Michaell Stanhope were condemned as consociates in the conspiracy of Somerset. Both reputed indifferently disposed to bad or good, yet neither of them of that temper as to dare any dangerous fact; either because they were so indeed, or because their fauour or alliance with the dutchesse of Somerset made them to be of lesse esteeme.

Garter King at armes was sent to the Lord Paget prisoner in the tower to take from him the garter and the George, and to discharge him of that order. The pretence of this dishonour was because he was said to be no gentleman of blood, neither by Father nor by Mother. The Garter and the George were forthwith bestowed vpon the Earle of Warwicke, eldest sonne to the Duke of Northumberland. [but was afterward restored to the Lord Paget againe.]²³⁰ About this time the order was almost wholly altered as by the statutes thereof then made it appeares.

After these times few matters of high nature or obseruable note happened in England during King Edwards life. Of these I will select such as I esteeme most fit for history, both as being publique, and as contained matter of some regard, not alwaies obseruing the just order of time, but sometime coherence or propinquity of matter.²³¹

Sir Philip Hobby was sent to pay 62,000²³² pounds at Antwerp, for paiment of which summe the King stood to diuers persons engaged. This done he went to the Regent, then lying at Brussels to declare vnto her certaine grieuances of the English merchants aduentures, but he receiued nothing but faire promises which proued deceiuable. Afterwards Mounsier de Couriers came from the Regent to the King to vnderstand more particularly the complaints of the Merchants, and therewith to desire that her subjects ships [Page 144] might safely take harbour in any of the Kings hauens. For the first a note of the merchants complaints was deliuered in writing, but answere was deferred for want of instructions, an vsuall pretence in like affaires. Touching the second, answere was made, that the King had giuen order that Flemmish shipps should not be molested in any of his hauens, which appeared in that they were there alwaies rescued from the pursuit and chase of the French. But hee thought it not fit that more should enter his hauens at once then he had power to gouerne. Assuredly the Merchant aduenturers haue beene often wronged and wringed to the quicke, but were neuer quicke and liuely in thankes to those by whose endeauours they were freed.

The same merchants exhibited a bill at the counsaile table against the Merchants of the Stilliard. After answere by those of the Stilliard, and reply by the aduenturers, it was conceiued vpon view of diuers Charters, that the Merchants of the Stilliard were no sufficient corporation, and that their number, names, and nation could not be knowen. Also that when they had forfeited their liberties, King Edward IV restored them vpon condition, that they should couer[233] no strangers goods which they had not obserued. And againe whereas at the beginning they shipped not aboue 80[234] cloathes after that 100, afterwards 1000, after that 6000, at that time 44,000 cloathes were shipped euery yeare in their names, and not aboue 1100 by all strangers besides, wherefore albeit certaine Embassadors from Hamborough and Lubeck spake much in their behalfe, yet a decree was made, that they had forfeited their liberties and were in the same condition with other strangers. And albeit they made great moanes afterwards, yet could they not procure this sentence to be reuersed.

A commission was granted to viii Bishops, viii other Diuines, viii Ciuilians, and viii common Lawyers, and in all xxxii to set forth ecclesiasticall lawes, agreeable to the nature both of the people and of the religion then established [Page 145] in the Church of England, but it tooke no effect. For neither the number of the commissioners being many, nor the quality of them being persons both in great offices and diuers farre remote could afford meetings for so great a businesse. Also the difference both of professions and of ends, did of necessity raise much difference in judgment.

The King had sixe Chaplaines in Ordinary, touching whose attendance in court an order was made, that two should remaine with the
King by turnes, and fower should trauaile in preaching abroad. The
first yeare two in Wales, and two in Lincolneshire,[235] the next yeare
two in the Marshes of Scotland and two in Yorkeshire. The third
yeare two in Deuonshire, and two in Hampshire. The fourth yeare
two in Northfolke, and Essex, and two in Kent and Sussex, and so
throw all the shires in England, which happily did not only serue for
a spirituall end, namely instruction in religion, but did also aduance
a temporall purpose of peaceable obedience. For as rude vntrained
mindes are not only easily drawen but inclineable of themselues to
sedition and tumult, so by learning and religion men are especially
both reduced and retained in ciuill quiet.

For better dispatch of businesse of diuers natures, the body of the
counsaile was diuided into seuerall commissions. Some were appointed for hearing those suits which were vsually brought before
the whole table, to send matters of justice to their proper courts, to
giue full deniall to such as they should not esteeme reasonable, to
certify what they thought meet to be granted, and vpon allowance
thereof to dispatch the parties. Others were appointed to consider
of penall lawes and proclamations in force and to quicken the execution of the most principall. These were directed first[236] to consider
what principall lawes and proclamations were most needfull to be
executed. Then to enquire into the countries how they were dis-
obeyed and first to punish greatest offendors, and afterwards to
proceede to the rest. Lastly that they should enquire what [Page
146] other disorders were either dangerous or offensiue in euery
shire, and either to punish the offendors or else to report their
judgement therein. Others were appointed to attend occurrences of
state at large, with whom the King did sit once euery weeke to heare
matters of greatest moment debated, because in these high passages
nothing was thought to be done truly with majesty, nothing agreeable
to the dignity of the state, but in the presence of the King. Generally
all the counsaile agreed that none of them should make suit to the
King for land or forfeitures aboue £20 or for reuersion of leases, or
any other extraordinary matter vntill the state of his Reuenewes
should be further knowen.

[Besides these commissions, another went forth for execution of
certaine statutes made in ye 4th yeare of King Henry VII, and in the

vii th and xxvii th yeares of King Henry VIII. Wherevpon instructions were giuen for enquirie what villages or howses had bin decayed, by reason of enclosures; what tillage had bin layd downe, and how manie ploughes cast vpp, by reason of the said enclosures: what landes had bin seuered from howses of husbandrie, whereby the same were ruined or decayed: what parkes were lately encloased or enlarged, and what arable ground is thereby layd to pasture: whether anie parson kept aboue 2000 sheepe; and what number may serue for his necessarie expence. Whether anie personne had taken in commons, or occupied aboue twoe tenementes of husbandry lying in one village; with other matters of the like nature.]²³⁷

Besides these commissions another went forth to ouersee and order the Kinges reuenewes, and to cut off superfluous charges, to ouersee all courts, especially those of new erection, as the court of augmentation, and of first fruits and tenths, and to prouide that the reuenewes were answered euery halfe yeare, another went forth for debts owing to the King, and to take accompt of paiments since the 35 of King Henry VIII, and in what manner the King had beene deceiued, either by not accompting or accompting falsely. Another also for taking away needlesse Boulwarkes, by vertue whereof, diuerse were dimolished vpon the sea coasts, in peace chargeable and little seruiceable in warre. [Lastly commissioners were appoincted to meete with commissioners of Scotland, for equal diuision of the debatable ground, whoe mett together, and settled that businesse in good manner.]²³⁸ And further for more orderly and speedy dispatch of causes, the King deliuered to his counsaile these Articles folowing.

1. That all suits petitions and common warrants deliuered to the priuy counsell be considered by them on mundaies in the afternoone and answered on saturdaies in the afternoone, and that those daies and no other be assigned to that purpose.

2. That such suits and petitions as pertaine to any courts of law, be referred to those courts where properly they are triable, others to be determined with expedition.

3. That in making warrants for money it be forseene, that [Page 147] they be not for such matters as may be dispatched by warrants dormant, least by such meanes accompts should be vncertaine.

4. That vpon Sundaies they intend publique affaires of the Realme, dispatch answeres to letters for good order of the state, and

make full dispatches of all things concluded the weeke before. Prouided that they be present at common praier.

5. That on Sunday night the Secretaries or one of them deliuer to the King a memoriall of such things as are to be debated by the priuy counsaile, and he to appoint certaine of them to be debated vpon seuerall daies, viz. Munday afternoone. Tuesday, wensday, Thursday, and Friday beforenoone.

6. That on friday afternoone they shall make a collection of such things as haue beene done the fower daies before, what they haue concluded and what the time suffered not to peruse. Also the principall reasons which moued them to conclude of such matters as seemed doubtfull.

7. That on Saturday before noone they present this collection to the King and enquire his pleasure vpon all things which they haue concluded, and also vpon all priuate suits.

[8. That on Sunday night againe the Kinge receiuing from the secretaries such matters as haue risen upon new occasion, with such matters as his counsaile haue left, either not debated or not determined; shall appoint what matters shall bee determined the weeke next following as vpon what dayes.]²³⁹

8. That none of the priuy counsell depart the court for longer time then two daies, vnlesse eight of the counsell remaine behind, and vnlesse the King haue notice thereof.

9. That they make no assembly in counsell vnlesse they be to the number of foure at the least.

10. That if they assemble to the number of fower, and vnder the number of sixe, then they may reason or examine the commodities or inconueniences of matters proposed, and make things plaine which seeme diffused at the first opening, and if they agree then at the next full assembly of sixe, a perfect conclusion thereof shall be made.

11. That if there be vnder fower and a matter arriseth requiring expedition, they shall declare it to the King, but not giue answere vnlesse it requires extraordinary hast.

12. That if such matters shall arise as it shall please the King to heare the same debated, warning shall be giuen that [Page 148] the more may be present.

13. That if such matter arise as cannot be ended without long debating, the counsaile shall not intermeddle with other causes vntill they haue concluded the same.

14. That no priuate suit be entermedled with great affaires, but shall be heard on Mundaies only.

15. That when matters for scantnesse of time be only discussed and not brought to an end, then it shall be noted to what point the businesse is brought, and what haue beene the principall reasons, that when it shall be treated againe it may the sooner come to conclusion.

16. That in tedious or difficult matters two or three or more may be appointed to prepare and report the same, that being lesse cumbrous and defuse they may the more easily be dispatched.

17. That no warrant for reward aboue £40, or businesse, or affaires aboue £100 passe but vnder the Kings signet.

18. That if vpon aduertisements or other occasions matters of great importance appeare which require hast, such matters shall be considered and determined, notwithstanding those Articles which appoint businesse for seuerall daies, so as this order be not generally or commonly broken.

Assuredly albeit the King declared both his judgment and his diligence and care of affaires of the realme. Yet is there one rule more (and not by him neglected) for all great officers, which if it be not sufficient in itselfe to hold matters in order, yet are no rules sufficient without it.

And this is to choose persons both for ability and integrity well reputed, albeit happily they be not alwaies vsed. For besides that these will be a rule to themselues, it is a great satisfaction to the people, and keepeth them both from murmuring and curious enquiring into counsailes of State, which is neuer good and often dangerous when they know or at least suppose matters to passe vnder such mens judgements.

In these times it was conceiued by many that by [Page 149] erecting of a Mart in England, the realme would be much enriched and made more famous, and lesse obnoxious to other countries. The time was then esteemed fit by reason of the warres betweene the Emperor and the French King. The places deemed most meete were Hull for the east countries, and Southampton for the South. London was thought no ill place, but Southampton was judged most conuenient for the first beginning. This matter detained the Lords of the counsell in a deliberation both serious and long, with great strength and variety of reasons on both sides, which because they may giue some light to the like question, which in times ensuing may happily againe be set on foot. I will here declare them in the same manner as they were collected by the King.

Against the Mart these objections were made.

1. That strangers could haue no accesse into England by land, which they had at Antwerp where the Mart then was.

2. That the ill working of English cloaths made them lesse esteemed abroad.

3. That the great quantity of English cloathes in Flanders would make them lesse desired from hence.

4. That the Merchants had then established their dwelling places at Antwerp.

5. That other Nations would forbeare their resort into England for a while vpon commandement of the Emperor.

6. That the deniall of the requests of the Merchants of the Stilliard would be a hindrance to the Mart if preuention were not vsed.

7. That the pouerty and smalnesse of Southampton would be a great impediment.

8. That the Riuer Rhene was more commodious for Antwerp then any riuer was for England.

Herevnto answere was made that at the time when the Mart should beginne at Southampton, the French King and the Almans would stop entercourse to Antwerp by land, so as nothing should passe that way but in great [Page 150] danger. Againe as Southampton wanteth the commodity of accesse of merchandise by land, so it hath the commodity that there can be no accesse of enimies by land, and if warres should be raised then the Nauie of England is sufficient to defend them. And further that trafique that cometh to Antwerp by land is almost only from the Venetians, who may with greater ease, and lesse danger transport their merchandises into England by sea. That the ill making of cloathes was fit to be redressed by the Parliament, then sitting, and the matter was then reduced to some ripenesse, the vpper house hauing one bill and the neither house another in good forwardnesse. Neither were they so ill made but that the Flemmings did easily desire them, offering rather to Pay the imposition of the Emperor then to be without them.

That it were necessarie that the passage of ships should be staied vntill the Mart should aduance to some ripenesse, and that cloathes should be bought with the Kinges money and conueied to Southampton to be there vttered at the Mart, which should helpe the inconuenience very well. That merchants neuer binde themselues to any mansion, which either to atchieue gaine or to auoide danger they will not readily forsake, for so they remoued from Bruges to Antwerp only for the English commodities. And therefore seeing they shall haue a good commodity by coming to Southampton, and be rid of great feare of danger both in their liues and goods, in forsaking Antwerp, there is little feare that they will be curious in making the change.

That the Emperor was then so neerely driuen, that neither was he willing to attend the impeachment of the Mart, neither could he at that time doe it, for the Flemmings and the Spaniards vnder him could more hardly be without the English, then the English without them, and therefore would hardly be brought to forebeare that trafique, and besides they liued then in feare of loosing all.

[Page 151] That it were good that for the present the Stilliard men were generally answered, and triall made whether by any gentle offer of some part of their liberties they might be brought to ship, and their wares vnto the mart. The French also might easily be drawen ouer, hauing [only][240] trafique at that time but with England. That these two might suffice to beginne a Mart.

That the merchants would make good shift for their lodging, and it is not the ability of the place that maketh a mart, but the resort of Merchants, as Spaniards, Almans, Italians, Flemmings, Venetians, Danes, in exchanging their commodities one with another. With whom also would concurre the Merchants of London, Bristowe, and other places of England, and some of the cloaths which should be carried thither at the first might be taken vp with the Kings money and there be vttered.

That Bruges where the Mart was before standeth not vpon the Rheene neither doth Antwerp where the Mart was then. Frankeford doth and may well serue for a faire for high Almaine, but Southampton serueth better for all countries vpon the sea, for few of these resort to Frankeford.

Herewith diuerse reasons were alleaged for the Mart, and namely that the vent of English cloathes would hereby be open in all times of warre, that the English merchants goods would be out of danger of strangers, and without feare of danger of arresting vpon euery light cause. That it would much enrich the Realme, because as a Market enricheth a towne, so doth a Mart enrich a Kingdome. That vpon occasion great summes of money might be borrowed of them who frequent the Mart. That the king might command a great number of strangers ships to serue in his warres. That warre being made all goods should be in the Kings danger. That the English should buy all things at the first hand of strangers. Wheras then the strangers sold their wares to the Flemings, and the Flemings to the English. That [Page 152] the townes towards the sea would hereby be made more populous, rich, beautifull and strong. That the merchants insteed of Tapistrie, points, glasses and other laces, would then bring in bullion, and other substantiall merchandizes to haue the English cloath, and tinne. That by this means the English should abate the power of their enimies, and not be enforced to borrow of Merchants but when they list, and that in no great quantity or summe.

The time was then esteemed most conuenient, because the warres betwixt the French and Emperor caused the Italians, Genowaies, Portugals, and Spaniards to forbeare their trade to Antwerp. The Prussians also and other East countries hauing 14 ships against the Emperor would not be very forward to aduenture thither. Againe the French inuading Lorraine, and menacing Flanders, and the Al-maines lying on the riuer of Rheene, did stop the course of merchants out of Italie, as well to Frankeford as to Antwerp. And further the putting of souldiers into Antwerp moued the Merchants to forbeare their trafique, and to looke to their safety. Also the breach which a late tempest had made, was like to make the channell vncertaine, and the hauen naught. Lastly the stop of the exchange to Lyons would make many Flemmings bankrupts. And because these na-tions cannot liue without a vent. These things decaying the Mart of Antwerp and Frankeford they would most willingly vpon erecting a free Mart resort to England.

And here the towne of Southampton was esteemed most fit because the Spaniards, Brittaines, Gascoins, Lombards, Genowaies, Normans, Italians, the Merchants of the Eastland, the Prussians, Danes, Swedens, and Norwegians might indifferently resort thither, and more easie than to Antwerpe. [Also Southampton is a better port then Antwerp.][241] And wheras the Flemmings hauing few commod-ities haue allured Merchants by their priuiledges to settle a Mart among them, much more easily should the English doe it hauing both oppurtunity and meanes, as cloath, tinne, seacoale lead, bellmettall and such other commodities, as few [Page 153] christian countries haue the like.

Lastly the meanes to establish this mart were contriued to be these. First that the English merchants should forbeare their resort for a mart or two beyond the seas vnder pretence of the impositions there charged vpon them. Then that proclamation should be made in diuerse parts of this Realme where Merchants chiefly resort, that there shalbe a free Mart kept at Southampton to beginne presently after whitsontide and to continue fiue weekes, so as it should be noe hindrance to St James faire at Bristow nor to Bartholomew faire in London. The priuiledges of which Mart should be expressed to be these.

That all men should haue free libertie for resort and returne without arresting, except in cases of treason, murther or felony. That for the time of the Mart all men should pay but halfe the custome due in other places of the Realme. That during the time noe shipping should be made from any place betweene Southwales and Essex but only to Southampton. That in Hampshire, Wiltshire, Sussex, Surry, Kent, Dorsetshire, and no bargaine should be made for wares during that time but only at that Mart. That a court should be erected to punish offendors [and endowed]²⁴² with liberties of good condition. That some one commodity as happily some one kind of cloath should be assigned as proper to the Mart. That some liberties must be giuen to the inhabitants of Southampton and some monies lent to them if it might be spared to beginne their Trafique. That ships should attend the safegard of Merchants so well as they could, and that if this Mart tooke good effect, another might be erected at Hull for the Northeast countries, to beginne presently after Sturbridge faire, so as they might returne before the great Ices stopped their seas.

Thus it was concluded but the execution was for a time delaied because the wooll fleete of 60 saile, was lately before departed for Antwerp, and could not possibly be called backe. But to make the first preparation because a Mart [Page 154] could not subsist without exchang, liberty was granted to the English merchants, to exchang and rechange money for money. As vpon this occasion this profitable purpose was first delaied, so afterwards it was altogether dashed, first by the Kinges sicknesse, after by his death.

Now albeit the King was both deepely in debt, and had many extraordinary occasions,²⁴³ yet in regard of the troublesome times he did forbeare to charge his subjects with such loanes and impositions as vsually in peace breed discontent, and in turbulent times disquiet, but he chose rather to deale with the Foulker in the low Countries for moneys vpon loane at a very high rate. And hereupon letters were directed from the lords of the counsell to the Foulker at Antwerp that he had receiued from the King 63,000 punds Flemmish in Februarie, and 24,000 in Aprill next before, which amounted to 87,000 pounds Flemmish. A faire summe to be paid in one year, especially in that busy world when it was necessarie to Princes not to be without money. Hereupon and for that they vnderstood that at that time he was well able to forbeare money, they aduised the King to pay to him only 5000 pounds of the £45,000 which then remained vnpaid, and to continue the rest at the vsuall yearly interest of £14 for euery hundred, wherewith they desired him to retaine good patience. Hereto the Foulker answered that as he had found faire dealings before, so he would rest content to deferre paiment of £30,000 so as £20,000 thereof might be well assured to be paid within some conuenient time. All this was presently agreed, and no lesse faithfully performed afterwards. And assuredly as God is the word and cannot but make good his word, so a Prince so much looseth of his dignity as hee declineth from his word.

About this time a garrison pay of £10,000 was sent to the Frontires of Scotland, and the like to Calais, and in the same yeere £5000 into Ireland, hereto if we adde the Kings great charges in fortification vpon both the frontires of [Page 155] Scotland and France the particulars whereof I omit as matters now altogether of no vse, it may easily be discerned that the hostility with Scotland and France and the inciuility of Ireland were a great part of the cause which held this frugall King thus diued in debt.

And for another means of raising of mony commissions went forth for selling chantry lands, and houses for paiment of the Kings debt giuen forth to be 251,000 pounds sterling at the least. Also to enquire of all Church goods either remaining in Cathedrall or parish Churches or embesled away, and namely of Jewels of gold and siluer or siluer crosses, candlesticks, censors, challicies, ready mony, coapes and other vestiments and reseruing to euery Church one Chalice, and couering for the Communion table, the residue to be applied to the benefit of the King. By their sales and enquiries the Kings wants, were somewhat relieued. And many persons, uery meane both for birth and ability of minde, and of no lesse place of emploiment, found means to aduance themselues to so great estate as they left their posterity ranged among the nobility of this realme.

Of these church purchasers, I haue seene many melt to nothing, and the residue shall be obserued either by riot or by improuidence to consume.

At the same time for more assured strength of the Borders vpon Scotland order was setled that no man in those parts should beare two offices at once, which not well obserued in later years hath much derogated both from the dignity and discharge of offices aswell in state as in some inferior places.

Another means for raising mony was practised no lesse pleasing to the [common]²⁴⁴ people then profitable to the commonwealth, and that was by enquiring after offences of officers in great place, who as by vnjust dealing they became most odious, so by justice in their punishments, the Prince acquireth both loue and applause. And so one Beamont Master of the Rolles was conuinced, that in his office of wardes [Page 156] he had purchased lands with the Kinges mony, also that he had lent aboue £700 of the Kinges mony, and forborne 11,000²⁴⁵ of the Kinges debts for his owne profit. Also that being Master of the Rolles he dealt corruptly in a case betweene the Duke of Suffolke, and the Lady Powes. For he bought the Ladies Tithe²⁴⁶ and caused an indenture to be forged from Charles Brandon the Duke a little before deceased, purposing²⁴⁷ a grant of the lands in question from Duke Charles to the Lady Powes. Also that he had concealed the felony of his seruant, who hauing stolne from him £200 he tooke the mony to himselfe againe. Hereupon he surrendred to the King all his offices, lands and goods in satisfaction aswell for the monies due by him to the King, as of the fines which his offences had merited, he was a man of a dull and heauy spirit, and therfore the more senslesly, deuoted in his sensuall auarice.

One Whalie receiuer of Yorkeshire acknowledged how he had lent the Kinges mony for gaine, how he euer paid one yeares reuenue with the arrerages of the yeare before, how he had bought the Kinges land with the Kinges mony, how he had made diuerse false accompts, how vpon fall of mony he borrowed diuerse summes, whereby he gained £500 at one crying downe. For these misdemeanors he surrendred his office and submitted himselfe to pay such fines as the King or his counsell should charge vpon him.

The Lord Paget Chancellor of the Duchie was conuinced[248] that he had sould the Kings Landes and timber woods without commission, that he had taken great fines for the Kings lands and applied them to his proper vse, and that he had made leases in reuersion for more then xxi years, for these offences he surrendred his office and submitted himselfe to be fined at the pleasure of the King. So his fine was gessed[249] at £6000 whereof 2000 were remitted vpon condition that the other 4000 should be paid within the compasse of that yeare.

This he endured with a manly patience as knowing [Page 157] right well that he held all the residue of his estate vpon curtesie of those who hated him at the heart. It was at the first suspected and afterwards expected by all that among other matters objected against the Lord Paget the chiefe or at least one should haue beene for contriuing to Banquet the Lords at his house, and vnder pretence thereof to take off their heads, which was the only cause for which the Duke of Somerset lost his head. But because no mention was made thereof, because about the same time the Lord Gray of Wilton, Bannister and Crane, and a little after the Earle of Arundell were freely discharged hauing beene imprisoned for this conspiracy, the conceit was taken that the Dukes head was the only aime, and that the residue were vsed but as a countenance of state to dazle the people.

Letters were sent to the gouernor of Gernesey, that diuine seruice should there be used according to the forme of the Church of England. A King of Armes named Vlster was newly instituted for Ireland, his prouince was all Ireland, and he was the first 4th King of Armes, the first herald appointed for Ireland.

Whilest these matters were in action the Emperors Embassador in England deliuered letters to the King from the Regent in the low Countries, importing that whereas the King was bound by a treaty betweene the Emperor and the Kinges Father at Lutrect[250] in the yeare 1542, that if the low Countries should be inuaded the King should aide him with 5000[251] foote, or 70 crownes a day during 4 monethes and that this aide should be performed within one moneth after request. For so much as the French King inuaded Luxembourg, the Emperor required aide of the King of England according to the effect of that treaty.

Herevpon order was giuen that if the Embassador did moue for answere to this letter, he should be told by two of the counsell, that during the Kinges progresse his counsell was dispersed, whose aduice he was desirous to heare. And further that the King had committed the same treaty to be perused by men whose judgments as he did much [Page 158] respect, so would he expect a time vntill their opinions might be heard. And in case that after this the Embassador should againe require an answere, then they should say that the King hauing lately wrestled out of most dangerous warres, wherewith his yong years were ouerburthened, he hoped well that the Emperor would not desire to thrust him into the like againe. That he had sworne amity with the French King which he could not with his honour breake, and therefore if the Emperor should deeme it so meete he would mediate a peace as a friend to both, which he should best effect by forbearing to vse hostility against either. And in case the Embassador should still perseuere to vrge the treaty they were lastly directed to answere that the King did not hold himselfe bound by that treaty, as both made by his Father and euidently prejudiciall to his realme, for albeit agreements of peace are perpetuall and bind the successor, yet it is not so in agreements of society and confederation. And this the Emperor did right well vnderstand, for when the King in his last warres desired to enter a new treaty with the Emperor, he returned answere that it should not need, for albeit the King were discharged by his Fathers death yet the Emperor was still bound. And againe the Emperor had not for his part performed the treaty, as well in hindring the carriage of horses, armor, and munition, which the King had prouided for his warres, as also in neglecting to send aide when the low Country of Calais was forraged, and therefore he did not justly demand performance thereof from the King.

I know it hath beene often in like sort answered, that treaties dissolue by death of those who made them, for so the Fidenates held themselues discharged of the league which they had made with Romulus after his death. And the Latines did the like after the death of Tullus, and likewise after the death of Ancus. The Etrurians affirmed the like after the death of Priscus. And the Sabines after the death of Seruius. And againe after that Tarquinius was [Page 159] cast out of state. I know also that the difference is great betweene a league of peace and a league of society and confederation. But I will not touch euery string of this question, which Hottoman[252] calleth a noble question, and much tossed and debated, partly because it consisteth of many knotty and thorny distinctions, wherein approued authors doe not well agree, but chiefely because at this time it fell not to be a difference betweene the Emperor and the King.

For when the Embassador first came for answere to this letter Mr Wotton and Mr Hobbie answered according to the first branch of their instructions, wherewith he departed well satisfied for the present, and before he called for answere againe one Stukely[253] arriued out of France and declared to the counsell how the French King being persuaded that Stukely would neuer returne into England because he departed without leaue vpon apprehension of the Duke of Somerset, his master bewraied to him that if he could procure peace with the Emperor, he intended to besiege Calais, and was in hope to carry the towne by way of the sand hills, and that from thence winning rice banke he might both famish the Towne, and beate the market place, how he further said that he intended to land in [England][254] about Falmouth because boulewarkes there might easily be wonne, and the people were for the most part Catholiques. And further how at the same time Mounsier de Guise should enter England by the way of Scotland, not only with good leaue, but with aide and conduct from the Scots.

Vpon this discouery the King assembled his counsell at Windesor, and entred with them into deliberation, whether it were either safe from him or to no disaduantage to rely so securely either vpon the strength or faith of France, as either to refuse or neglect to afford aide vnto the Emperor, and thereby happily incurre his hostility.

Many were of opinion that the King should condescend to aide the Emperor. First for that if the King were [Page 160] desirous to hold the Emperor bound by the treaty made with the Kinges father he must also be obliged thereby. Otherwise it was a lame halting league and could not possibly goe vpright. Then for that if the Emperor should not be aided the house of Burgundie was like to be deuoured by the French, whereby their greatnesse might grow dreadfull especially to England. Then for that againe the French King had drawen the Turke into Christendome, and therefore was to be resisted as a common enimy. And further in case the Emperor vpon extremity should compose agreement with the French, the danger to England would be double. First vpon offence taken by the Emperor, then vpon the French Kings old disposition edged by euery new displeasure wherein the deuotion of the Bishop of Rome would not be wanting. And againe the English Merchants were so ill intreated in the Empire, the Realme was so much [endamaged][255] in honour and in wealth as some remedy was to be sought, and none better then by giuing aide. Lastly the French Kings proceedings were no lesse doubtfull then fearfull, not only in regard of Stukelies report (not altogether to be neglected) but by reason of his breaking and firing diuers English ships the auncient strength and fortresses of the realme.

Others were of aduice that the Emperors demands of aide should be denied. First for that it would be too chargeable and almost impossible for the English to performe. Then for that when the Emperor should die the whole weight of the warre would roule vpon the English. And further the Germaine Protestants would be offended herewith, and conceiue some doubts of their owne estates. Lastly there was hope that the amity with France would not long continue but amend, and that the embassadors then lately sent would repaire all harmes done by the French upon English shipps.

Betweene both these the King stroke a midling judgment, so to aide the Emperor against the French King as other Christian princes should also adjoine, and that for no [Page 161] other cause but as a common enimy for drawing the Turkes forces vpon them.

That hereby as the cause was common so would there be more parties to it. And this also would moderate the charge of aiding the Emperor according to the treaty, and whensoeuer the Emperor should die or breake off, it was likely that some of those Princes and parties should remaine so as the King should not stand alone. Moreouer this friendship would much advance the Kinges other affaires in Germany, and finally it would be honourable to breake with the French King vpon this common quarrell.

Against this advise of the King, two objections were made, one that the treaty must be entertained with so many that it could not be speedily or secretly concluded. The other that in case the purpose should be discouered and not concluded the French might be prouoked thereby to practise the like confederation [with all Catholicks][256] against the English.

All these the King did knit vp in this conclusion, first that the treaty should be made only with the Emperor, and by the Emperors means with other Princes. Secondly that the Emperors acceptance should be well vnderstood before any treaty were either entered or entertained against the French.

Herevpon letters were dispatched to Mr Morison the Kinges Embassador with the Emperor whereby he was directed to declare to the Emperor how the King touched with pitty at the invasion of Christian countries by the Turkes, would willingly joine with him and other States of the Empire (in case the Emperor could bring it to passe) in some league against the Turkes and against their confederats. But caution was giuen that he should not once mention the French King nor answere any mention made of him, only to say that his commission extended no further. But if the Emperor would send a messenger into England he should happily know more.

Herewith and because time beateth out truth letters [Page 162] were sent to Mr Pickering the Kinges Embassador in France to know whether Stukely had acquainted him with any of those matters which he had disclosed in England. And with what familiarity the French King vsed him or by what other circumstances he could conceiue his report to be true. Herewith also the Lord Gray was chosen deputy of Calais, and the Lord Wentworth[257] remoued as one whose youth and want of experience, was held vnfit to gouerne that charge in turbulent times. On the other side Sir Nicholas Wentworth was remoued from being Porter of the towne by reason of his old age, but had an hundred pounds yearly pension assigned him for his life.[258] Also by abating needlesse expences to be the better enabled against charge the seuerall tables for young Lords, for the masters of Requests, and for Sergeants at armes were laid downe, and diuerse extraordinary allowances were taken away. And further because the King was to make paiment of £48,000 beyond the seas, and had but £14,000 towards the summe 300 of the chiefe Merchants aduenturers granted to him a lone of £40,000 for three moneths, to be leuied from the cloaths which they were then to transport after the rate of 20 shillings for euery cloath.[259] But these Aduenturers went not vpon any aduenture because at that shipping 40,000 broad cloaths were by them transported.

Whilest these matters were in action[260] two Lawyers arriued in England with direction from the French King to declare what matters had beene determined against the English by the French Kings counsell, and vpon what reasons and also what matters were then depending, and what care and diligence was vsed in those dispatches. They were much commended by all for their modest behauiour, and their sweet eloquence much delighted the King who againe in a short speech first thanked the French King for his desire to giue him satisfaction, then commended them for well performing their charge, but for the substance of their businesse he referred them to London, where [Page 163] some of his counsell should commune thereof fully with them.   Here Mr Secretary Peeter, and Mr Watton, and Sir Thomas Smith laid before them the grieuances of the English merchants, whose losses by the French exceeded the summe of £50,000. To this the Embassadors gaue little answere, but said they would make report thereof at their returne into France, affirming that they had no commission but only to declare the manner and causes of judiciall proceedings.

Presently after their returne Mounsier Villandry was sent againe in post to the King to declare vnto him that albeit Mr Sydneies, and Mr Winters matters went justly against them, yet because they were the Kings seruants, and one of them in place neere his person, the French King was content freely to giue to Mr Sydney his ship and all his goods in her, and to Mr Winter his ship and all his owne goods. But this offer the King refused affirming that he required nothing freely, but expected justice and expedition. Villandry shewed further that the King his master was desirous that the ordinances and customes of England and France touching Marine affaires might be reduced into one forme, without any difference betweene them. Whereto answere was made that the English ordinances for marine affaires were no other then the ciuill lawes and certaine auntient additions of the Realme, wherein they could conceiue no reason or conueniency of change, hauing long continued without reproofe. After this Villandry brought forth two proclamations not long before published in France and very aduantageable for the English, for the which he had a letter of thankes to the King his master. Lastly, which was [indeed][261] the maine of his message, and whereto all other were but insinuations he desired that certaine Frenchmen taken vpon the coast of England might be released. Hereto he receiued answere that they were Pirats, and that some of them should by justice be punished, and some might happily by clemency [Page 164] be spared, so with this dispatch he returned for France.

But before it was conceiued he could be fully at home he came againe to the English court, and there declared to the King, how the King his master would deliuer 4 shipps against which judgment had beene giuen. And that hee would appoint men of good sort and sufficiency to heare the English Merchants at Paris, and that he would alter his ordinances for marine affaires, of which emendations he then sent a copy to the King. The King appointed his Secretaries to consider therof. And after some passages of time Villandry had his answere. That the King intended not be receiuing fower ships freely to prejudice his right in the rest. That the appointing of an inferior counsell to heare Merchants at Paris after former tedious suits in a higher court, he thought would be but dilatory and so to little purpose, because the inferior counsell would neuer vndoe that (albeit good cause should appeare) which had bin judged by a higher counsell. That the new ordinances he liked no better then he did the olde, and therfore desired no other then the customes which of late times had beene vsed in France, and then continued in force betweene England and the low countries. Lastly he desired no more words but deeds.

And now were letters returned from Mr Pickering out of France, whereby he aduertised the King how Stukely neuer discouered any of those speeches to him, which since he had charged vpon the French King. And further that he neuer was either in credite or conuersant with the French King or with the Constable, nor euer resorted vnto them except once when he was interpreter betweene the Constable and certaine English [prisoners],[262], wherfore as it was very like so did he verily belieue that as the French King was alwaies close and reserued amongst his best knowne friends, so would he not be open and vncircumspect to impart a matter of such import to a meere stranger and in a most vnseasonable time.

[Page 165] Hereupon Stukely was examined againe, and then finding it dangerous alike to confesse a truth or stand to a ly, he became more vnconstant and variable then he was before, wherfore he was committed to the Tower, and notice was giuen to the French Kings Embassador of all those proceedings, to the intent that he might acquaint his master with them. Letters were also sent to the Kings Embassador in France, directing him to aduertise the French King of all these matters, and that for two speciall ends. One to manifest the Kings confidence in his amity with France, the other to bring the French King into suspition against all English fugitiues who resorted daily to his court. And so because no better person was the author, incredible fables were not belieued. But herevpon some began to discourse that the accusations against the Duke of

Somerset were no lesse improbable, and vpon the credict of no better persons, and therefore might happily be no lesse vntrue. But the difference is great betweene both the persons, and the facts of a soueraigne Prince and of a subject.

And now when the French King vnderstood aswell the imputation which Stukely had raised as his imprisonment. First he deepely protested his innocence in his particular and his generall sincere meaning for preseruing amity with England. Then he much blamed Stukelies villany, and no lesse thanked the King aswell for that he had not afforded a credulous eare to such mischeiuous devises, wherein the tender touch of his estate might happily haue excused his error as for his Princely manner in acquainting him therwith.

On the other side when Mr Morrison the Kings Embassador with the Emperor, had opened the matters giuen him in charge, touching a league against the Turke, and against his confederats. The Emperor much thanked the King for his gentle offer, and promised to procure the Regent to send ouer some persons of credite to understand the Kings further meaning. Soone after Mr Thomas Gresham came [Page 166] from Antwerp into England, and declared to the counsell how Mounsier Longie the Emperors Treasurer in Flanders was sent to him from the Regent with a packet of letters which the Burgundians had intercepted in Bullonois sent as it was said from the Dowager of Scotland, wherein she set forth how she had imprisoned George Paris an Irishman because she vnderstood that vpon grant of his pardon he had a meaning to come into England, and how she had sent Oconners sonne into Ireland to giue encouragement to the Irish Lords. Also he shewed instructions giuen about 4 years before vpon the fall of the Admirall of France, to a gentleman then coming from England, that if any were in England of the Admiralls faction he should doe his best to excite a trouble.[263]

The deputy of Ireland was at that time ready to transport into England. But vpon this aduertisement Sir Henry Knowles was sent in post to stay him there, yet with caution that he should pretend to stay vpon his owne occasions, and therevpon deferred his departure from weeke to weeke, least the true reason should be discerned. Letters of thankes were also sent to the Regent for this gentle ouerture. And the messenger was directed to vse pleasing words in the deliuery of the letter, and to wish a further amity betweene the two states. And further to acquaint her with the French Kings practise in waging 5000 Scottish footmen, and 500 horsemen, and how he tooke vp £100,000 by exchange at Lubecke, whereby the conjecture was evident that he had some meaning against the Emperor in the spring then next following. Doubtlesse the aduertisement of neighbour Princes are alwaies much to be regarded, for that they receiue intelligence from better Authors and surer grounds then persons of inferior note and sort.

About this time one of the Earle of Tyrones men was committed to the tower for making an vntrue complaint against the deputy and counsell of Ireland. And for bruting abroad how the Duke of Northumberland and the [Page 167] Earle of Pembrooke were fallen into quarrell, and one of them against the other in the field.

In Aprill in the 6th yeare of the raigne of the King [1552], he fell sicke of the Measles, wherof in short time he well recouered, afterwards he sickned of the small poxe, which breaking kindly from him, was thought would proue a means to clense his body from such vnhealthfull humors as commonly occasion long sicknesse or death. And herof he also so perfectly recouered that in the sommer next following he rode his progresse with greater magnificence then euer before. For whether it were to maintaine his majesty or to manifest the feare which had beene formerly impressed, he caried with him a band of 320 men,[264] which made vp his whole traine aboue the number of 4000 horse. But because this multitude was burthensome to the Country through which he passed, which did afford little meadow or pasture, because also it seemed to bewray distrust as if the King should thinke that he rather marched among dangerous rebells then tooke his pleasure among faithfull and quiet disposed subjects, about the middest of his progresse the greatest part was discharged. For furnishing the charge of this progresse 500 pound weight of gold was coined with 1500 pounds sterling.

Soone after the King did complaine of a continuall infirmity of body, yet rather as an indisposition in health then any set sicknesse.

And about that time certaine prodigies were seene either as messengers or signes of some imminent and eminent euill. At Middleton eleuen miles from Oxford a woman brought forth a female child which had two bodies from the nauill vpward, so vnited at the nauill as when they were laid in length the one stretched directly opposite to the other, from the nauill downward it was but one, it liued weakly 18 daies, and then both bodies died together. Vpon birth of such monsters the Grecians, and after them the Romans did vse diuerse sorts of expiations, and to goe [Page 168] about their principall citties, with many solemne ceremonies and sacrafices, supposing hereby that wrath from heauen was menaced against them. At Quinborough three great Dolphins were taken, and a few daies following at Blackwall sixe, which were brought to London, the least in bignesse exceeding any horse. After this, three great fishes were taken at Grauesend called Whirlepooles and drawen [up to the king]²⁶⁵ vpon the Kings bridge at Westminster. These accidents the more rarely they happen, the more onimous are they commonly esteemed, either because they are so indeed or because they are neuer obserued but when sad euents doe ensue.

In January about the beginning of the 7th yeare of the Kings raigne [1553] his sicknesse did more apparantly shew it selfe, especially by the symptome of a tough strong streining cough. All the medicines and diet which could be prescribed together with the helpes both of his yong age, and of the rising time of the yeare, were so farre either from curing or abating his griefe, that it daily encreased by dangerous degrees, and it was not only a violence of the cough that did infect him, but therewith a weaknesse and faintnes of spirit, which shewed plainly that his vitall parts were most strongly and strangely assaulted, and the talke hereof among the people was so much the more because²⁶⁶ through an opinion obscurely raised but running as most absurd,²⁶⁷ that his sicknesse grew by a slow working poison. Vpon this cause it happened that a Parliament beginning vpon the first day of March was vpon the last of the same moneth dissolued.

And now the danger of the Kings sicknesse was much lamented, not only by his owne people but by strangers abroad, because his curtesy and wisdome had begot to him such loue, that he was no lesse honoured by those who heard of him, then of those who conuersed with him. For he was famous in all places by reason of his foresight and judgment in affaires, and did so well temper the greatnes [Page 169] of his estate both with modestie and with grauitie, that he auoided enuie by the one, and contempt by the other. Some compared him with greatest persons that had beene, both for warre and peace, because in the like pitch of yeares, none of them attained to the like perfections. Haply hee did not appeare in souldiery so great, but that was because he was not so rash, being also drawne backe from his pursutes abroad by domesticall disorders and diuisions, both amongst the people and Nobilitie of his Realme, by reason whereof he scarce seemed well setled in his Chaire of Estate, and yet his fortunes were alwayes Victorious.

It hapned during his sicknesse that Doctor Ridley Bishop of London, preached before him, and in his Sermon much commended workes of charitie, which as they were a dutie for all men to performe, so most especially for men in most especiall dignitie and place, as well in regard of their large abilities, as for that they were much obliged to giue examples of goodnesse to others: the same day after dinner the King sent for him priuatly into the Gallery at White-Hall, caused him to sit in a chaire by him, would not permit him to remaine vncouered, and then after courteous thankes, he reported all the principall points of his Sermon, and further added; I tooke my selfe to be especially touched by your speech, as well in regard of the abilities which God hath giuen me, as in regard of the example, which from mee hee will require, for as in the Kingdome I am next vnder God, so must I most neerely approach to him in goodnesse and in mercie, for as our miseries stand most in need from him, so are we the greatest debtors; debtors to all that are miserable and shall be the greatest accomptants of our dispensation therein. And therefore, my Lord, as you haue giuen me (I thanke you) this generall exhortation, so direct me, I intreat you, by what particular actions I may this way best discharge my dutie.

The Bishop partly astonished, and partly ouerjoyed with these speeches, was strucke into a sad silence for a time, at [Page 170] last teares and words breaking forth together, he declared to the King, so as he little expected such a question, so was he not furnished with a present answer, for this matter had a great mixture of a ciuill gouernment, wherein he conceiued that the Citizens of London had best experience, as ouerburthened with multitudes of poore, not only of their owne, but from all parts of the Realme besides, and therefore as they best know both the qualitie of such people, and the inconueniences which they occasion, so could they best aduise what remedies were fittest: wherefore, if the King were pleased to afford his Letters to that effect, he would confer with them, and in very short time returne with answer. The King forthwith caused his Letters to be written, and would not suffer the Bishop to depart vntill hee had firmed them with his hand and Signet, and enjoyned the Bishop to be the messenger, imposing great charge for expedition.

The Bishop hasted with his Letters to the Lord Maior, who presently assembled certaine Aldermen, and foure and twentie Commissioners, by which aduice the poore were cast into three companies and sorts, some were poore by impotencie of nature, as young fatherlesse children, old decrepit persons, Ideots, Criples and such like; others are poore by [casualtie],[268] as wounded souldiers; diseased and sicke persons, and the like; the third sort are the poore by idlenesse or vnthriftinesse, as riotous spenders, vagabonds, loyterers, lewd strumpets and their companions, that the first of these were to be educated and maintained, the second to be cured and releeued, and the third to be chastised and reduced to good order.

When this was presented to the King, he gaue to the Citie for education and maintenance of the first sort of poore, the Gray-Friers Church neere Newgate market, with all the reuenues thereto belonging; for cure and releefe of the second sort, he gaue Saint Bartholomewes neere Smithfield; for correction of the third, hee appointed his house at Bridewell, the ancient Mansion of many English Kings, and [Page 171] which not long before had beene repaired and beautified by Henry VIII, for the entertainment of the great Emperour Charles V, for increase of maintenance of their places, together with the new re-edified Hospitall of Saint Thomas in Southwark, the King gaue seuen hundred and fifty[269] markes yearely out of the rents of the Hospitall of Saint John Baptist, or the Sauoy, with all the bedding and furniture at that time belonging to that place, and when the charter of this gift was presented vnto him with a blanke space for lands to be afterward receiued in Mortmaine, to a yearly valew without further licence, the King presently with his owne hand filled vp the void space with these words (foure thousand markes by yeare) this done with reuerent gesture and speech, he thanked God for prolonging his life to finish that businesse; and so hee was the first Founder of those three pious workes, which by many additions are now growne to be the most absolute and famous of that kinde in Europe.

The Kings sicknesse daily increased, and so did the Duke of Northumberlands diligence about him; for he was little absent from the King, and had alwayes some well assured to espie how the state of his health changed euery houre, and the more joyfull hee was at the heart, the more sorrowfull appearance did he outwardly make, whether any tokens of poyson did appeare, reports are various, certainly his Physitians discerned an inuincible malignitie in his disease, and the suspition did the more increase, for that the complaint being chiefly from the lights, a part as of no quicke sense, so no seat for any sharpe disease, yet his sicknesse towards the end grew highly extreme; but the Duke regarded not much the muttering multitude, knowing right well that rumours grow stale and vanish, with time, and yet somewhat either to abate or delay them for the present, hee caused speeches to be spread abroad, that the King was well recouered in health, which was readily belieued, as most desired to be true.

[Page 172] Hereupon all persons expressed joy in their countenance and speech, which they inlarged by telling the newes to others whom they incountred, who haply had heard it often before, and as the report increased, so therewith increased also the joy: Thus whilest euery man beleeued, and no man knew, it was made more credible by religious persons, who openly in Churches gaue publike thankes for the Kings recouery.

But when the speech of his danger was againe [received],²⁷⁰ and as in newes, it happeneth, the more stopped, the more increased to the worse, then as if the second time he had beene lost, the people did immoderatly breake forth into passions, complaining, that for this cause his two Vncles had beene taken away, for this cause the most faithfull of his Nobilitie and of his Councell were disgraced and remoued from Court; this was the reason that such were placed next his person, who were most assuredly disposed either to commit or permit any mischiefe, that then it did appeare, that it was not vainly conjectured some yeares before by men of judgement and fore-sight, that after Somersets death the King should not long enjoy his life. To qualifie these and some broader speeches, it was thought conuenient that the King sometimes should shew himselfe abroad, albeit, little either with his pleasure or for his health, yet a thing which in long consuming sicknesses, euen to the last period of life, men are often able to doe.

Whilest the King remained thus grieuously sicke, diuers notable mariages were solemnized at once in Durham place, The Lord Guldford, fourth sonne to the Duke of Northumberland, married Lady Jane, the Duke of Suffolkes eldest daughter, by Frances daughter to Mary second sister to King Henry VIII: also the Earl of Pembrokes eldest sonne married the Lady Katherine, the Duke of

Suffolkes [second][271] daughter by the said Lady Frances, who then was liuing: and Martin Kayes, Gentleman Porter, married Marie the third daughter of the Duke of Suffolke, by the said [Page 173] Lady Frances: lastly, the Lord Hastings, sonne to the Earle of Huntington, tooke to wife Katherine youngest daughter to the Duke of Northumberland; hereupon the common people vpon a disposition to interpret all Northumberlands actions to the worst, left nothing vnspoken which might serue to stirre their hatred against the Duke, or pitie towards the King: but the Duke was nothing moued hereat, for being equally obstinate both in purpose and desire, and mounting his hopes aboue the pitch of reason, he resolued then to dissemble no longer, but began openly to play his game.

For albeit the Lady Jane married to his fourth sonne, had not right to the succession of the Crowne, for that shee was excluded, first, by the two Ladies Mary and Elizabeth, daughters of King Henry the eighth; next, by the issue of Lady Margret married into Scotland, eldest sister to King Henry VIII: lastly, by her owne mother, the Ladie Frances, who then was liuing, yet Northumberland, sottishly mad with ouer great fortune, procured the King by his Letters Patents vnder the great Seale of England, to appoint the Lady Jane to succeed him in the inheritance of the Crowne; in this contriuance he vsed the aduice of two especially, Lord chiefe Justice Montague, who drew the Letters Patents, and Secretary Cecil [many of whose actions afterwards affected litle matter of praise][272]: these furnished the Patent with diuers reasons, whereof some were of Law and some of policie in State: The pretensions of Law were these, that albeit the Crowne of the Realme, by an Act of the fiue and thirtieth of King Henry VIII, was in default of his issue of his body, and of the body of Edward his sonne lawfully begotten, limited to remaine to the Lady Mary, his eldest daughter, and to the heires of her body lawfully begotten; and in default of such issue, the remainder thereof to the Lady Elizabeth, his second daughter, and to the heires of her body lawfully begotten, vnder such conditions as should be limited by the said King vnder his Letters Patents, vnder the great Seale, or by his last Will in writing, signed with his hand; yet because the said limitations were made [Page 174] to persons illegitimate, both the marriages betweene King Henry VIII and their seuerall mothers, being vndone by sentences of diuorce, and the seuerall diuorcements ratified by authoritie of Parliament in the eight and thirtieth yeare of King Henry VIII, which Act remained then in force, both the Lady Mary and the Lady Elizabeth were thereby disabled to claime the Crowne, or any honours or hereditaments as heires to King Edward VI or any other person.

And againe, the said two Ladies, Mary and Elizabeth, being but of the halfe bloud to King Edward, albeit they had beene borne in lawfull matrimony, yet by the ancient Lawes of the Realme they were not inheritable to him by descent, and had no capacitie in any degree to receiue any inheritance from him.

The reasons or pretexts of necessitie to the State were these: In case the Ladie Mary and the Lady Elizabeth should enjoy the Crowne, they would assuredly joyne in marriage with some stranger, who would reduce this noble and free Realme into the seruitude of the Bishop of Rome, and thereby bring in forren [persons],[273] customes and Lawes, abolishing those whereupon the rights of all natiue subjects depend, and haply the whole body of the Realme should hereby be annexed as a member to some other greater Kingdome, to the vtter subuersion of the ancient dignitie and Estate thereof, [and further upon this forreine marriage and the consequences thereof,][274] the people were not vnlike to elect a King of some priuate Stocke, a popular and seditious man, peraduenture one who to countenance his own vnworthinesse and obscurity, would little regard what contumely he cast vpon the falling Family of the Kings before him; wherefore he[275] held it the most prouident aduice, that the King by his authoritie should designe, not only his next Successour, but others also in reuersion, that the Crowne might not be subject to rifling, but remaine to those whom hee loued, and who humoured[276] him best.

These reasons did more easily sinke into the Kings [Page 175] judgement, partly by meanes of the great affection which he bare to the Religion that he had established, of the change whereof he was assuredly perswaded in case the Lady Mary his sister should succeed, and partly by reason of the entire loue hee bare to his Cosin the Ladie Jane, a woman of the most rare and incomparable perfections: For besides her excellent beautie adorned with all varietie of vertues, as a cleere skie with starres, as a princely Diadem with jewels, shee was most deare to the King in regard both of her religion and of her education in the knowledge of the liberall Sciences, and skill in Languages, for in Theologie, in Philosophie, in all liberall Arts, in the Latine and Greeke tongues, and in the Vulgar Languages of diuers neere Nations; shee farre exceeded all of her sex, and any of her yeares, vnlesse haply the King himselfe.

Hereupon the King consented that Letters Patents should be drawne, importing that in case the King should die with out issue of his bodie lawfully begotten, then the Imperiall Crowne of England and Ireland, with his title to the Crown of France, and all things to them belonging should remaine and come to the eldest sonne of the Ladie Frances, daughter to the Ladie Mary, youngest sister to Henry VIII, in case such issue should be borne into the world, during the life of King Edward and after to the heires male of the said issue, and in like sort from sonne to sonne of the said Ladie Frances lawfully begotten, as they should be in prioritie of birth, and borne during the Kings life; and in default of such sonnes and of heires male of euery such sonne lawfully begotten, that then the said Crowne and all the premises should remaine and come to the Lady Jane, eldest daughter to the said Ladie Frances, and the heirs males of her lawfully begotten, and for default of such issue the said Crowne to remaine to the Lady Katherine; second daughter to the said Lady Frances, with diuers other remainders, ouer which as they were vainly appointed, so are they needlesse to be repeated.

[Page 176] These Letters were dated the one and twentieth of June. in the seuenth yeare of King Edwards raign [1553], and by him signed when he was in great debilitie of body, and afterwards passed vnder the great Seale of England. And albeit the course contriuance was almost visible, first, for that such prouision was made for the Issue male of the said Lady Frances who neither at that time had any, and was commonly reputed to be past yeares of child-bearing: secondly, for that in case, that beyond the ordinary course of nature she should conceiue, the hope was desperate that the King should liue vntill the birth.

Lastly, for that her children borne, and to be borne, were so carefully and orderly remembred, and no mention made of her selfe, from whom their title must be deriued, yet these Letters were subscribed by all the Priuie Counsellours, the greatest part both of number and power of the Nobilitie of the Realme, the Bishops, the Kings learned Counsell, and all the Judges at the Common Law, except only Sir James Holles,[277] one of the Justices of the Common Pleas, a man well obserued to be both religious and vpright, who worthily refused to subscribe, and was vnworthily requited by Queene Mary afterwards.

It is very like that some of these were guided with respect of their particular interest, for that they were possessed of diuers lands which once pertained to Monasteries, Chantries, and other religions houses not long before dissolued, of these they held themselues in some danger to lose, in case religion should change to the ancient forme, which by succession of Queene Mary they did euidently fore-see.

Others were drawne partly by feare, and partly by obligation to the Duke of Northumberland, who then was exceeding potent, and almost absolute in gouernment of the State, and supposed able to make any title good, either by his authoritie, or by his sword. [Assuredly his power was dreadful, for as he was easy to enterteine displeasure, so was he strong to reteine it, a cunning dissembler for a tyme, but a sure paymaster in the end.][278]

Now whether a King may lawfully dispose by his will, or otherwise, of a Kingdome that hath beene long carried in [Page 177] one forme of succession contrary to that ancient forme I haue largely discoursed in my History of the three Norman Kings, about the beginning of the raigne of King William II; but certaine it is, that when kingdomes haue customably beene carried by right of succession, according to proximitie of bloud, the violation of which course hath alwayes beene either very vaine, or with dangerous consequence, it hath alwayes beene like the breaking of a band which holdeth a sheafe of arrowes together, like a rupture in bankes, which bindeth a riuer within its proper channell, or like a casting down of a pale, wherewith deere or other beasts are inclosed: It was neuer done, but either no effect ensued, or bloudie disorders, or haply both, and the Duke by piercing his ambitious purpose with his vnjust policie, did no otherwise than often doth a foolish, greedie gamester, who by stealing a card to win a stake, forfeits the whole rest.

But hauing thus in his owne opinion assured his owne deuices, nothing remained but that the King should not longer suruiue, lest haply his sickly judgement might be over-ruled by sounder aduice; his disease was violent, but his physitians conceiued some hope of recouery, in case he might be remoued to change of healthfull aire, which infirmities of the vitall parts, the seat of his sicknesse, is of greatest moment for the cure.

But hereto the Councell would not consent, so he continued without either any sensible mending, or impairing for a time. At the last a Gentlewoman, vnworthy to be named, but accounted to be a schoole mistresse for the purpose, offered her seruice assuredly to cure him, in case he were committed wholly to her hand; hereto the Physitians would in no case afford their aduice, because as she could give no reason, either of the nature of the disease, or of the part afflicted, so shee would not declare the meanes whereby shee intended to worke the cure.

After some shew of deliberation among the Councell it [Page 178] was resolued that the Physitians should be discharged, and the cure committed to her alone: the apparant defect both of her judgement and experience, joyned to the weightinesse of the aduenture, caused many to maruell, and some deeply to suspect that shee was but an instrument of mischiefe; this surmise was strongly confirmed within a very short time ensuing when the King did fall into desperate extremities, his vitall parts were mortally stuffed, which brought him to a difficultie of speech and of breath, his legs swelled, his pulse failed, his skin changed colour, and many other horrid symptomes appeared.

Then were the Physitians called againe, who espying him in that fearefull estate departed from him with a sad silence, leauing him to the miserable mercy of neere approaching death, some of these whispered among their priuate friends, that they were called for fashion only, but neither their aduice nor appliances[279] were any deale regarded,[280] but the King had beene ill dealt with more than once, and that when by the benefit, both of his youth and of carefull meanes, there was faire means[281] of his recouery he was againe more strongly ouerlaid.

Yet as crueltie and wrong neuer stand secure, so the Duke thought one thing more expedient for assuring his designes, and that was to draw the Lady Mary wholly into his power: to this purpose Letters were directed to her in the Kings name from the Councell, willing her forthwith to resort to the King, as well to be a comfort to him in his sicknesse, as to see all matters well ordered about him; the Ladie suspecting no lurking mischiefe, addressed herselfe with all speed to the journey, expressing great joy, that either her company or her seruice, should be esteemed needfull[282] to the King; but as she was vpon the way, and within halfe a daies journey of London, her foot readie to slip into the snare, shee receiued aduice both of the Kings desperate estate, and of the Dukes designments against her wherevpon she returned in haste to her house at Houeden,[283] where in a short time shee [Page 179] heard how vnprofitable her journey would haue beene to London.

So the King hauing long wrastled with a lingring and tormenting sicknesse, at the last his spirits yeelded to the malice of his disease, which as with great patience hee did endure, so with no lesse pietie did he end it; many feruent prayers hee made, both for himselfe and for the people of his Realmes, and some when he was esteemed almost past sense, and so spent his last breath in committing his sweet soule into the Almighties hands which had created it.

He died at Greenwich vpon Thursday the sixth day of July, in the yeare 1553 and in the seuenteenth yeare of his age, when he had raigned six yeares, fiue moneths and nine dayes; two dayes his death was concealed, to open a straight way for the Dukes crooked purposes; his body was buried vpon the ninth of August in the same yeare, in the Chappell of Saint Peters Church in Westminster, and laid neere to the body of King Henry VII, his Grand-father. [Page 180]

THIS HISTORY I HAVE

BVILT FOR THE

MONUMENT OF HIS

VNPERISHABLE FAME.

FINIS[284]

Notes

1. Hieronymus Cardano
2. Trinity MS; 1630 edition gives incorrect date of October 17.
3. Trinity MS.
4. Marginal notes opposite paragraph:
   Plin. lib. 7, cap. 9
   Plin. 16
   Fest. lib. 3
   Solin. ca 4
   rer. mem.
5. Marginal notes opposite paragraph:
   Prob. in epit. 1. 10
   Valerii
   Liv. dec. 1
   lib. 2
   Sil. Ital. lib. 13
   Hermo.
   in castig.
   Plin. loco cod.
6. Harl. and Trinity MSS.
7. Marginal note opposite paragraph: Lib. 10
8. Marginal note opposite line: Lib. 7
9. Folger MS.
10. Marginal note opposite line: Lib. 7. c. 53
11. Harl. and Trinity MSS; 1630 edition has "estate," Folger MS, "realme."
12. Folger MS.
13. Harl., Trinity, and Ogden MSS; 1630 edition has "searre."
14. Folger MS.
15. Harl. MS; omitted in 1630 edition.
16. William Paulet
17. Joan Bocher and George van Paris
18. Folger MS; this manuscript omits subsequent phrase about madness.
19. "Importunate" in Folger MS.
20. Harl. MS.
21. "Rovers" in Folger MS.
22. Folger MS.
23. Harl. MS.
24. Lennox.
25. "Not" in Folger MS.

26. Folger MS.
27. Folger and Harl. MSS.
28. "Twoe" in Folger MS.
29. Folger and Harl. MSS.
30. Solway Moss
31. "Forte" in Folger MS.
32. Folger MS reads: "John Dudley Earle of Warwicke was a man of ancient nobility and in high estimacon with the poeple, eyther for his vertues, or appearances of vertues, for hee vsed liberalitie towardes his friendes, and (in stead thereof) to strangers courtesie and affabilitie. Hee was of faire stature, and comely countenance but of . . ."
33. Folger MS adds the following: "Hee allwayes encreased both in estimacon with the Prince, and authoritie in the state; doubtful whether by fatall destinie whereby some rise in fauour and some decline; or whether hauing made full proofe of his abilities, hee chose a course free from daunger, betweene stiffe stubbornesse and filthie flatterie."
34. Folger MS reads: "hauing the art also by vaine promises and hopes, to drawe the people to what he listed, . . ."
35. In Folger MS the paragraph ends with this sentence: "I haue wrott of these twoe persones more largely in this place, because during the reigne of Kinge Edward, they were the principall actors in euery Scene."
36. "Shottes" in Folger MS.
37. "Shott" in Folger MS.
38. Marginal notes:
Caes. 2
Gallic.
Conest. 6
Deut. 20
39. Folger MS reads: "The Governor of Scotland was somewhat appalled, as neither funished at that time with forraine aide, nor much trusting his forces at home 'for both the Protestants and the Catholicks were discontented at his vncertainties. And the friendes of the exile Leuinus whom the Gouernour had hardly entreated, did beare a sharpe hatred against him. Notwithstanding hee sent his herehaultes' through all parts."
40. "2000" in Folger MS.
41. Odgen MS; "returned" in 1630 edition.
42. "Confusion" in Odgen MS.
43. Harl. MS.
44. Folger and Ogden MSS; "advantage" in 1630 edition.
45. Harl. MS has marginal notes opposite the Latin references:
Liuie. lib. 1
Plut. in Sertorio
Plut. in Aug
cedren
Guicc. 28
46. A night attack

47. "Flight" in Folger MS.

48. Harl. MS; "vallye" in 1630 edition.

49. Harl. MS.

50. Folger MS adds details of military action missing in printed editions.

51. Folger and Harl. MSS.

52. "Riders" in Folger MS.

53. Folger MS (fos. 21v, 22r) gives a more detailed account of these events.

54. See William Patten, "The Late Expedition into Scotland," in *Tudor Tracts: 1532-1588*, edited by A. F. Pollard, which reads: ". . . the Lord of Yester: Hobby Hambleton [Hamilton], Captain of Dunbar, the Master of Sampoole [Semple]: the Laird of Wimmes . . ." (127).

55. Folger MS (fos. 22v-24v) gives a slightly different account of events on pages 37-39.

56. Harl. MS.

57. Harl., Ogden, and Trinity MSS.

58. Folger and Trinity MSS.

59. Marginal note in Folger MS: "lib. 52"; probably Cassius Dio. See Cassius Dio, *The Roman History: The Reign of Augustus*, trans. Ian Scott-Kilvert (London, 1987).

60. Folger, Harl., and Ogden MSS; 1630 edition has "lost."

61. Harl. MS.

62. Folger, Ogden, and Trinity MSS; 1630 edition has "a company of."

63. "Two third" in Harl. MS.

64. "Base breath of the vulgar people" in Folger MS.

65. Folger and Trinity MSS; 1630 edition has "intempestuous."

66. "Enboldned" in Ogden MS.

67. "Parliament" in Harl. MS; Trinity and Ogden MSS and 1636 edition are as 1630 edition.

68. Trinity MS.

69. All MSS; 1630 edition has "brackes."

70. St. Mynettes.

71. Hume

72. Brian O'Connor and Patrick O'More

73. Folger MS.

74. Folger, Ogden, and Trinity MSS; 1630 and 1636 editions have "distinguish."

75. Folger MS adds "Soone after commissioners went forth to determine differences touching enclosures."

76. Honiton

77. Folger MS reads: Humphrey Arundell, "gouernor of the Mount, a man both for courage and comelinesse of persone well esteemed, Robert Bochame and seaven other priestes. . . ."

78. All MSS; "laiers" in 1630 edition.

79. Additions from Harl. MS.

80. Trinity MS.

81. Ogden MS has "liberty."

82. Folger MS omits reference to tax on sheep and cattle.

83. Harl. MS.

84. Trinity and Ogden MSS; 1630 edition has "assailed."

85. Ottery St. Mary

86. Trinity and Ogden MSS; 1630 edition has "valued."

87. Folger MS.

88. "200" in Ogden MS.

89. Travers

90. Clyst St. Mary

91. Harl. MS; 1630 and 1636 editions have "Euiland."

92. Clyst Heath

93. Trinity MS; 1630 and 1636 editions have "vague."

94. Hethersett

95. Folger MS.

96. Harl. and Trinity MSS; 1630 edition has "38s 4d."

97. Trinity MS; 1630 edition has "require."

98. Harl. MS; 1630 edition reads: "fine workemen I warrant you, who can so closely carry their dealings, that then men only discouer them, how harmelesse counsailes were fit for tame fooles . . ."

99. Mousehold Heath

100. Trinity and Ogden MSS.

101. Harl. MS reads: "in time of disorder religion and enclosures . . ."

102. Harl. MS; 1630 edition reads "they concerned themselues . . ."

103. Folger and Harl. MSS.

104. Harl. MS reads: ". . . their sureties that they would violentlie take his authoritie into their hands."

105. All MSS; 1630 and 1636 editions have "side."

106. All MSS; 1630 and 1636 editions have "2000."

107. Ogden MS; 1630 edition has "neither."

108. Trinity and Ogden MSS have "streightnes."

109. "Gray" in Folger MS.

110. Harl. MS.

111. Odgen MS; 1630 edition has "chafed."

112. Folger and Harl. MS.

113. Harl. MS reads: ". . . rather by faire means then by force, he would . . ."

114. The preceding sentence is missing in Folger MS where the paragraph ends as follows: "The like exceptions I haue often heard against bloudie executions frequently vsed in Paules churchyard."

115. "A yeoman" in Folger MS.

116. Trinity MS. One who vexatiously raises or incites to litigation.

117. Harl. MS; 1630 edition reads "and that present they vnderstood to be the time . . ."

118. Harl. MS; 1630 edition has "wild."

119. 1636 edition; "peice" in 1630 edition.

120. Folger MS gives a more favorable description of Lord Sudley: "Lord Sudley did exceed him both in courage and comlinesse of personne and in fine courtly behauior both were so . . ."

121. "Myned" in Ogden MS.
122. Ogden MS; 1630 edition has "pitty."
123. Ogden MS.
124. Folger MS.
125. "Destroy the King" in Folger MS.
126. Harl. MS.
127. Folger MS.
128. Harl. MS reads: "time could haue byn in probabilitie required."
129. Harl. MS has in margin:
    Shawe
    Barlowe
    and others
130. In margin: Cap. 25. Cap. 29 in Harl. MS. The reference is to Sirach.
131. In margin: Gen. 3.17.
132. Ogden MS reads: "many might be conjectured but few knew."
133. Sir William Petre
134. In Folger MS only the Earl of Warwick sent for the mayor.
135. "No high" in Harl. MS; Newberry copy describes Lord Rich only as "a man of quicke and liuely deliuery of speech."
136. Harl. MS.
137. "Reason" in Harl. MS.
138. 1630 edition reads: "which were knowne to be of an inestimable value, that it might well be said euen as he had giuen forth."
139. Durham.
140. "Boutie-sale" in Harl. MS.
141. Harl. and Trinity MSS.
142. Ogden MS and 1636 edition.
143. All MSS.
144. All MSS; 1630 edition has "country."
145. "The aldermen" in Folger MS.
146. Ogden MS and 1636 edition; 1630 edition has "them."
147. Ogden MS and 1636 edition; 1630 edition has "dispressed."
148. Folger MS.
149. "Consideringe" in Ogden MS.
150. Newberry copy reads "a man of spirit enough."
151. All MSS; 1630 edition has "guardes."
152. Harl. MS has "misdemeanors."
153. "Quiet" in Ogden MS.
154. "3" in Ogden MS.
155. Ogden MS and 1636 edition.
156. Folger MS.
157. "Surveigh" in Harl. MS.
158. Guernsey
159. Newberry copy omits "being of base gold and fearing the touch."
160. Harl. MS.
161. Trinity MS and 1636 edition; 1630 edition has "vice."

162. Folger MS adds the following: "Nowe the Earle of Warwick was little pleased that the Duke was not onely thus restored, but did daylie rise to a good degree, both of fauor and authoritie in the court."

163. Harl. MS; 1630 edition has "shorte."

164. Folger MS.

165. "5000" in Trinity MS.

166. "Offence" in Harl. MS.

167. "8000" in Trinity MS.

168. Harl. MS.

169. "25" in Harl. MS.

170. Harl. MS.

171. Folger, Harl., and Trinity MSS; 1630 and 1636 editions have "clime."

172. "20,000" in Harl. MS.

173. "312,000" in Harl. MS.

174. Harl. and Trinity MSS and 1636 edition; 1630 edition has "treatise."

175. Harl. MS.

176. "The Lord Pagett" in Harl. MS.

177. Harl. and Trinity MSS.

178. "2,000,000" in Trinity MS.

179. See W. K. Jordan, ed., *The Chronicle and Political Papers of King Edward VI*: ". . . if the Scots razed Lauder, etc., we should raze Roxburgh and Eyemouth" (22).

180. Folger MS reads: "They were encountred at Blackheath by diuers noble men, all the kinges pentioners, and aboue 100 gentlmen brauely mounted, who did accompanie them."

181. In margin: "Or happely yeare."

182. Harl. MS; 1630 and 1636 editions have "bande."

183. Folger and Harl. MSS; 1630 edition reads "more faithfull then they were, the King had eares enough."

184. Osmunds, or iron bars of superior quality.

185. Trinity MS.

186. "6d" in Harl. MS.

187. "2d" in Harl. and Trinity MSS.

188. Folger MS adds: "they might bee suffred to trafficke as if they were in peace."

189. Sir Anthony St. Leger

190. Folger MS.

191. Harl. MS and 1636 edition.

192. Folger and Harl. MSS.

193. Folger MS.

194. Folger MS.

195. Sir John Borthwick

196. Folger MS.

197. "36" in Folger, Harl., and Trinity MSS.

198. Folger and Trinity MSS and 1636 edition; 1630 edition has "150,000."

199. Folger and Harl. MSS; 1630 edition has "they."

200. Harl. and Trinity MSS.

201. Trinity MS.
202. "Heavinesse" in Folger MS.
203. Folger, Harl., and Trinity MSS and 1636 edition.
204. "Prosperitie" in Folger MS.
205. Folger, Harl., and Trinity MSS; 1630 edition has "yeares."
206. Folger and Trinity MSS.
207. Richard Whalley
208. Folger MS.
209. Folger MS; "detection" in 1630 edition.
210. Folger MS.
211. Folger and Trinity MSS and 1636 edition; 1630 edition has "especiall."
212. Folger and Trinity MSS and 1636 edition.
213. Folger MS.
214. Trinity MS; 1630 edition has "crew"; "misconstruction" in Harl. MS.
215. Folger and Trinity MSS; "fast" in 1630 edition.
216. "3 Henrie 7" in Folger, Harl., and Trinity MSS.
217. Folger MS.
218. "Bartevile" in Harl. and Trinity MSS. See Jordan, ed., *The Chronicle and Political Papers of King Edward VI*, 100.
219. Folger and Harl. MSS and 1636 edition; Trinity MS has "many."
220. Harl. MS reads "a man still famous."
221. Folger and Harl. MSS; "conuert" in 1630 edition.
222. Folger, Harl., and Trinity MSS; 1630 edition has "title."
223. "Verily it was fitt hee should bee wary of men, bloudy, populare, and rich" in Folger MS.
224. Folger MS reads: "people greedy for novelties."
225. Folger and Trinity MSS.
226. Folger and Harl. MSS; 1630 and 1636 editions have "deserued."
227. Folger MS.
228. Harl. and Trinity MSS; "yeares" in 1630 edition.
229. Folger and Harl. MSS.
230. Folger and Harl. MSS.
231. In Folger MS the paragraph ends: "But the chiefest I will briefly sett downe; not always obseruing the coherence of the time, but somtimes of the businesse."
232. "63,000" in Folger and Harl. MSS.
233. "Colour" in Harl. MS.
234. "8" in Folger MS.
235. "And twoe in Lanchashire" in Folger MS.
236. Harl. and Trinity MSS read: "to certifie what penall lawes and proclamations were not needful to be executed."
237. Folger MS, fo. 78v.
238. Folger MS.
239. Folger MS. Subsequent entries are numbered 9 through 19.
240. Trinity MS; "one" in 1630 edition; "no" in 1636 edition.
241. Harl. MS.
242. Harl. MS.

243. Harl. MS reads: "of expence that ordinarie supplies for his subjects could not suffice wherein also in regard of the times he was somewhat sparing and therefore did deale with the Foulker."

244. Harl. MS.

245. "110,000" in Trinity MS.

246. 1630 and 1636 editions; Folger, Harl., and Trinity MSS have "title."

247. "Purporting" in Harl. and Trinity MSS.

248. "Convicted" in Folger MS.

249. "Sessed" in Trinity MS.

250. Utrecht

251. "500" in Harl. MS.

252. Francois Hotman

253. Thomas Stuckley

254. Harl. MS; 1630 and 1636 editions and Trinity MS have "some angle of Scotland about Falmouth . . ."

255. Harl. MS; 1630 and 1636 editions and Trinity MS have "engaged."

256. Harl. MS; "with all Papistes" in Folger MS.

257. See Jordan, ed., *The Chronicle and Political Papers of King Edward VI*: "The Lord Grey was chosen Deputy of Calais in the Lord Willoughby's place, who was thought unmeet for it" (144).

258. Folger MS adds: "and one [Sir Thomas] Cotton was appointed in his place."

259. Folger MS reads: "the rate of 20 shillings the cloath for they caried at that shipping 40,000 broad cloathes." Last sentence of paragraph is missing in Folger MS.

260. "Question" in Harl. MS.

261. Folger, Harl., and Trinity MSS; 1630 and 1636 editions have "indited."

262. Trinity MS; 1630 and 1636 editions have "pioners."

263. "Tumult" in Harl. MS.

264. Folger MS (fo. 80v.) reads: "a band of 320 men, as if hee had marched amongst daungerous rebells." The king discharged all "except 150."

265. Trinity MS.

266. Harl. and Trinity MSS read: "the more heavie through an opinion . . ."

267. "Assured" in Harl. MS.

268. "Faculty" in 1630 and 1636 editions.

269. "700" in Harl. and Trinity MSS.

270. Trinity MS; 1630 and 1636 editions have "reuiued."

271. Harl. and Trinity MSS and 1636 edition; 1630 edition has "eldest."

272. Harl. and Trinity MSS.

273. Harl. MS.

274. Harl. and Trinity MSS.

275. "They" in Harl. MS.

276. "Honored" in Trinity MS.

277. Hales

278. Harl. and Trinity MSS.

279. "Applications" in Harl. MS.

280. "Rewarded" in Trinity MS.

281. "Hope" in Harl. and Trinity MSS.
282. "Useful" in Trinity MS.
283. Hunsdon, Hertfordshire
284. The last four lines are omitted in the 1636 edition.

Select Bibliography

SIR JOHN HAYWARD

Anderson, Judith H. *Biographical Truth: The Representation of Historical Persons in Tudor-Stuart Writing*. New Haven, Conn.: Yale Univ. Press, 1984.

Benjamin, Edwin B. "Sir John Hayward and Tacitus." *Review of English Studies* NS 8 (1957): 275–76.

Bruce, John, ed. *Annals of the First Four Years of the Reign of Queen Elizabeth, by Sir John Hayward*. London, 1840.

Camden, William. *Remains Concerning Britain*. Ed. R. D. Dunn. Toronto: Univ. of Toronto Press, 1984.

The Carl H. Pforzheimer Library: English Literature 1475–1700. Ed. C. H. Pforzheimer. 3 vols. New York: Morrill Press, 1940.

Cogswell, Thomas. *The Blessed Revolution: English Politics and the Coming of War, 1621–1624*. Cambridge: Cambridge Univ. Press, 1989.

Collins, S. L. *From Divine Cosmos to Sovereign State*. Oxford: Oxford Univ. Press, 1989.

Dowling, Margaret. "Sir John Hayward's Troubles over His *Life* of Henry IV." *The Library* 4th ser., 11 (1930–31): 212–24.

Evans, Joan. *A History of the Society of Antiquaries*. Oxford: Clarendon, 1956.

Evans, John X. ed. *The Works of Roger Williams*. Oxford: Clarendon, 1972.

Fox, Levi, ed. *English Historical Scholarship in the Sixteenth and Seventeenth Centuries*. Oxford: Dugdale Society, 1956.

Galloway, Bruce. *The Union of England and Scotland: 1603–1608*. Edinburgh: J. Donald, 1986.

Garraty, John. *The Nature of Biography*. New York: Knopf, 1957.

Goldberg, S. L. "Sir John Hayward, 'Politic Historian.'" *Review of English Studies* NS, 6 (1955): 233–44.

Hervey, M. F. S. *The Life, Correspondence and Collections of Thomas Howard Earl of Arundel*. Cambridge: Cambridge Univ. Press, 1921.

Hill, L. M. *Bench and Bureaucracy: The Public Career of Sir Julius Caesar, 1580–1636*. Palo Alto: Stanford Univ. Press, 1988.

Jackson, W. A. "Counterfeit Printing in Jacobean Times." *The Library* 4th ser., 15 (1934): 364–76.

James, M. R., ed. *The Western Manuscripts in the Library of Trinity College, Cambridge.* 4 vols. Cambridge: Cambridge Univ. Press, 1902.

Kendall, P. M. *The Art of Biography.* New York: Norton, 1965.

Knafla, L. *Law and Politics in Jacobean England.* Cambridge: Cambridge Univ. Press, 1977.

Levack, Brian P. *The Civil Lawyers in England, 1603–1641: A Political Study.* Oxford: Clarendon, 1973.

———. *The Formation of the British State.* Oxford: Clarendon, 1987.

Levy, F. J. "Hayward, Daniel and the Beginnings of Politic History in England." *Huntington Library Quarterly* 50 (1987): 1–34.

———. *Tudor Historical Thought.* San Marino, Calif.: Huntington Library, 1967.

Manning, John J., ed. *The First and Second Parts of John Hayward's The Life and Raigne of King Henrie IIII.* London: Royal Historical Society, 1991.

Plomer, Henry R. "Eliot's Court Press: Decorated Blocks and Initials." *The Library* 4th ser., 3 (1922): 194–209.

———. "The Eliot's Court Printing House, 1584–1674." *The Library* 4th ser., 2 (1921): 175–84.

Russell, Conrad. *Parliaments and English Politics, 1621–1629.* Oxford: Oxford Univ. Press, 1979.

Scarfe, Norman. "Sir John Hayward: An Elizabethan Historian, His Life and Disappointments." *Suffolk Institute of Archaeology* 25 (1952): 79–97.

Shapiro, Barbara J. *Probability and Certainty in Seventeenth-Century England.* Princeton: Princeton Univ. Press, 1983.

Sharpe, Kevin. *Sir Robert Cotton: 1586–1631.* Oxford: Oxford Univ. Press, 1979.

Sharpe, Kevin and Steven N. Zwicker, eds. *Politics of Discourse: The Literature and History of Seventeenth-Century England.* Berkeley: Univ. of California Press, 1987.

Sommerville, J. P. *Politics and Ideology in England, 1603–1640.* London: Longman, 1986.

Squibb, G. D. *Doctors' Commons: A History of the College of Advocates and Doctors of Law.* Oxford: Oxford Univ. Press, 1977.

Stauffer, Donald A. *English Biography before 1700.* Cambridge, Mass.: Harvard Univ. Press, 1930.

Strong, Roy C. *Henry, Prince of Wales and England's Lost Renaissance.* New York: Thames and Hudson, 1986.

Strype, John. "Animadversions" in vol. 2, part 2 of *Ecclesiastical Memorials.* Oxford: 1822.

Todd, Margo. *Christian Humanism and the Puritan Social Order.* Cambridge: Cambridge Univ. Press, 1987.

White, Helen C. *English Devotional Literature: Prose, 1600–1640.* Madison: Univ. of Wisconsin Press, 1931.

Wilson, Elkin C. *Prince Henry and English Literature.* Ithaca, N.Y.: Cornell Univ. Press, 1946.

Woolf, D. R. *The Idea of History in Early Stuart England.* Toronto: Univ. of Toronto Press, 1990.

REIGN OF EDWARD VI

Beer, Barrett L. "Northumberland: The Myth of the Wicked Duke and the Historical John Dudley." *Albion* 11 (1979): 1–14.

———. *Northumberland: The Political Career of John Dudley, Earl of Warwick and Duke of Northumberland.* Kent, Ohio: Kent State Univ. Press, 1973.

———. *Rebellion and Riot: Popular Disorder in England during the Reign of Edward VI.* Kent, Ohio: Kent State Univ. Press, 1982.

Bush, M. L. *The Government Policy of Protector Somerset.* Montreal: McGill-Queen's Univ. Press, 1975.

Elton, G. R. *Reform and Reformation: England, 1509–1558.* Cambridge, Mass.: Harvard Univ. Press, 1977.

Guy, John. *Tudor England.* Oxford: Oxford Univ. Press, 1990.

Hoak, Dale E. *The King's Council in the Reign of Edward VI.* Cambridge: Cambridge Univ. Press, 1976.

———. "Rehabilitating the Duke of Northumberland: Politics and Political Control, 1549–53." In *The Mid-Tudor Polity c. 1540–1560,* edited by Robert Tittler and Jennifer Loach. Totowa, N.J.: Rowman and Littlefield, 1980.

Jordan, W. K. *Edward VI: The Young King.* London: George Allen and Unwin, 1968.

———. *Edward VI: The Threshold of Power.* London: George Allen and Unwin, 1970.

———, ed. *The Chronicle and Political Papers of King Edward VI.* Ithaca, N.Y.: Cornell Univ. Press, 1966.

Pollard, A. F. *England under Protector Somerset.* London, 1900.

———, ed. *Tudor Tracts, 1532–1588.* New York: E. P. Dutton, n.d.

Index

The Life and Raigne of King Edward the Sixth
was composed in 10½-point Caslon 540 leaded 2½ points
on an IBM PC-based system using Ventura Publisher with Linotronic output
by Inari Information Services, Inc.;
with Caslon 471 Swash caps set by TSI, Inc.;
printed by sheet-fed offset on
60-pound Glatfelter Natural acid-free stock,
Smyth sewn and bound over 88-point binder's boards in
Holliston Roxite cloth
by BookCrafters, Inc.;
designed by Will Underwood;
and published by
The Kent State University Press
KENT, OHIO 44242

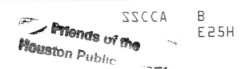